DATABASE DRIVEN ASP.NET WITH CODE BEHIND USING VB.NET

Powering the ASP using Microsoft.Jet.OLEDB.4.0

Richard Edwards

THE DEVIL IS IN THE DETAILS

Let's do more than make a standard user experience

Let's try something a little bit different with this book. Instead of just using ASP tags like this:

```
<html xmlns="http://www.w3.org/1999/xhtml">
<head runat="server">
    <title></title>
</head>
<body>
    <form id="form1" runat="server">
    <div>
    <asp:Table runat="server">
    <asp:TableHeaderRow>
    <asp:TableHeaderCell></asp:TableHeaderCell>
    </asp:TableHeaderRow>
    <asp:TableRow>
    <asp:TableCell></asp:TableCell>
    </asp:TableRow>
    </asp:Table>
    </div>
    </form>
</body>
</html>
```

Let's add some additional tags not part of the ASP.Net rule book:

```html
<html xmlns="http://www.w3.org/1999/xhtml">
<head runat="server">
    <title>Products</title>
</head>
<body>
    <form id="form1" runat="server">
    <div>
    <asp:Table runat="server">
    <asp:TableHeaderRow>
    <asp:TableHeaderCell style="text-align:left;">A
message</asp:TableHeaderCell>
    </asp:TableHeaderRow>
    <asp:TableRow>
    <asp:TableCell><input style="text-align:left;" type="text"
value="Hello World"/></asp:TableCell>
    </asp:TableRow>
    </asp:Table>
    </div>
    </form>
</body>
</html>
```

And that comes out looking like this:

A message

Hello World

Which I guess is okay, but that won't win you any awards either. Right?
So, let's add some style.

```
<style type='text/css'>
th
{
   BORDER-RIGHT: #999999 2px solid;
   PADDING-RIGHT: 6px;
   PADDING-LEFT: 6px;
   FONT-WEIGHT: Bold;
   PADDING-BOTTOM: 6px;
   COLOR: #600000;
```

```css
    PADDING-TOP: 6px;
    BORDER-BOTTOM: #999 2px solid;
    BACKGROUND-COLOR: #eeeeee;
    FONT-FAMILY: Cambria, serif;
    FONT-SIZE: 16px;
    text-align: right;
    white-Space: nowrap;
}
td
{
    BORDER-RIGHT: #999999 3px solid;
    PADDING-RIGHT: 6px;
    PADDING-LEFT: 6px;
    FONT-WEIGHT: Normal;
    PADDING-BOTTOM: 6px;
    COLOR: navy;
    LINE-HEIGHT: 14px;
    PADDING-TOP: 6px;
    BORDER-BOTTOM: #999 1px solid;
    BACKGROUND-COLOR: #eeeeee;
    FONT-FAMILY: Cambria, serif;
    FONT-SIZE: 12px;
    text-align: left;
    white-Space: nowrap;
}
.div
{
    BORDER-RIGHT: #999999 3px solid;
    PADDING-RIGHT: 6px;
    PADDING-LEFT: 6px;
    FONT-WEIGHT: Normal;
    PADDING-BOTTOM: 6px;
    COLOR: white;
    PADDING-TOP: 6px;
    BORDER-BOTTOM: #999 1px solid;
    BACKGROUND-COLOR: navy;
    FONT-FAMILY: Cambria, serif;
    FONT-SIZE: 10px;
    text-align: left;
    white-Space: nowrap;
```

```css
}
.span
{
    BORDER-RIGHT: #999999 3px solid;
    PADDING-RIGHT: 3px;
    PADDING-LEFT: 3px;
    FONT-WEIGHT: Normal;
    PADDING-BOTTOM: 3px;
    COLOR: white;
    PADDING-TOP: 3px;
    BORDER-BOTTOM: #999 1px solid;
    BACKGROUND-COLOR: navy;
    FONT-FAMILY: Cambria, serif;
    FONT-SIZE: 10px;
    text-align: left;
    white-Space: nowrap;
    display: inline-block;
    width: 100%;
}
.textarea
{
    BORDER-RIGHT: #999999 3px solid;
    PADDING-RIGHT: 3px;
    PADDING-LEFT: 3px;
    FONT-WEIGHT: Normal;
    PADDING-BOTTOM: 3px;
    COLOR: white;
    PADDING-TOP: 3px;
    BORDER-BOTTOM: #999 1px solid;
    BACKGROUND-COLOR: navy;
    FONT-FAMILY: Cambria, serif;
    FONT-SIZE: 10px;
    text-align: left;
    white-Space: nowrap;
    width: 100%;
}
.select
{
    BORDER-RIGHT: #999999 3px solid;
    PADDING-RIGHT: 6px;
```

```css
    PADDING-LEFT: 6px;
    FONT-WEIGHT: Normal;
    PADDING-BOTTOM: 6px;
    COLOR: white;
    PADDING-TOP: 6px;
    BORDER-BOTTOM: #999 1px solid;
    BACKGROUND-COLOR: navy;
    FONT-FAMILY: Cambria, serif;
    FONT-SIZE: 10px;
    text-align: left;
    white-Space: nowrap;
    width: 100%;
}
input
{
    BORDER-RIGHT: #999999 1px solid;
    PADDING-RIGHT: 1px;
    PADDING-LEFT: 1px;
    FONT-WEIGHT: Normal;
    PADDING-BOTTOM: 1px;
    COLOR: White;
    PADDING-TOP: 1px;
    BORDER-BOTTOM: #999 1px solid;
    BACKGROUND-COLOR: #888800;
    FONT-FAMILY: Cambria, serif;
    FONT-SIZE: 12px;
    text-align: left;
    display: table-cell;
    white-Space: nowrap;
    width: auto;
}
</style>
```

Once added, the page gets run again:

Now, that is something I can live with. But the green looks too much like Army green. Perhaps, a different background color?

Okay, that looks better. The blue complements the red and white.

And now, a confession. Ever since I worked on a Content Management Program for the Games Group at Microsoft back in 2006, I have developed an interest for different and unique ways to display information through ASP and HTML. Only problem is, things like the VML and a lot of really cool design patterns we had back then to use and be creative with, well, they became obsolete.

Some of it is coming back in the form of CSS stylesheets and that helps. This is an example of that kind of view but in a newer browser:

ProductID	ProductName	SupplierID	CategoryID	QuantityPerUnit	UnitPrice	UnitsInStock	UnitsOnOrder	ReorderLevel	Discontinued
	Chai	1	1	10 boxes x 20 bags	18	39	0	10	False
	Chang	1	1	24 - 12 oz bottles	19	17	40	25	False
	Aniseed Syrup	1	2	12 - 550 ml bottles	10	13	70	25	False
	Chef Anton's Cajun Seasoning	2	2	48 - 6 oz jars	22	53	0	0	False
	Chef Anton's Gumbo Mix	2	2	36 boxes	21.35	0	0	0	True
	Grandma's Boysenberry	3	2	12 - 8 oz jars	25	120	0	25	False
	Uncle Bob's Organic Dried	3	7	12 - 1 lb pkgs	30	15	0	10	False
	Northwoods Cranberry S	3	2	12 - 12 oz jars	40	6	0	0	False
	Mishi Kobe Niku	4	6	18 - 500 g pkgs	97	29	0	0	True
10		4	8	12 - 200 ml jars	31	31	0	0	False

This is the same view in an older browser:

ProductID	ProductName	SupplierID	CategoryID	QuantityPerUnit	UnitPrice	UnitsInStock	UnitsOnOrder	ReorderLevel	Discontinued
1	Chai	1	1	10 boxes x 20 bags	18	39	0	10	False
2	Chang	1	1	24 - 12 oz bottles	19	17	40	25	False
3	Aniseed Syrup	1	2	12 - 550 ml bottles	10	13	70	25	False
4	Chef Anton's Cajun Seasoning	2	7	48 - 6 oz jars	22	53	0	0	False
5	Chef Anton's Gumbo Mix	2	2	36 boxes	21.35	0	0	0	True
6	Grandma's Boysenberry Spread	3	2	12 - 8 oz jars	25	120	0	25	False
7	Uncle Bob's Organic Dried Pears	3	7	12 - 1 lb pkgs	30	15	0	10	False
8	Northwoods Cranberry Sauce	3	2	12 - 12 oz jars	40	6	0	0	False

Time to move on to drive this page with data.

STATIC VERSES DYNAMIC RENDERING

Both get the same job done

When you want to use ASP tags this book stated with, they have to be scribed inside the ASPX Form before it gets run.

For anyone who has worked with these forms, that statement may seem obvious, trite and, indeed, laughable.

I have my reason for stating it. The asp code inside the form can be put into the form anytime. Even after production. A concept that is as important – at least to me – as creating web pages and adding them to a website every time a change needs to be made.

Take a look at the following code:

```
Public Class Form1

    Private Sub Form1_Load(ByVal sender As System.Object, ByVal e As System.EventArgs) Handles MyBase.Load

        Dim fso As Object = CreateObject("Scripting.FileSystemObject")
        Dim txtstream As Object = fso.OpenTextFile(Application.StartupPath & "\Products.aspx", 2, True, -2)
        txtstream.WriteLine("<html xmlns=""http://www.w3.org/1999/xhtml"">")
        txtstream.WriteLine("<head runat=""server"">")
        txtstream.WriteLine("   <title>Products</title>")
        txtstream.WriteLine("<style type='text/css'>")
        txtstream.WriteLine("body")
        txtstream.WriteLine("{")
        txtstream.WriteLine("   BORDER-TOP: navy 1px solid;")
        txtstream.WriteLine("   BORDER-LEFT: navy 1px solid;")
        txtstream.WriteLine("   BORDER-RIGHT: navy 1px solid;")
        txtstream.WriteLine("   BORDER-BOTTOM: navy 1px solid;")
        txtstream.WriteLine("   PADDING-RIGHT: 1px;")
        txtstream.WriteLine("   PADDING-LEFT: 1px;")
        txtstream.WriteLine("   FONT-WEIGHT: Normal;")
        txtstream.WriteLine("   PADDING-BOTTOM: 1px;")
        txtstream.WriteLine("   COLOR: black;")
        txtstream.WriteLine("   PADDING-TOP: 1px;")
```

```
txtstream.WriteLine("     BORDER-BOTTOM: #999 1px solid;")
txtstream.WriteLine("     BACKGROUND-COLOR: ButtonFace;")
txtstream.WriteLine("     FONT-FAMILY: Cambria, serif;")
txtstream.WriteLine("     FONT-SIZE: 12px;")
txtstream.WriteLine("     text-align: left;")
txtstream.WriteLine("     display: table-cell;")
txtstream.WriteLine("     white-Space: nowrap;")
txtstream.WriteLine("     width: auto;")
txtstream.WriteLine("     height: auto;")
txtstream.WriteLine("}")
txtstream.WriteLine("Table")
txtstream.WriteLine("{")
txtstream.WriteLine("     BORDER-TOP: navy 1px solid;")
txtstream.WriteLine("     BORDER-LEFT: navy 1px solid;")
txtstream.WriteLine("     BORDER-RIGHT: navy 1px solid;")
txtstream.WriteLine("     BORDER-BOTTOM: navy 1px solid;")
txtstream.WriteLine("     PADDING-RIGHT: 1px;")
txtstream.WriteLine("     PADDING-LEFT: 1px;")
txtstream.WriteLine("     FONT-WEIGHT: Normal;")
txtstream.WriteLine("     PADDING-BOTTOM: 1px;")
txtstream.WriteLine("     COLOR: black;")
txtstream.WriteLine("     PADDING-TOP: 1px;")
txtstream.WriteLine("     BORDER-BOTTOM: #999 1px solid;")
txtstream.WriteLine("     BACKGROUND-COLOR: ButtonFace;")
txtstream.WriteLine("     FONT-FAMILY: Cambria, serif;")
txtstream.WriteLine("     FONT-SIZE: 12px;")
txtstream.WriteLine("     text-align: left;")
txtstream.WriteLine("     display: table-cell;")
txtstream.WriteLine("     white-Space: nowrap;")
txtstream.WriteLine("     width: auto;")
txtstream.WriteLine("     height: auto;")
txtstream.WriteLine("}")
txtstream.WriteLine("th")
txtstream.WriteLine("{")
txtstream.WriteLine("     BORDER-RIGHT: #999999 2px solid;")
txtstream.WriteLine("     PADDING-RIGHT: 6px;")
txtstream.WriteLine("     PADDING-LEFT: 6px;")
txtstream.WriteLine("     FONT-WEIGHT: Bold;")
txtstream.WriteLine("     PADDING-BOTTOM: 6px;")
txtstream.WriteLine("     COLOR: #600000;")
txtstream.WriteLine("     PADDING-TOP: 6px;")
txtstream.WriteLine("     BORDER-BOTTOM: #999 2px solid;")
txtstream.WriteLine("     BACKGROUND-COLOR: #eeeeee;")
txtstream.WriteLine("     FONT-FAMILY: Cambria, serif;")
txtstream.WriteLine("     FONT-SIZE: 16px;")
txtstream.WriteLine("     text-align: right;")
txtstream.WriteLine("     white-Space: nowrap;")
txtstream.WriteLine("}")
txtstream.WriteLine("td")
txtstream.WriteLine("{")
txtstream.WriteLine("     BORDER-RIGHT: #999999 3px solid;")
txtstream.WriteLine("     PADDING-RIGHT: 6px;")
txtstream.WriteLine("     PADDING-LEFT: 6px;")
txtstream.WriteLine("     FONT-WEIGHT: Normal;")
txtstream.WriteLine("     PADDING-BOTTOM: 6px;")
txtstream.WriteLine("     COLOR: navy;")
txtstream.WriteLine("     LINE-HEIGHT: 14px;")
txtstream.WriteLine("     PADDING-TOP: 6px;")
txtstream.WriteLine("     BORDER-BOTTOM: #999 1px solid;")
txtstream.WriteLine("     BACKGROUND-COLOR: #eeeeee;")
txtstream.WriteLine("     FONT-FAMILY: Cambria, serif;")
txtstream.WriteLine("     FONT-SIZE: 12px;")
txtstream.WriteLine("     text-align: left;")
txtstream.WriteLine("     white-Space: nowrap;")
txtstream.WriteLine("}")
txtstream.WriteLine(".div")
```

```
txtstream.WriteLine("{")
txtstream.WriteLine("    BORDER-RIGHT: #999999 3px solid;")
txtstream.WriteLine("    PADDING-RIGHT: 6px;")
txtstream.WriteLine("    PADDING-LEFT: 6px;")
txtstream.WriteLine("    FONT-WEIGHT: Normal;")
txtstream.WriteLine("    PADDING-BOTTOM: 6px;")
txtstream.WriteLine("    COLOR: white;")
txtstream.WriteLine("    PADDING-TOP: 6px;")
txtstream.WriteLine("    BORDER-BOTTOM: #999 1px solid;")
txtstream.WriteLine("    BACKGROUND-COLOR: navy;")
txtstream.WriteLine("    FONT-FAMILY: Cambria, serif;")
txtstream.WriteLine("    FONT-SIZE: 10px;")
txtstream.WriteLine("    text-align: left;")
txtstream.WriteLine("    white-Space: nowrap;")
txtstream.WriteLine("}")
txtstream.WriteLine(".span")
txtstream.WriteLine("{")
txtstream.WriteLine("    BORDER-RIGHT: #999999 3px solid;")
txtstream.WriteLine("    PADDING-RIGHT: 3px;")
txtstream.WriteLine("    PADDING-LEFT: 3px;")
txtstream.WriteLine("    FONT-WEIGHT: Normal;")
txtstream.WriteLine("    PADDING-BOTTOM: 3px;")
txtstream.WriteLine("    COLOR: white;")
txtstream.WriteLine("    PADDING-TOP: 3px;")
txtstream.WriteLine("    BORDER-BOTTOM: #999 1px solid;")
txtstream.WriteLine("    BACKGROUND-COLOR: navy;")
txtstream.WriteLine("    FONT-FAMILY: Cambria, serif;")
txtstream.WriteLine("    FONT-SIZE: 10px;")
txtstream.WriteLine("    text-align: left;")
txtstream.WriteLine("    white-Space: nowrap;")
txtstream.WriteLine("    display: inline-block;")
txtstream.WriteLine("    width: 100%;")
txtstream.WriteLine("}")
txtstream.WriteLine(".textarea")
txtstream.WriteLine("{")
txtstream.WriteLine("    BORDER-RIGHT: #999999 3px solid;")
txtstream.WriteLine("    PADDING-RIGHT: 3px;")
txtstream.WriteLine("    PADDING-LEFT: 3px;")
txtstream.WriteLine("    FONT-WEIGHT: Normal;")
txtstream.WriteLine("    PADDING-BOTTOM: 3px;")
txtstream.WriteLine("    COLOR: white;")
txtstream.WriteLine("    PADDING-TOP: 3px;")
txtstream.WriteLine("    BORDER-BOTTOM: #999 1px solid;")
txtstream.WriteLine("    BACKGROUND-COLOR: navy;")
txtstream.WriteLine("    FONT-FAMILY: Cambria, serif;")
txtstream.WriteLine("    FONT-SIZE: 10px;")
txtstream.WriteLine("    text-align: left;")
txtstream.WriteLine("    white-Space: nowrap;")
txtstream.WriteLine("    width: 100%;")
txtstream.WriteLine("}")
txtstream.WriteLine(".Select")
txtstream.WriteLine("{")
txtstream.WriteLine("    BORDER-RIGHT: #999999 3px solid;")
txtstream.WriteLine("    PADDING-RIGHT: 6px;")
txtstream.WriteLine("    PADDING-LEFT: 6px;")
txtstream.WriteLine("    FONT-WEIGHT: Normal;")
txtstream.WriteLine("    PADDING-BOTTOM: 6px;")
txtstream.WriteLine("    COLOR: white;")
txtstream.WriteLine("    PADDING-TOP: 6px;")
txtstream.WriteLine("    BORDER-BOTTOM: #999 1px solid;")
txtstream.WriteLine("    BACKGROUND-COLOR: navy;")
txtstream.WriteLine("    FONT-FAMILY: Cambria, serif;")
txtstream.WriteLine("    FONT-SIZE: 10px;")
txtstream.WriteLine("    text-align: left;")
txtstream.WriteLine("    white-Space: nowrap;")
txtstream.WriteLine("    width: 100%;")
```

```vb
txtstream.WriteLine("}")
txtstream.WriteLine("input")
txtstream.WriteLine("{")
txtstream.WriteLine("    BORDER-RIGHT: #999999 1px solid;")
txtstream.WriteLine("    PADDING-RIGHT: 1px;")
txtstream.WriteLine("    PADDING-LEFT: 1px;")
txtstream.WriteLine("    FONT-WEIGHT: Normal;")
txtstream.WriteLine("    PADDING-BOTTOM: 1px;")
txtstream.WriteLine("    COLOR: White;")
txtstream.WriteLine("    PADDING-TOP: 1px;")
txtstream.WriteLine("    BORDER-BOTTOM: #999 1px solid;")
txtstream.WriteLine("    BACKGROUND-COLOR: navy;")
txtstream.WriteLine("    FONT-FAMILY: Cambria, serif;")
txtstream.WriteLine("    FONT-SIZE: 12px;")
txtstream.WriteLine("    text-align: left;")
txtstream.WriteLine("    display: table-cell;")
txtstream.WriteLine("    white-Space: nowrap;")
txtstream.WriteLine("    width: auto;")
txtstream.WriteLine("}")
txtstream.WriteLine("</style>")
txtstream.WriteLine("</head>")
txtstream.WriteLine("<body>")
txtstream.WriteLine("    <form id=""form1"" runat=""server"">")
txtstream.WriteLine("        <div>")
txtstream.WriteLine("            <asp:Table ID=""Table1"" runat=""Server"">")


Dim cnstr As String = "Provider=Microsoft.Jet.OLEDB.4.0;Data Source=C:\nwind.mdb;"
Dim strQuery As String = "Select * From Products"
Dim cn As System.Data.OleDb.OleDbConnection = New System.Data.OleDb.OleDbConnection()
cn.ConnectionString = cnstr
cn.Open()

Dim cmd As System.Data.OleDb.OleDbCommand = New System.Data.OleDb.OleDbCommand()
cmd.Connection = cn
cmd.CommandType = CommandType.Text
cmd.CommandText = strQuery
cmd.ExecuteNonQuery()

Dim da As System.Data.OleDb.OleDbDataAdapter = New System.Data.OleDb.OleDbDataAdapter(cmd)
Dim ds As System.Data.DataSet = New System.Data.DataSet()
da.Fill(ds)

txtstream.WriteLine("                <asp:TableHeaderRow>")
For x As Integer = 0 To ds.Tables(0).Columns.Count - 1
    txtstream.WriteLine("                    <asp:TableHeaderCell style=""text-align:left;"">" +
ds.Tables(0).Columns(x).Caption + "</asp:TableHeaderCell>")
    Next
txtstream.WriteLine("                </asp:TableHeaderRow>")
For y As Integer = 0 To ds.Tables(0).Rows.Count - 1
    txtstream.WriteLine("                <asp:TableRow>")
    For x As Integer = 0 To ds.Tables(0).Columns.Count - 1
        Try
            txtstream.WriteLine("                    <asp:TableCell style=""text-align:left;"">" +
ds.Tables(0).Rows(y).Item(ds.Tables(0).Columns(x).Caption).ToString() + "</asp:TableCell>")
        Catch ex As Exception
            txtstream.WriteLine("                    <asp:TableCell style=""text-align:left;""></asp:TableCell>")
        End Try

    Next
    txtstream.WriteLine("                </asp:TableRow>")
Next
txtstream.WriteLine("            </asp:Table>")
txtstream.WriteLine("        </div>")
txtstream.WriteLine("    </form>")
txtstream.WriteLine("</body>")
```

```
        txtstream.WriteLine("</html>")
        txtstream.Close()


    End Sub

End Class
```

And that produces this:

```
<html xmlns="http://www.w3.org/1999/xhtml">
<head id="Head1" runat="server">
<title>Products</title>
<style type='text/css'>
body
{
    BORDER-TOP: navy 1px solid;
    BORDER-LEFT: navy 1px solid;
    BORDER-RIGHT: navy 1px solid;
    BORDER-BOTTOM: navy 1px solid;
    PADDING-RIGHT: 1px;
    PADDING-LEFT: 1px;
    FONT-WEIGHT: Normal;
    PADDING-BOTTOM: 1px;
    COLOR: black;
    PADDING-TOP: 1px;
    BORDER-BOTTOM: #999 1px solid;
    BACKGROUND-COLOR: ButtonFace;
    FONT-FAMILY: Cambria, serif;
    FONT-SIZE: 12px;
    text-align: left;
    display: table-cell;
    white-Space: nowrap;
    width: auto;
    height: auto;
}
Table
{
    BORDER-TOP: navy 1px solid;
    BORDER-LEFT: navy 1px solid;
    BORDER-RIGHT: navy 1px solid;
    BORDER-BOTTOM: navy 1px solid;
    PADDING-RIGHT: 1px;
    PADDING-LEFT: 1px;
    FONT-WEIGHT: Normal;
    PADDING-BOTTOM: 1px;
    COLOR: black;
    PADDING-TOP: 1px;
    BORDER-BOTTOM: #999 1px solid;
    BACKGROUND-COLOR: ButtonFace;
    FONT-FAMILY: Cambria, serif;
    FONT-SIZE: 12px;
    text-align: left;
    display: table-cell;
    white-Space: nowrap;
    width: auto;
    height: auto;
}
th
{
    BORDER-RIGHT: #999999 2px solid;
    PADDING-RIGHT: 6px;
    PADDING-LEFT: 6px;
    FONT-WEIGHT: Bold;
    PADDING-BOTTOM: 6px;
```

```css
    COLOR: #600000;
    PADDING-TOP: 6px;
    BORDER-BOTTOM: #999 2px solid;
    BACKGROUND-COLOR: #eeeeee;
    FONT-FAMILY: Cambria, serif;
    FONT-SIZE: 16px;
    text-align: right;
    white-Space: nowrap;
}
td
{
    BORDER-RIGHT: #999999 3px solid;
    PADDING-RIGHT: 6px;
    PADDING-LEFT: 6px;
    FONT-WEIGHT: Normal;
    PADDING-BOTTOM: 6px;
    COLOR: navy;
    LINE-HEIGHT: 14px;
    PADDING-TOP: 6px;
    BORDER-BOTTOM: #999 1px solid;
    BACKGROUND-COLOR: #eeeeee;
    FONT-FAMILY: Cambria, serif;
    FONT-SIZE: 12px;
    text-align: left;
    white-Space: nowrap;
}
.div
{
    BORDER-RIGHT: #999999 3px solid;
    PADDING-RIGHT: 6px;
    PADDING-LEFT: 6px;
    FONT-WEIGHT: Normal;
    PADDING-BOTTOM: 6px;
    COLOR: white;
    PADDING-TOP: 6px;
    BORDER-BOTTOM: #999 1px solid;
    BACKGROUND-COLOR: navy;
    FONT-FAMILY: Cambria, serif;
    FONT-SIZE: 10px;
    text-align: left;
    white-Space: nowrap;
}
.span
{
    BORDER-RIGHT: #999999 3px solid;
    PADDING-RIGHT: 3px;
    PADDING-LEFT: 3px;
    FONT-WEIGHT: Normal;
    PADDING-BOTTOM: 3px;
    COLOR: white;
    PADDING-TOP: 3px;
    BORDER-BOTTOM: #999 1px solid;
    BACKGROUND-COLOR: navy;
    FONT-FAMILY: Cambria, serif;
    FONT-SIZE: 10px;
    text-align: left;
    white-Space: nowrap;
    display: inline-block;
    width: 100%;
}
.textarea
{
    BORDER-RIGHT: #999999 3px solid;
    PADDING-RIGHT: 3px;
    PADDING-LEFT: 3px;
    FONT-WEIGHT: Normal;
```

```
          PADDING-BOTTOM: 3px;
          COLOR: white;
          PADDING-TOP: 3px;
          BORDER-BOTTOM: #999 1px solid;
          BACKGROUND-COLOR: navy;
          FONT-FAMILY: Cambria, serif;
          FONT-SIZE: 10px;
          text-align: left;
          white-Space: nowrap;
          width: 100%;
}
.Select
{
          BORDER-RIGHT: #999999 3px solid;
          PADDING-RIGHT: 6px;
          PADDING-LEFT: 6px;
          FONT-WEIGHT: Normal;
          PADDING-BOTTOM: 6px;
          COLOR: white;
          PADDING-TOP: 6px;
          BORDER-BOTTOM: #999 1px solid;
          BACKGROUND-COLOR: navy;
          FONT-FAMILY: Cambria, serif;
          FONT-SIZE: 10px;
          text-align: left;
          white-Space: nowrap;
          width: 100%;
}
input
{
          BORDER-RIGHT: #999999 1px solid;
          PADDING-RIGHT: 1px;
          PADDING-LEFT: 1px;
          FONT-WEIGHT: Normal;
          PADDING-BOTTOM: 1px;
          COLOR: White;
          PADDING-TOP: 1px;
          BORDER-BOTTOM: #999 1px solid;
          BACKGROUND-COLOR: navy;
          FONT-FAMILY: Cambria, serif;
          FONT-SIZE: 12px;
          text-align: left;
          display: table-cell;
          white-Space: nowrap;
          width: auto;
}
</style>
</head>
<body>
    <form id="form1" runat="server">
        <div>
          <asp:Table ID="Table1" runat="Server">
             <asp:TableHeaderRow>
               <asp:TableHeaderCell style="text-align:left;">ProductID</asp:TableHeaderCell>
               <asp:TableHeaderCell style="text-align:left;">ProductName</asp:TableHeaderCell>
               <asp:TableHeaderCell style="text-align:left;">SupplierID</asp:TableHeaderCell>
               <asp:TableHeaderCell style="text-align:left;">CategoryID</asp:TableHeaderCell>
               <asp:TableHeaderCell style="text-align:left;">QuantityPerUnit</asp:TableHeaderCell>
               <asp:TableHeaderCell style="text-align:left;">UnitPrice</asp:TableHeaderCell>
               <asp:TableHeaderCell style="text-align:left;">UnitsInStock</asp:TableHeaderCell>
               <asp:TableHeaderCell style="text-align:left;">UnitsOnOrder</asp:TableHeaderCell>
               <asp:TableHeaderCell style="text-align:left;">ReorderLevel</asp:TableHeaderCell>
               <asp:TableHeaderCell style="text-align:left;">Discontinued</asp:TableHeaderCell>
             </asp:TableHeaderRow>
          <asp:TableRow>
             <asp:TableCell style="text-align:left;">1</asp:TableCell>
```

```
    <asp:TableCell style="text-align:left;">Chai</asp:TableCell>
    <asp:TableCell style="text-align:left;">1</asp:TableCell>
    <asp:TableCell style="text-align:left;">1</asp:TableCell>
    <asp:TableCell style="text-align:left;">10 boxes x 20 bags</asp:TableCell>
    <asp:TableCell style="text-align:left;">18</asp:TableCell>
    <asp:TableCell style="text-align:left;">39</asp:TableCell>
    <asp:TableCell style="text-align:left;">0</asp:TableCell>
    <asp:TableCell style="text-align:left;">10</asp:TableCell>
    <asp:TableCell style="text-align:left;">False</asp:TableCell>
</asp:TableRow>
<asp:TableRow>
    <asp:TableCell style="text-align:left;">2</asp:TableCell>
    <asp:TableCell style="text-align:left;">Chang</asp:TableCell>
    <asp:TableCell style="text-align:left;">1</asp:TableCell>
    <asp:TableCell style="text-align:left;">1</asp:TableCell>
    <asp:TableCell style="text-align:left;">24 - 12 oz bottles</asp:TableCell>
    <asp:TableCell style="text-align:left;">19</asp:TableCell>
    <asp:TableCell style="text-align:left;">17</asp:TableCell>
    <asp:TableCell style="text-align:left;">40</asp:TableCell>
    <asp:TableCell style="text-align:left;">25</asp:TableCell>
    <asp:TableCell style="text-align:left;">False</asp:TableCell>
</asp:TableRow>
<asp:TableRow>
    <asp:TableCell style="text-align:left;">3</asp:TableCell>
    <asp:TableCell style="text-align:left;">Aniseed Syrup</asp:TableCell>
    <asp:TableCell style="text-align:left;">1</asp:TableCell>
    <asp:TableCell style="text-align:left;">2</asp:TableCell>
    <asp:TableCell style="text-align:left;">12 - 550 ml bottles</asp:TableCell>
    <asp:TableCell style="text-align:left;">10</asp:TableCell>
    <asp:TableCell style="text-align:left;">13</asp:TableCell>
    <asp:TableCell style="text-align:left;">70</asp:TableCell>
    <asp:TableCell style="text-align:left;">25</asp:TableCell>
    <asp:TableCell style="text-align:left;">False</asp:TableCell>
</asp:TableRow>
<asp:TableRow>
    <asp:TableCell style="text-align:left;">4</asp:TableCell>
    <asp:TableCell style="text-align:left;">Chef Anton's Cajun Seasoning</asp:TableCell>
    <asp:TableCell style="text-align:left;">2</asp:TableCell>
    <asp:TableCell style="text-align:left;">2</asp:TableCell>
    <asp:TableCell style="text-align:left;">48 - 6 oz jars</asp:TableCell>
    <asp:TableCell style="text-align:left;">22</asp:TableCell>
    <asp:TableCell style="text-align:left;">53</asp:TableCell>
    <asp:TableCell style="text-align:left;">0</asp:TableCell>
    <asp:TableCell style="text-align:left;">0</asp:TableCell>
    <asp:TableCell style="text-align:left;">False</asp:TableCell>
</asp:TableRow>
<asp:TableRow>
    <asp:TableCell style="text-align:left;">5</asp:TableCell>
    <asp:TableCell style="text-align:left;">Chef Anton's Gumbo Mix</asp:TableCell>
    <asp:TableCell style="text-align:left;">2</asp:TableCell>
    <asp:TableCell style="text-align:left;">2</asp:TableCell>
    <asp:TableCell style="text-align:left;">36 boxes</asp:TableCell>
    <asp:TableCell style="text-align:left;">21.35</asp:TableCell>
    <asp:TableCell style="text-align:left;">0</asp:TableCell>
    <asp:TableCell style="text-align:left;">0</asp:TableCell>
    <asp:TableCell style="text-align:left;">0</asp:TableCell>
    <asp:TableCell style="text-align:left;">True</asp:TableCell>
</asp:TableRow>
<asp:TableRow>
    <asp:TableCell style="text-align:left;">6</asp:TableCell>
    <asp:TableCell style="text-align:left;">Grandma's Boysenberry Spread</asp:TableCell>
    <asp:TableCell style="text-align:left;">3</asp:TableCell>
    <asp:TableCell style="text-align:left;">2</asp:TableCell>
    <asp:TableCell style="text-align:left;">12 - 8 oz jars</asp:TableCell>
    <asp:TableCell style="text-align:left;">25</asp:TableCell>
    <asp:TableCell style="text-align:left;">120</asp:TableCell>
```

```
          <asp:TableCell style="text-align:left;">0</asp:TableCell>
          <asp:TableCell style="text-align:left;">25</asp:TableCell>
          <asp:TableCell style="text-align:left;">False</asp:TableCell>
      </asp:TableRow>
      <asp:TableRow>
          <asp:TableCell style="text-align:left;">7</asp:TableCell>
          <asp:TableCell style="text-align:left;">Uncle Bob's Organic Dried Pears</asp:TableCell>
          <asp:TableCell style="text-align:left;">3</asp:TableCell>
          <asp:TableCell style="text-align:left;">7</asp:TableCell>
          <asp:TableCell style="text-align:left;">12 - 1 lb pkgs.</asp:TableCell>
          <asp:TableCell style="text-align:left;">30</asp:TableCell>
          <asp:TableCell style="text-align:left;">15</asp:TableCell>
          <asp:TableCell style="text-align:left;">0</asp:TableCell>
          <asp:TableCell style="text-align:left;">10</asp:TableCell>
          <asp:TableCell style="text-align:left;">False</asp:TableCell>
      </asp:TableRow>
      <asp:TableRow>
          <asp:TableCell style="text-align:left;">8</asp:TableCell>
          <asp:TableCell style="text-align:left;">Northwoods Cranberry Sauce</asp:TableCell>
          <asp:TableCell style="text-align:left;">3</asp:TableCell>
          <asp:TableCell style="text-align:left;">2</asp:TableCell>
          <asp:TableCell style="text-align:left;">12 - 12 oz jars</asp:TableCell>
          <asp:TableCell style="text-align:left;">40</asp:TableCell>
          <asp:TableCell style="text-align:left;">6</asp:TableCell>
          <asp:TableCell style="text-align:left;">0</asp:TableCell>
          <asp:TableCell style="text-align:left;">0</asp:TableCell>
          <asp:TableCell style="text-align:left;">False</asp:TableCell>
      </asp:TableRow>
      <asp:TableRow>
          <asp:TableCell style="text-align:left;">9</asp:TableCell>
          <asp:TableCell style="text-align:left;">Mishi Kobe Niku</asp:TableCell>
          <asp:TableCell style="text-align:left;">4</asp:TableCell>
          <asp:TableCell style="text-align:left;">6</asp:TableCell>
          <asp:TableCell style="text-align:left;">18 - 500 g pkgs.</asp:TableCell>
          <asp:TableCell style="text-align:left;">97</asp:TableCell>
          <asp:TableCell style="text-align:left;">29</asp:TableCell>
          <asp:TableCell style="text-align:left;">0</asp:TableCell>
          <asp:TableCell style="text-align:left;">0</asp:TableCell>
          <asp:TableCell style="text-align:left;">True</asp:TableCell>
      </asp:TableRow>
      <asp:TableRow>
          <asp:TableCell style="text-align:left;">10</asp:TableCell>
          <asp:TableCell style="text-align:left;">Ikura</asp:TableCell>
          <asp:TableCell style="text-align:left;">4</asp:TableCell>
          <asp:TableCell style="text-align:left;">8</asp:TableCell>
          <asp:TableCell style="text-align:left;">12 - 200 ml jars</asp:TableCell>
          <asp:TableCell style="text-align:left;">31</asp:TableCell>
          <asp:TableCell style="text-align:left;">31</asp:TableCell>
          <asp:TableCell style="text-align:left;">0</asp:TableCell>
          <asp:TableCell style="text-align:left;">0</asp:TableCell>
          <asp:TableCell style="text-align:left;">False</asp:TableCell>
      </asp:TableRow>
      <asp:TableRow>
          <asp:TableCell style="text-align:left;">11</asp:TableCell>
          <asp:TableCell style="text-align:left;">Queso Cabrales</asp:TableCell>
          <asp:TableCell style="text-align:left;">5</asp:TableCell>
          <asp:TableCell style="text-align:left;">4</asp:TableCell>
          <asp:TableCell style="text-align:left;">1 kg pkg.</asp:TableCell>
          <asp:TableCell style="text-align:left;">21</asp:TableCell>
          <asp:TableCell style="text-align:left;">22</asp:TableCell>
          <asp:TableCell style="text-align:left;">30</asp:TableCell>
          <asp:TableCell style="text-align:left;">30</asp:TableCell>
          <asp:TableCell style="text-align:left;">False</asp:TableCell>
      </asp:TableRow>
      <asp:TableRow>
          <asp:TableCell style="text-align:left;">12</asp:TableCell>
```

```
          <asp:TableCell style="text-align:left;">Queso Manchego La Pastora</asp:TableCell>
          <asp:TableCell style="text-align:left;">5</asp:TableCell>
          <asp:TableCell style="text-align:left;">4</asp:TableCell>
          <asp:TableCell style="text-align:left;">10 - 500 g pkgs.</asp:TableCell>
          <asp:TableCell style="text-align:left;">38</asp:TableCell>
          <asp:TableCell style="text-align:left;">86</asp:TableCell>
          <asp:TableCell style="text-align:left;">0</asp:TableCell>
          <asp:TableCell style="text-align:left;">0</asp:TableCell>
          <asp:TableCell style="text-align:left;">False</asp:TableCell>
      </asp:TableRow>
      <asp:TableRow>
          <asp:TableCell style="text-align:left;">13</asp:TableCell>
          <asp:TableCell style="text-align:left;">Konbu</asp:TableCell>
          <asp:TableCell style="text-align:left;">6</asp:TableCell>
          <asp:TableCell style="text-align:left;">8</asp:TableCell>
          <asp:TableCell style="text-align:left;">2 kg box</asp:TableCell>
          <asp:TableCell style="text-align:left;">6</asp:TableCell>
          <asp:TableCell style="text-align:left;">24</asp:TableCell>
          <asp:TableCell style="text-align:left;">0</asp:TableCell>
          <asp:TableCell style="text-align:left;">5</asp:TableCell>
          <asp:TableCell style="text-align:left;">False</asp:TableCell>
      </asp:TableRow>
      <asp:TableRow>
          <asp:TableCell style="text-align:left;">14</asp:TableCell>
          <asp:TableCell style="text-align:left;">Tofu</asp:TableCell>
          <asp:TableCell style="text-align:left;">6</asp:TableCell>
          <asp:TableCell style="text-align:left;">7</asp:TableCell>
          <asp:TableCell style="text-align:left;">40 - 100 g pkgs.</asp:TableCell>
          <asp:TableCell style="text-align:left;">23.25</asp:TableCell>
          <asp:TableCell style="text-align:left;">35</asp:TableCell>
          <asp:TableCell style="text-align:left;">0</asp:TableCell>
          <asp:TableCell style="text-align:left;">0</asp:TableCell>
          <asp:TableCell style="text-align:left;">False</asp:TableCell>
      </asp:TableRow>
      <asp:TableRow>
          <asp:TableCell style="text-align:left;">15</asp:TableCell>
          <asp:TableCell style="text-align:left;">Genen Shouyu</asp:TableCell>
          <asp:TableCell style="text-align:left;">6</asp:TableCell>
          <asp:TableCell style="text-align:left;">2</asp:TableCell>
          <asp:TableCell style="text-align:left;">24 - 250 ml bottles</asp:TableCell>
          <asp:TableCell style="text-align:left;">15.5</asp:TableCell>
          <asp:TableCell style="text-align:left;">39</asp:TableCell>
          <asp:TableCell style="text-align:left;">0</asp:TableCell>
          <asp:TableCell style="text-align:left;">5</asp:TableCell>
          <asp:TableCell style="text-align:left;">False</asp:TableCell>
      </asp:TableRow>
      <asp:TableRow>
          <asp:TableCell style="text-align:left;">16</asp:TableCell>
          <asp:TableCell style="text-align:left;">Pavlova</asp:TableCell>
          <asp:TableCell style="text-align:left;">7</asp:TableCell>
          <asp:TableCell style="text-align:left;">3</asp:TableCell>
          <asp:TableCell style="text-align:left;">32 - 500 g boxes</asp:TableCell>
          <asp:TableCell style="text-align:left;">17.45</asp:TableCell>
          <asp:TableCell style="text-align:left;">29</asp:TableCell>
          <asp:TableCell style="text-align:left;">0</asp:TableCell>
          <asp:TableCell style="text-align:left;">10</asp:TableCell>
          <asp:TableCell style="text-align:left;">False</asp:TableCell>
      </asp:TableRow>
      <asp:TableRow>
          <asp:TableCell style="text-align:left;">17</asp:TableCell>
          <asp:TableCell style="text-align:left;">Alice Mutton</asp:TableCell>
          <asp:TableCell style="text-align:left;">7</asp:TableCell>
          <asp:TableCell style="text-align:left;">6</asp:TableCell>
          <asp:TableCell style="text-align:left;">20 - 1 kg tins</asp:TableCell>
          <asp:TableCell style="text-align:left;">39</asp:TableCell>
          <asp:TableCell style="text-align:left;">0</asp:TableCell>
```

```
    <asp:TableCell style="text-align:left;">0</asp:TableCell>
    <asp:TableCell style="text-align:left;">0</asp:TableCell>
    <asp:TableCell style="text-align:left;">True</asp:TableCell>
 </asp:TableRow>
 <asp:TableRow>
    <asp:TableCell style="text-align:left;">18</asp:TableCell>
    <asp:TableCell style="text-align:left;">Carnarvon Tigers</asp:TableCell>
    <asp:TableCell style="text-align:left;">7</asp:TableCell>
    <asp:TableCell style="text-align:left;">8</asp:TableCell>
    <asp:TableCell style="text-align:left;">16 kg pkg.</asp:TableCell>
    <asp:TableCell style="text-align:left;">62.5</asp:TableCell>
    <asp:TableCell style="text-align:left;">42</asp:TableCell>
    <asp:TableCell style="text-align:left;">0</asp:TableCell>
    <asp:TableCell style="text-align:left;">0</asp:TableCell>
    <asp:TableCell style="text-align:left;">False</asp:TableCell>
 </asp:TableRow>
 <asp:TableRow>
    <asp:TableCell style="text-align:left;">19</asp:TableCell>
    <asp:TableCell style="text-align:left;">Teatime Chocolate Biscuits</asp:TableCell>
    <asp:TableCell style="text-align:left;">8</asp:TableCell>
    <asp:TableCell style="text-align:left;">3</asp:TableCell>
    <asp:TableCell style="text-align:left;">10 boxes x 12 pieces</asp:TableCell>
    <asp:TableCell style="text-align:left;">9.2</asp:TableCell>
    <asp:TableCell style="text-align:left;">25</asp:TableCell>
    <asp:TableCell style="text-align:left;">0</asp:TableCell>
    <asp:TableCell style="text-align:left;">5</asp:TableCell>
    <asp:TableCell style="text-align:left;">False</asp:TableCell>
 </asp:TableRow>
 <asp:TableRow>
    <asp:TableCell style="text-align:left;">20</asp:TableCell>
    <asp:TableCell style="text-align:left;">Sir Rodney's Marmalade</asp:TableCell>
    <asp:TableCell style="text-align:left;">8</asp:TableCell>
    <asp:TableCell style="text-align:left;">3</asp:TableCell>
    <asp:TableCell style="text-align:left;">30 gift boxes</asp:TableCell>
    <asp:TableCell style="text-align:left;">81</asp:TableCell>
    <asp:TableCell style="text-align:left;">40</asp:TableCell>
    <asp:TableCell style="text-align:left;">0</asp:TableCell>
    <asp:TableCell style="text-align:left;">0</asp:TableCell>
    <asp:TableCell style="text-align:left;">False</asp:TableCell>
 </asp:TableRow>
 <asp:TableRow>
    <asp:TableCell style="text-align:left;">21</asp:TableCell>
    <asp:TableCell style="text-align:left;">Sir Rodney's Scones</asp:TableCell>
    <asp:TableCell style="text-align:left;">8</asp:TableCell>
    <asp:TableCell style="text-align:left;">3</asp:TableCell>
    <asp:TableCell style="text-align:left;">24 pkgs. x 4 pieces</asp:TableCell>
    <asp:TableCell style="text-align:left;">10</asp:TableCell>
    <asp:TableCell style="text-align:left;">3</asp:TableCell>
    <asp:TableCell style="text-align:left;">40</asp:TableCell>
    <asp:TableCell style="text-align:left;">5</asp:TableCell>
    <asp:TableCell style="text-align:left;">False</asp:TableCell>
 </asp:TableRow>
 <asp:TableRow>
    <asp:TableCell style="text-align:left;">22</asp:TableCell>
    <asp:TableCell style="text-align:left;">Gustaf's Knäckebröd</asp:TableCell>
    <asp:TableCell style="text-align:left;">9</asp:TableCell>
    <asp:TableCell style="text-align:left;">5</asp:TableCell>
    <asp:TableCell style="text-align:left;">24 - 500 g pkgs.</asp:TableCell>
    <asp:TableCell style="text-align:left;">21</asp:TableCell>
    <asp:TableCell style="text-align:left;">104</asp:TableCell>
    <asp:TableCell style="text-align:left;">0</asp:TableCell>
    <asp:TableCell style="text-align:left;">25</asp:TableCell>
    <asp:TableCell style="text-align:left;">False</asp:TableCell>
 </asp:TableRow>
 <asp:TableRow>
    <asp:TableCell style="text-align:left;">23</asp:TableCell>
```

```
<asp:TableCell style="text-align:left;">Tunnbröd</asp:TableCell>
<asp:TableCell style="text-align:left;">9</asp:TableCell>
<asp:TableCell style="text-align:left;">5</asp:TableCell>
<asp:TableCell style="text-align:left;">12 - 250 g pkgs.</asp:TableCell>
<asp:TableCell style="text-align:left;">9</asp:TableCell>
<asp:TableCell style="text-align:left;">61</asp:TableCell>
<asp:TableCell style="text-align:left;">0</asp:TableCell>
<asp:TableCell style="text-align:left;">25</asp:TableCell>
<asp:TableCell style="text-align:left;">False</asp:TableCell>
</asp:TableRow>
<asp:TableRow>
<asp:TableCell style="text-align:left;">24</asp:TableCell>
<asp:TableCell style="text-align:left;">Guaraná Fantástica</asp:TableCell>
<asp:TableCell style="text-align:left;">10</asp:TableCell>
<asp:TableCell style="text-align:left;">1</asp:TableCell>
<asp:TableCell style="text-align:left;">12 - 355 ml cans</asp:TableCell>
<asp:TableCell style="text-align:left;">4.5</asp:TableCell>
<asp:TableCell style="text-align:left;">20</asp:TableCell>
<asp:TableCell style="text-align:left;">0</asp:TableCell>
<asp:TableCell style="text-align:left;">0</asp:TableCell>
<asp:TableCell style="text-align:left;">True</asp:TableCell>
</asp:TableRow>
<asp:TableRow>
<asp:TableCell style="text-align:left;">25</asp:TableCell>
<asp:TableCell style="text-align:left;">NuNuCa Nuß-Nougat-Creme</asp:TableCell>
<asp:TableCell style="text-align:left;">11</asp:TableCell>
<asp:TableCell style="text-align:left;">3</asp:TableCell>
<asp:TableCell style="text-align:left;">20 - 450 g glasses</asp:TableCell>
<asp:TableCell style="text-align:left;">14</asp:TableCell>
<asp:TableCell style="text-align:left;">76</asp:TableCell>
<asp:TableCell style="text-align:left;">0</asp:TableCell>
<asp:TableCell style="text-align:left;">30</asp:TableCell>
<asp:TableCell style="text-align:left;">False</asp:TableCell>
</asp:TableRow>
<asp:TableRow>
<asp:TableCell style="text-align:left;">26</asp:TableCell>
<asp:TableCell style="text-align:left;">Gumbär Gummibärchen</asp:TableCell>
<asp:TableCell style="text-align:left;">11</asp:TableCell>
<asp:TableCell style="text-align:left;">3</asp:TableCell>
<asp:TableCell style="text-align:left;">100 - 250 g bags</asp:TableCell>
<asp:TableCell style="text-align:left;">31.23</asp:TableCell>
<asp:TableCell style="text-align:left;">15</asp:TableCell>
<asp:TableCell style="text-align:left;">0</asp:TableCell>
<asp:TableCell style="text-align:left;">0</asp:TableCell>
<asp:TableCell style="text-align:left;">False</asp:TableCell>
</asp:TableRow>
<asp:TableRow>
<asp:TableCell style="text-align:left;">27</asp:TableCell>
<asp:TableCell style="text-align:left;">Schoggi Schokolade</asp:TableCell>
<asp:TableCell style="text-align:left;">11</asp:TableCell>
<asp:TableCell style="text-align:left;">3</asp:TableCell>
<asp:TableCell style="text-align:left;">100 - 100 g pieces</asp:TableCell>
<asp:TableCell style="text-align:left;">43.9</asp:TableCell>
<asp:TableCell style="text-align:left;">49</asp:TableCell>
<asp:TableCell style="text-align:left;">0</asp:TableCell>
<asp:TableCell style="text-align:left;">30</asp:TableCell>
<asp:TableCell style="text-align:left;">False</asp:TableCell>
</asp:TableRow>
<asp:TableRow>
<asp:TableCell style="text-align:left;">28</asp:TableCell>
<asp:TableCell style="text-align:left;">Rössle Sauerkraut</asp:TableCell>
<asp:TableCell style="text-align:left;">12</asp:TableCell>
<asp:TableCell style="text-align:left;">7</asp:TableCell>
<asp:TableCell style="text-align:left;">25 - 825 g cans</asp:TableCell>
<asp:TableCell style="text-align:left;">45.6</asp:TableCell>
<asp:TableCell style="text-align:left;">26</asp:TableCell>
```

```
    <asp:TableCell style="text-align:left;">0</asp:TableCell>
    <asp:TableCell style="text-align:left;">0</asp:TableCell>
    <asp:TableCell style="text-align:left;">True</asp:TableCell>
  </asp:TableRow>
  <asp:TableRow>
    <asp:TableCell style="text-align:left;">29</asp:TableCell>
    <asp:TableCell style="text-align:left;">Thüringer Rostbratwurst</asp:TableCell>
    <asp:TableCell style="text-align:left;">12</asp:TableCell>
    <asp:TableCell style="text-align:left;">6</asp:TableCell>
    <asp:TableCell style="text-align:left;">50 bags x 30 sausgs.</asp:TableCell>
    <asp:TableCell style="text-align:left;">123.79</asp:TableCell>
    <asp:TableCell style="text-align:left;">0</asp:TableCell>
    <asp:TableCell style="text-align:left;">0</asp:TableCell>
    <asp:TableCell style="text-align:left;">0</asp:TableCell>
    <asp:TableCell style="text-align:left;">True</asp:TableCell>
  </asp:TableRow>
  <asp:TableRow>
    <asp:TableCell style="text-align:left;">30</asp:TableCell>
    <asp:TableCell style="text-align:left;">Nord-Ost Matjeshering</asp:TableCell>
    <asp:TableCell style="text-align:left;">13</asp:TableCell>
    <asp:TableCell style="text-align:left;">8</asp:TableCell>
    <asp:TableCell style="text-align:left;">10 - 200 g glasses</asp:TableCell>
    <asp:TableCell style="text-align:left;">25.89</asp:TableCell>
    <asp:TableCell style="text-align:left;">10</asp:TableCell>
    <asp:TableCell style="text-align:left;">0</asp:TableCell>
    <asp:TableCell style="text-align:left;">15</asp:TableCell>
    <asp:TableCell style="text-align:left;">False</asp:TableCell>
  </asp:TableRow>
  <asp:TableRow>
    <asp:TableCell style="text-align:left;">31</asp:TableCell>
    <asp:TableCell style="text-align:left;">Gorgonzola Telino</asp:TableCell>
    <asp:TableCell style="text-align:left;">14</asp:TableCell>
    <asp:TableCell style="text-align:left;">4</asp:TableCell>
    <asp:TableCell style="text-align:left;">12 - 100 g pkgs</asp:TableCell>
    <asp:TableCell style="text-align:left;">12.5</asp:TableCell>
    <asp:TableCell style="text-align:left;">0</asp:TableCell>
    <asp:TableCell style="text-align:left;">70</asp:TableCell>
    <asp:TableCell style="text-align:left;">20</asp:TableCell>
    <asp:TableCell style="text-align:left;">False</asp:TableCell>
  </asp:TableRow>
  <asp:TableRow>
    <asp:TableCell style="text-align:left;">32</asp:TableCell>
    <asp:TableCell style="text-align:left;">Mascarpone Fabioli</asp:TableCell>
    <asp:TableCell style="text-align:left;">14</asp:TableCell>
    <asp:TableCell style="text-align:left;">4</asp:TableCell>
    <asp:TableCell style="text-align:left;">24 - 200 g pkgs.</asp:TableCell>
    <asp:TableCell style="text-align:left;">32</asp:TableCell>
    <asp:TableCell style="text-align:left;">9</asp:TableCell>
    <asp:TableCell style="text-align:left;">40</asp:TableCell>
    <asp:TableCell style="text-align:left;">25</asp:TableCell>
    <asp:TableCell style="text-align:left;">False</asp:TableCell>
  </asp:TableRow>
  <asp:TableRow>
    <asp:TableCell style="text-align:left;">33</asp:TableCell>
    <asp:TableCell style="text-align:left;">Geitost</asp:TableCell>
    <asp:TableCell style="text-align:left;">15</asp:TableCell>
    <asp:TableCell style="text-align:left;">4</asp:TableCell>
    <asp:TableCell style="text-align:left;">500 g</asp:TableCell>
    <asp:TableCell style="text-align:left;">2.5</asp:TableCell>
    <asp:TableCell style="text-align:left;">112</asp:TableCell>
    <asp:TableCell style="text-align:left;">0</asp:TableCell>
    <asp:TableCell style="text-align:left;">20</asp:TableCell>
    <asp:TableCell style="text-align:left;">False</asp:TableCell>
  </asp:TableRow>
  <asp:TableRow>
    <asp:TableCell style="text-align:left;">34</asp:TableCell>
```

```
    <asp:TableCell style="text-align:left;">Sasquatch Ale</asp:TableCell>
    <asp:TableCell style="text-align:left;">16</asp:TableCell>
    <asp:TableCell style="text-align:left;">1</asp:TableCell>
    <asp:TableCell style="text-align:left;">24 - 12 oz bottles</asp:TableCell>
    <asp:TableCell style="text-align:left;">14</asp:TableCell>
    <asp:TableCell style="text-align:left;">111</asp:TableCell>
    <asp:TableCell style="text-align:left;">0</asp:TableCell>
    <asp:TableCell style="text-align:left;">15</asp:TableCell>
    <asp:TableCell style="text-align:left;">False</asp:TableCell>
</asp:TableRow>
<asp:TableRow>
    <asp:TableCell style="text-align:left;">35</asp:TableCell>
    <asp:TableCell style="text-align:left;">Steeleye Stout</asp:TableCell>
    <asp:TableCell style="text-align:left;">16</asp:TableCell>
    <asp:TableCell style="text-align:left;">1</asp:TableCell>
    <asp:TableCell style="text-align:left;">24 - 12 oz bottles</asp:TableCell>
    <asp:TableCell style="text-align:left;">18</asp:TableCell>
    <asp:TableCell style="text-align:left;">20</asp:TableCell>
    <asp:TableCell style="text-align:left;">0</asp:TableCell>
    <asp:TableCell style="text-align:left;">15</asp:TableCell>
    <asp:TableCell style="text-align:left;">False</asp:TableCell>
</asp:TableRow>
<asp:TableRow>
    <asp:TableCell style="text-align:left;">36</asp:TableCell>
    <asp:TableCell style="text-align:left;">Inlagd Sill</asp:TableCell>
    <asp:TableCell style="text-align:left;">17</asp:TableCell>
    <asp:TableCell style="text-align:left;">8</asp:TableCell>
    <asp:TableCell style="text-align:left;">24 - 250 g  jars</asp:TableCell>
    <asp:TableCell style="text-align:left;">19</asp:TableCell>
    <asp:TableCell style="text-align:left;">112</asp:TableCell>
    <asp:TableCell style="text-align:left;">0</asp:TableCell>
    <asp:TableCell style="text-align:left;">20</asp:TableCell>
    <asp:TableCell style="text-align:left;">False</asp:TableCell>
</asp:TableRow>
<asp:TableRow>
    <asp:TableCell style="text-align:left;">37</asp:TableCell>
    <asp:TableCell style="text-align:left;">Gravad lax</asp:TableCell>
    <asp:TableCell style="text-align:left;">17</asp:TableCell>
    <asp:TableCell style="text-align:left;">8</asp:TableCell>
    <asp:TableCell style="text-align:left;">12 - 500 g pkgs.</asp:TableCell>
    <asp:TableCell style="text-align:left;">26</asp:TableCell>
    <asp:TableCell style="text-align:left;">11</asp:TableCell>
    <asp:TableCell style="text-align:left;">50</asp:TableCell>
    <asp:TableCell style="text-align:left;">25</asp:TableCell>
    <asp:TableCell style="text-align:left;">False</asp:TableCell>
</asp:TableRow>
<asp:TableRow>
    <asp:TableCell style="text-align:left;">38</asp:TableCell>
    <asp:TableCell style="text-align:left;">Côte de Blaye</asp:TableCell>
    <asp:TableCell style="text-align:left;">18</asp:TableCell>
    <asp:TableCell style="text-align:left;">1</asp:TableCell>
    <asp:TableCell style="text-align:left;">12 - 75 cl bottles</asp:TableCell>
    <asp:TableCell style="text-align:left;">263.5</asp:TableCell>
    <asp:TableCell style="text-align:left;">17</asp:TableCell>
    <asp:TableCell style="text-align:left;">0</asp:TableCell>
    <asp:TableCell style="text-align:left;">15</asp:TableCell>
    <asp:TableCell style="text-align:left;">False</asp:TableCell>
</asp:TableRow>
<asp:TableRow>
    <asp:TableCell style="text-align:left;">39</asp:TableCell>
    <asp:TableCell style="text-align:left;">Chartreuse verte</asp:TableCell>
    <asp:TableCell style="text-align:left;">18</asp:TableCell>
    <asp:TableCell style="text-align:left;">1</asp:TableCell>
    <asp:TableCell style="text-align:left;">750 cc per bottle</asp:TableCell>
    <asp:TableCell style="text-align:left;">18</asp:TableCell>
    <asp:TableCell style="text-align:left;">69</asp:TableCell>
```

```
      <asp:TableCell style="text-align:left;">0</asp:TableCell>
      <asp:TableCell style="text-align:left;">5</asp:TableCell>
      <asp:TableCell style="text-align:left;">False</asp:TableCell>
    </asp:TableRow>
    <asp:TableRow>
      <asp:TableCell style="text-align:left;">40</asp:TableCell>
      <asp:TableCell style="text-align:left;">Boston Crab Meat</asp:TableCell>
      <asp:TableCell style="text-align:left;">19</asp:TableCell>
      <asp:TableCell style="text-align:left;">8</asp:TableCell>
      <asp:TableCell style="text-align:left;">24 - 4 oz tins</asp:TableCell>
      <asp:TableCell style="text-align:left;">18.4</asp:TableCell>
      <asp:TableCell style="text-align:left;">123</asp:TableCell>
      <asp:TableCell style="text-align:left;">0</asp:TableCell>
      <asp:TableCell style="text-align:left;">30</asp:TableCell>
      <asp:TableCell style="text-align:left;">False</asp:TableCell>
    </asp:TableRow>
    <asp:TableRow>
      <asp:TableCell style="text-align:left;">41</asp:TableCell>
      <asp:TableCell style="text-align:left;">Jack's New England Clam Chowder</asp:TableCell>
      <asp:TableCell style="text-align:left;">19</asp:TableCell>
      <asp:TableCell style="text-align:left;">8</asp:TableCell>
      <asp:TableCell style="text-align:left;">12 - 12 oz cans</asp:TableCell>
      <asp:TableCell style="text-align:left;">9.65</asp:TableCell>
      <asp:TableCell style="text-align:left;">85</asp:TableCell>
      <asp:TableCell style="text-align:left;">0</asp:TableCell>
      <asp:TableCell style="text-align:left;">10</asp:TableCell>
      <asp:TableCell style="text-align:left;">False</asp:TableCell>
    </asp:TableRow>
    <asp:TableRow>
      <asp:TableCell style="text-align:left;">42</asp:TableCell>
      <asp:TableCell style="text-align:left;">Singaporean Hokkien Fried Mee</asp:TableCell>
      <asp:TableCell style="text-align:left;">20</asp:TableCell>
      <asp:TableCell style="text-align:left;">5</asp:TableCell>
      <asp:TableCell style="text-align:left;">32 - 1 kg pkgs.</asp:TableCell>
      <asp:TableCell style="text-align:left;">14</asp:TableCell>
      <asp:TableCell style="text-align:left;">26</asp:TableCell>
      <asp:TableCell style="text-align:left;">0</asp:TableCell>
      <asp:TableCell style="text-align:left;">0</asp:TableCell>
      <asp:TableCell style="text-align:left;">True</asp:TableCell>
    </asp:TableRow>
    <asp:TableRow>
      <asp:TableCell style="text-align:left;">43</asp:TableCell>
      <asp:TableCell style="text-align:left;">Ipoh Coffee</asp:TableCell>
      <asp:TableCell style="text-align:left;">20</asp:TableCell>
      <asp:TableCell style="text-align:left;">1</asp:TableCell>
      <asp:TableCell style="text-align:left;">16 - 500 g tins</asp:TableCell>
      <asp:TableCell style="text-align:left;">46</asp:TableCell>
      <asp:TableCell style="text-align:left;">17</asp:TableCell>
      <asp:TableCell style="text-align:left;">10</asp:TableCell>
      <asp:TableCell style="text-align:left;">25</asp:TableCell>
      <asp:TableCell style="text-align:left;">False</asp:TableCell>
    </asp:TableRow>
    <asp:TableRow>
      <asp:TableCell style="text-align:left;">44</asp:TableCell>
      <asp:TableCell style="text-align:left;">Gula Malacca</asp:TableCell>
      <asp:TableCell style="text-align:left;">20</asp:TableCell>
      <asp:TableCell style="text-align:left;">2</asp:TableCell>
      <asp:TableCell style="text-align:left;">20 - 2 kg bags</asp:TableCell>
      <asp:TableCell style="text-align:left;">19.45</asp:TableCell>
      <asp:TableCell style="text-align:left;">27</asp:TableCell>
      <asp:TableCell style="text-align:left;">0</asp:TableCell>
      <asp:TableCell style="text-align:left;">15</asp:TableCell>
      <asp:TableCell style="text-align:left;">False</asp:TableCell>
    </asp:TableRow>
    <asp:TableRow>
      <asp:TableCell style="text-align:left;">45</asp:TableCell>
```

```
        <asp:TableCell style="text-align:left;">Røgede sild</asp:TableCell>
        <asp:TableCell style="text-align:left;">21</asp:TableCell>
        <asp:TableCell style="text-align:left;">8</asp:TableCell>
        <asp:TableCell style="text-align:left;">1k pkg.</asp:TableCell>
        <asp:TableCell style="text-align:left;">9.5</asp:TableCell>
        <asp:TableCell style="text-align:left;">5</asp:TableCell>
        <asp:TableCell style="text-align:left;">70</asp:TableCell>
        <asp:TableCell style="text-align:left;">15</asp:TableCell>
        <asp:TableCell style="text-align:left;">False</asp:TableCell>
    </asp:TableRow>
    <asp:TableRow>
        <asp:TableCell style="text-align:left;">46</asp:TableCell>
        <asp:TableCell style="text-align:left;">Spegesild</asp:TableCell>
        <asp:TableCell style="text-align:left;">21</asp:TableCell>
        <asp:TableCell style="text-align:left;">8</asp:TableCell>
        <asp:TableCell style="text-align:left;">4 - 450 g glasses</asp:TableCell>
        <asp:TableCell style="text-align:left;">12</asp:TableCell>
        <asp:TableCell style="text-align:left;">95</asp:TableCell>
        <asp:TableCell style="text-align:left;">0</asp:TableCell>
        <asp:TableCell style="text-align:left;">0</asp:TableCell>
        <asp:TableCell style="text-align:left;">False</asp:TableCell>
    </asp:TableRow>
    <asp:TableRow>
        <asp:TableCell style="text-align:left;">47</asp:TableCell>
        <asp:TableCell style="text-align:left;">Zaanse koeken</asp:TableCell>
        <asp:TableCell style="text-align:left;">22</asp:TableCell>
        <asp:TableCell style="text-align:left;">3</asp:TableCell>
        <asp:TableCell style="text-align:left;">10 - 4 oz boxes</asp:TableCell>
        <asp:TableCell style="text-align:left;">9.5</asp:TableCell>
        <asp:TableCell style="text-align:left;">36</asp:TableCell>
        <asp:TableCell style="text-align:left;">0</asp:TableCell>
        <asp:TableCell style="text-align:left;">0</asp:TableCell>
        <asp:TableCell style="text-align:left;">False</asp:TableCell>
    </asp:TableRow>
    <asp:TableRow>
        <asp:TableCell style="text-align:left;">48</asp:TableCell>
        <asp:TableCell style="text-align:left;">Chocolade</asp:TableCell>
        <asp:TableCell style="text-align:left;">22</asp:TableCell>
        <asp:TableCell style="text-align:left;">3</asp:TableCell>
        <asp:TableCell style="text-align:left;">10 pkgs.</asp:TableCell>
        <asp:TableCell style="text-align:left;">12.75</asp:TableCell>
        <asp:TableCell style="text-align:left;">15</asp:TableCell>
        <asp:TableCell style="text-align:left;">70</asp:TableCell>
        <asp:TableCell style="text-align:left;">25</asp:TableCell>
        <asp:TableCell style="text-align:left;">False</asp:TableCell>
    </asp:TableRow>
    <asp:TableRow>
        <asp:TableCell style="text-align:left;">49</asp:TableCell>
        <asp:TableCell style="text-align:left;">Maxilaku</asp:TableCell>
        <asp:TableCell style="text-align:left;">23</asp:TableCell>
        <asp:TableCell style="text-align:left;">3</asp:TableCell>
        <asp:TableCell style="text-align:left;">24 - 50 g pkgs.</asp:TableCell>
        <asp:TableCell style="text-align:left;">20</asp:TableCell>
        <asp:TableCell style="text-align:left;">10</asp:TableCell>
        <asp:TableCell style="text-align:left;">60</asp:TableCell>
        <asp:TableCell style="text-align:left;">15</asp:TableCell>
        <asp:TableCell style="text-align:left;">False</asp:TableCell>
    </asp:TableRow>
    <asp:TableRow>
        <asp:TableCell style="text-align:left;">50</asp:TableCell>
        <asp:TableCell style="text-align:left;">Valkoinen suklaa</asp:TableCell>
        <asp:TableCell style="text-align:left;">23</asp:TableCell>
        <asp:TableCell style="text-align:left;">3</asp:TableCell>
        <asp:TableCell style="text-align:left;">12 - 100 g bars</asp:TableCell>
        <asp:TableCell style="text-align:left;">16.25</asp:TableCell>
        <asp:TableCell style="text-align:left;">65</asp:TableCell>
```

```
      <asp:TableCell style="text-align:left;">0</asp:TableCell>
      <asp:TableCell style="text-align:left;">30</asp:TableCell>
      <asp:TableCell style="text-align:left;">False</asp:TableCell>
  </asp:TableRow>
  <asp:TableRow>
      <asp:TableCell style="text-align:left;">51</asp:TableCell>
      <asp:TableCell style="text-align:left;">Manjimup Dried Apples</asp:TableCell>
      <asp:TableCell style="text-align:left;">24</asp:TableCell>
      <asp:TableCell style="text-align:left;">7</asp:TableCell>
      <asp:TableCell style="text-align:left;">50 - 300 g pkgs.</asp:TableCell>
      <asp:TableCell style="text-align:left;">53</asp:TableCell>
      <asp:TableCell style="text-align:left;">20</asp:TableCell>
      <asp:TableCell style="text-align:left;">0</asp:TableCell>
      <asp:TableCell style="text-align:left;">10</asp:TableCell>
      <asp:TableCell style="text-align:left;">False</asp:TableCell>
  </asp:TableRow>
  <asp:TableRow>
      <asp:TableCell style="text-align:left;">52</asp:TableCell>
      <asp:TableCell style="text-align:left;">Filo Mix</asp:TableCell>
      <asp:TableCell style="text-align:left;">24</asp:TableCell>
      <asp:TableCell style="text-align:left;">5</asp:TableCell>
      <asp:TableCell style="text-align:left;">16 - 2 kg boxes</asp:TableCell>
      <asp:TableCell style="text-align:left;">7</asp:TableCell>
      <asp:TableCell style="text-align:left;">38</asp:TableCell>
      <asp:TableCell style="text-align:left;">0</asp:TableCell>
      <asp:TableCell style="text-align:left;">25</asp:TableCell>
      <asp:TableCell style="text-align:left;">False</asp:TableCell>
  </asp:TableRow>
  <asp:TableRow>
      <asp:TableCell style="text-align:left;">53</asp:TableCell>
      <asp:TableCell style="text-align:left;">Perth Pasties</asp:TableCell>
      <asp:TableCell style="text-align:left;">24</asp:TableCell>
      <asp:TableCell style="text-align:left;">6</asp:TableCell>
      <asp:TableCell style="text-align:left;">48 pieces</asp:TableCell>
      <asp:TableCell style="text-align:left;">32.8</asp:TableCell>
      <asp:TableCell style="text-align:left;">0</asp:TableCell>
      <asp:TableCell style="text-align:left;">0</asp:TableCell>
      <asp:TableCell style="text-align:left;">0</asp:TableCell>
      <asp:TableCell style="text-align:left;">True</asp:TableCell>
  </asp:TableRow>
  <asp:TableRow>
      <asp:TableCell style="text-align:left;">54</asp:TableCell>
      <asp:TableCell style="text-align:left;">Tourtière</asp:TableCell>
      <asp:TableCell style="text-align:left;">25</asp:TableCell>
      <asp:TableCell style="text-align:left;">6</asp:TableCell>
      <asp:TableCell style="text-align:left;">16 pies</asp:TableCell>
      <asp:TableCell style="text-align:left;">7.45</asp:TableCell>
      <asp:TableCell style="text-align:left;">21</asp:TableCell>
      <asp:TableCell style="text-align:left;">0</asp:TableCell>
      <asp:TableCell style="text-align:left;">10</asp:TableCell>
      <asp:TableCell style="text-align:left;">False</asp:TableCell>
  </asp:TableRow>
  <asp:TableRow>
      <asp:TableCell style="text-align:left;">55</asp:TableCell>
      <asp:TableCell style="text-align:left;">Pâté chinois</asp:TableCell>
      <asp:TableCell style="text-align:left;">25</asp:TableCell>
      <asp:TableCell style="text-align:left;">6</asp:TableCell>
      <asp:TableCell style="text-align:left;">24 boxes x 2 pies</asp:TableCell>
      <asp:TableCell style="text-align:left;">24</asp:TableCell>
      <asp:TableCell style="text-align:left;">115</asp:TableCell>
      <asp:TableCell style="text-align:left;">0</asp:TableCell>
      <asp:TableCell style="text-align:left;">20</asp:TableCell>
      <asp:TableCell style="text-align:left;">False</asp:TableCell>
  </asp:TableRow>
  <asp:TableRow>
      <asp:TableCell style="text-align:left;">56</asp:TableCell>
```

```
            <asp:TableCell style="text-align:left;">Gnocchi di nonna Alice</asp:TableCell>
            <asp:TableCell style="text-align:left;">26</asp:TableCell>
            <asp:TableCell style="text-align:left;">5</asp:TableCell>
            <asp:TableCell style="text-align:left;">24 - 250 g pkgs.</asp:TableCell>
            <asp:TableCell style="text-align:left;">38</asp:TableCell>
            <asp:TableCell style="text-align:left;">21</asp:TableCell>
            <asp:TableCell style="text-align:left;">10</asp:TableCell>
            <asp:TableCell style="text-align:left;">30</asp:TableCell>
            <asp:TableCell style="text-align:left;">False</asp:TableCell>
        </asp:TableRow>
        <asp:TableRow>
            <asp:TableCell style="text-align:left;">57</asp:TableCell>
            <asp:TableCell style="text-align:left;">Ravioli Angelo</asp:TableCell>
            <asp:TableCell style="text-align:left;">26</asp:TableCell>
            <asp:TableCell style="text-align:left;">5</asp:TableCell>
            <asp:TableCell style="text-align:left;">24 - 250 g pkgs.</asp:TableCell>
            <asp:TableCell style="text-align:left;">19.5</asp:TableCell>
            <asp:TableCell style="text-align:left;">36</asp:TableCell>
            <asp:TableCell style="text-align:left;">0</asp:TableCell>
            <asp:TableCell style="text-align:left;">20</asp:TableCell>
            <asp:TableCell style="text-align:left;">False</asp:TableCell>
        </asp:TableRow>
        <asp:TableRow>
            <asp:TableCell style="text-align:left;">58</asp:TableCell>
            <asp:TableCell style="text-align:left;">Escargots de Bourgogne</asp:TableCell>
            <asp:TableCell style="text-align:left;">27</asp:TableCell>
            <asp:TableCell style="text-align:left;">8</asp:TableCell>
            <asp:TableCell style="text-align:left;">24 pieces</asp:TableCell>
            <asp:TableCell style="text-align:left;">13.25</asp:TableCell>
            <asp:TableCell style="text-align:left;">62</asp:TableCell>
            <asp:TableCell style="text-align:left;">0</asp:TableCell>
            <asp:TableCell style="text-align:left;">20</asp:TableCell>
            <asp:TableCell style="text-align:left;">False</asp:TableCell>
        </asp:TableRow>
        <asp:TableRow>
            <asp:TableCell style="text-align:left;">59</asp:TableCell>
            <asp:TableCell style="text-align:left;">Raclette Courdavault</asp:TableCell>
            <asp:TableCell style="text-align:left;">28</asp:TableCell>
            <asp:TableCell style="text-align:left;">4</asp:TableCell>
            <asp:TableCell style="text-align:left;">5 kg pkg.</asp:TableCell>
            <asp:TableCell style="text-align:left;">55</asp:TableCell>
            <asp:TableCell style="text-align:left;">79</asp:TableCell>
            <asp:TableCell style="text-align:left;">0</asp:TableCell>
            <asp:TableCell style="text-align:left;">0</asp:TableCell>
            <asp:TableCell style="text-align:left;">False</asp:TableCell>
        </asp:TableRow>
        <asp:TableRow>
            <asp:TableCell style="text-align:left;">60</asp:TableCell>
            <asp:TableCell style="text-align:left;">Camembert Pierrot</asp:TableCell>
            <asp:TableCell style="text-align:left;">28</asp:TableCell>
            <asp:TableCell style="text-align:left;">4</asp:TableCell>
            <asp:TableCell style="text-align:left;">15 - 300 g rounds</asp:TableCell>
            <asp:TableCell style="text-align:left;">34</asp:TableCell>
            <asp:TableCell style="text-align:left;">19</asp:TableCell>
            <asp:TableCell style="text-align:left;">0</asp:TableCell>
            <asp:TableCell style="text-align:left;">0</asp:TableCell>
            <asp:TableCell style="text-align:left;">False</asp:TableCell>
        </asp:TableRow>
        <asp:TableRow>
            <asp:TableCell style="text-align:left;">61</asp:TableCell>
            <asp:TableCell style="text-align:left;">Sirop d'érable</asp:TableCell>
            <asp:TableCell style="text-align:left;">29</asp:TableCell>
            <asp:TableCell style="text-align:left;">2</asp:TableCell>
            <asp:TableCell style="text-align:left;">24 - 500 ml bottles</asp:TableCell>
            <asp:TableCell style="text-align:left;">28.5</asp:TableCell>
            <asp:TableCell style="text-align:left;">113</asp:TableCell>
```

```
    <asp:TableCell style="text-align:left;">0</asp:TableCell>
    <asp:TableCell style="text-align:left;">25</asp:TableCell>
    <asp:TableCell style="text-align:left;">False</asp:TableCell>
  </asp:TableRow>
  <asp:TableRow>
    <asp:TableCell style="text-align:left;">62</asp:TableCell>
    <asp:TableCell style="text-align:left;">Tarte au sucre</asp:TableCell>
    <asp:TableCell style="text-align:left;">29</asp:TableCell>
    <asp:TableCell style="text-align:left;">3</asp:TableCell>
    <asp:TableCell style="text-align:left;">48 pies</asp:TableCell>
    <asp:TableCell style="text-align:left;">49.3</asp:TableCell>
    <asp:TableCell style="text-align:left;">17</asp:TableCell>
    <asp:TableCell style="text-align:left;">0</asp:TableCell>
    <asp:TableCell style="text-align:left;">0</asp:TableCell>
    <asp:TableCell style="text-align:left;">False</asp:TableCell>
  </asp:TableRow>
  <asp:TableRow>
    <asp:TableCell style="text-align:left;">63</asp:TableCell>
    <asp:TableCell style="text-align:left;">Vegie-spread</asp:TableCell>
    <asp:TableCell style="text-align:left;">7</asp:TableCell>
    <asp:TableCell style="text-align:left;">2</asp:TableCell>
    <asp:TableCell style="text-align:left;">15 - 625 g jars</asp:TableCell>
    <asp:TableCell style="text-align:left;">43.9</asp:TableCell>
    <asp:TableCell style="text-align:left;">24</asp:TableCell>
    <asp:TableCell style="text-align:left;">0</asp:TableCell>
    <asp:TableCell style="text-align:left;">5</asp:TableCell>
    <asp:TableCell style="text-align:left;">False</asp:TableCell>
  </asp:TableRow>
  <asp:TableRow>
    <asp:TableCell style="text-align:left;">64</asp:TableCell>
    <asp:TableCell style="text-align:left;">Wimmers gute Semmelknödel</asp:TableCell>
    <asp:TableCell style="text-align:left;">12</asp:TableCell>
    <asp:TableCell style="text-align:left;">5</asp:TableCell>
    <asp:TableCell style="text-align:left;">20 bags x 4 pieces</asp:TableCell>
    <asp:TableCell style="text-align:left;">33.25</asp:TableCell>
    <asp:TableCell style="text-align:left;">22</asp:TableCell>
    <asp:TableCell style="text-align:left;">80</asp:TableCell>
    <asp:TableCell style="text-align:left;">30</asp:TableCell>
    <asp:TableCell style="text-align:left;">False</asp:TableCell>
  </asp:TableRow>
  <asp:TableRow>
    <asp:TableCell style="text-align:left;">65</asp:TableCell>
    <asp:TableCell style="text-align:left;">Louisiana Fiery Hot Pepper Sauce</asp:TableCell>
    <asp:TableCell style="text-align:left;">2</asp:TableCell>
    <asp:TableCell style="text-align:left;">2</asp:TableCell>
    <asp:TableCell style="text-align:left;">32 - 8 oz bottles</asp:TableCell>
    <asp:TableCell style="text-align:left;">21.05</asp:TableCell>
    <asp:TableCell style="text-align:left;">76</asp:TableCell>
    <asp:TableCell style="text-align:left;">0</asp:TableCell>
    <asp:TableCell style="text-align:left;">0</asp:TableCell>
    <asp:TableCell style="text-align:left;">False</asp:TableCell>
  </asp:TableRow>
  <asp:TableRow>
    <asp:TableCell style="text-align:left;">66</asp:TableCell>
    <asp:TableCell style="text-align:left;">Louisiana Hot Spiced Okra</asp:TableCell>
    <asp:TableCell style="text-align:left;">2</asp:TableCell>
    <asp:TableCell style="text-align:left;">2</asp:TableCell>
    <asp:TableCell style="text-align:left;">24 - 8 oz jars</asp:TableCell>
    <asp:TableCell style="text-align:left;">17</asp:TableCell>
    <asp:TableCell style="text-align:left;">4</asp:TableCell>
    <asp:TableCell style="text-align:left;">100</asp:TableCell>
    <asp:TableCell style="text-align:left;">20</asp:TableCell>
    <asp:TableCell style="text-align:left;">False</asp:TableCell>
  </asp:TableRow>
  <asp:TableRow>
    <asp:TableCell style="text-align:left;">67</asp:TableCell>
```

```
<asp:TableCell style="text-align:left;">Laughing Lumberjack Lager</asp:TableCell>
<asp:TableCell style="text-align:left;">16</asp:TableCell>
<asp:TableCell style="text-align:left;">1</asp:TableCell>
<asp:TableCell style="text-align:left;">24 - 12 oz bottles</asp:TableCell>
<asp:TableCell style="text-align:left;">14</asp:TableCell>
<asp:TableCell style="text-align:left;">52</asp:TableCell>
<asp:TableCell style="text-align:left;">0</asp:TableCell>
<asp:TableCell style="text-align:left;">10</asp:TableCell>
<asp:TableCell style="text-align:left;">False</asp:TableCell>
</asp:TableRow>
<asp:TableRow>
<asp:TableCell style="text-align:left;">68</asp:TableCell>
<asp:TableCell style="text-align:left;">Scottish Longbreads</asp:TableCell>
<asp:TableCell style="text-align:left;">8</asp:TableCell>
<asp:TableCell style="text-align:left;">3</asp:TableCell>
<asp:TableCell style="text-align:left;">10 boxes x 8 pieces</asp:TableCell>
<asp:TableCell style="text-align:left;">12.5</asp:TableCell>
<asp:TableCell style="text-align:left;">6</asp:TableCell>
<asp:TableCell style="text-align:left;">10</asp:TableCell>
<asp:TableCell style="text-align:left;">15</asp:TableCell>
<asp:TableCell style="text-align:left;">False</asp:TableCell>
</asp:TableRow>
<asp:TableRow>
<asp:TableCell style="text-align:left;">69</asp:TableCell>
<asp:TableCell style="text-align:left;">Gudbrandsdalsost</asp:TableCell>
<asp:TableCell style="text-align:left;">15</asp:TableCell>
<asp:TableCell style="text-align:left;">4</asp:TableCell>
<asp:TableCell style="text-align:left;">10 kg pkg.</asp:TableCell>
<asp:TableCell style="text-align:left;">36</asp:TableCell>
<asp:TableCell style="text-align:left;">26</asp:TableCell>
<asp:TableCell style="text-align:left;">0</asp:TableCell>
<asp:TableCell style="text-align:left;">15</asp:TableCell>
<asp:TableCell style="text-align:left;">False</asp:TableCell>
</asp:TableRow>
<asp:TableRow>
<asp:TableCell style="text-align:left;">70</asp:TableCell>
<asp:TableCell style="text-align:left;">Outback Lager</asp:TableCell>
<asp:TableCell style="text-align:left;">7</asp:TableCell>
<asp:TableCell style="text-align:left;">1</asp:TableCell>
<asp:TableCell style="text-align:left;">24 - 355 ml bottles</asp:TableCell>
<asp:TableCell style="text-align:left;">15</asp:TableCell>
<asp:TableCell style="text-align:left;">15</asp:TableCell>
<asp:TableCell style="text-align:left;">10</asp:TableCell>
<asp:TableCell style="text-align:left;">30</asp:TableCell>
<asp:TableCell style="text-align:left;">False</asp:TableCell>
</asp:TableRow>
<asp:TableRow>
<asp:TableCell style="text-align:left;">71</asp:TableCell>
<asp:TableCell style="text-align:left;">Fløtemysost</asp:TableCell>
<asp:TableCell style="text-align:left;">15</asp:TableCell>
<asp:TableCell style="text-align:left;">4</asp:TableCell>
<asp:TableCell style="text-align:left;">10 - 500 g pkgs.</asp:TableCell>
<asp:TableCell style="text-align:left;">21.5</asp:TableCell>
<asp:TableCell style="text-align:left;">26</asp:TableCell>
<asp:TableCell style="text-align:left;">0</asp:TableCell>
<asp:TableCell style="text-align:left;">0</asp:TableCell>
<asp:TableCell style="text-align:left;">False</asp:TableCell>
</asp:TableRow>
<asp:TableRow>
<asp:TableCell style="text-align:left;">72</asp:TableCell>
<asp:TableCell style="text-align:left;">Mozzarella di Giovanni</asp:TableCell>
<asp:TableCell style="text-align:left;">14</asp:TableCell>
<asp:TableCell style="text-align:left;">4</asp:TableCell>
<asp:TableCell style="text-align:left;">24 - 200 g pkgs.</asp:TableCell>
<asp:TableCell style="text-align:left;">34.8</asp:TableCell>
<asp:TableCell style="text-align:left;">14</asp:TableCell>
```

```
        <asp:TableCell style="text-align:left;">0</asp:TableCell>
        <asp:TableCell style="text-align:left;">0</asp:TableCell>
        <asp:TableCell style="text-align:left;">False</asp:TableCell>
    </asp:TableRow>
    <asp:TableRow>
        <asp:TableCell style="text-align:left;">73</asp:TableCell>
        <asp:TableCell style="text-align:left;">Röd Kaviar</asp:TableCell>
        <asp:TableCell style="text-align:left;">17</asp:TableCell>
        <asp:TableCell style="text-align:left;">8</asp:TableCell>
        <asp:TableCell style="text-align:left;">24 - 150 g jars</asp:TableCell>
        <asp:TableCell style="text-align:left;">15</asp:TableCell>
        <asp:TableCell style="text-align:left;">101</asp:TableCell>
        <asp:TableCell style="text-align:left;">0</asp:TableCell>
        <asp:TableCell style="text-align:left;">5</asp:TableCell>
        <asp:TableCell style="text-align:left;">False</asp:TableCell>
    </asp:TableRow>
    <asp:TableRow>
        <asp:TableCell style="text-align:left;">74</asp:TableCell>
        <asp:TableCell style="text-align:left;">Longlife Tofu</asp:TableCell>
        <asp:TableCell style="text-align:left;">4</asp:TableCell>
        <asp:TableCell style="text-align:left;">7</asp:TableCell>
        <asp:TableCell style="text-align:left;">5 kg pkg.</asp:TableCell>
        <asp:TableCell style="text-align:left;">10</asp:TableCell>
        <asp:TableCell style="text-align:left;">4</asp:TableCell>
        <asp:TableCell style="text-align:left;">20</asp:TableCell>
        <asp:TableCell style="text-align:left;">5</asp:TableCell>
        <asp:TableCell style="text-align:left;">False</asp:TableCell>
    </asp:TableRow>
    <asp:TableRow>
        <asp:TableCell style="text-align:left;">75</asp:TableCell>
        <asp:TableCell style="text-align:left;">Rhönbräu Klosterbier</asp:TableCell>
        <asp:TableCell style="text-align:left;">12</asp:TableCell>
        <asp:TableCell style="text-align:left;">1</asp:TableCell>
        <asp:TableCell style="text-align:left;">24 - 0.5 l bottles</asp:TableCell>
        <asp:TableCell style="text-align:left;">7.75</asp:TableCell>
        <asp:TableCell style="text-align:left;">125</asp:TableCell>
        <asp:TableCell style="text-align:left;">0</asp:TableCell>
        <asp:TableCell style="text-align:left;">25</asp:TableCell>
        <asp:TableCell style="text-align:left;">False</asp:TableCell>
    </asp:TableRow>
    <asp:TableRow>
        <asp:TableCell style="text-align:left;">76</asp:TableCell>
        <asp:TableCell style="text-align:left;">Lakkalikööri</asp:TableCell>
        <asp:TableCell style="text-align:left;">23</asp:TableCell>
        <asp:TableCell style="text-align:left;">1</asp:TableCell>
        <asp:TableCell style="text-align:left;">500 ml</asp:TableCell>
        <asp:TableCell style="text-align:left;">18</asp:TableCell>
        <asp:TableCell style="text-align:left;">57</asp:TableCell>
        <asp:TableCell style="text-align:left;">0</asp:TableCell>
        <asp:TableCell style="text-align:left;">20</asp:TableCell>
        <asp:TableCell style="text-align:left;">False</asp:TableCell>
    </asp:TableRow>
    <asp:TableRow>
        <asp:TableCell style="text-align:left;">77</asp:TableCell>
        <asp:TableCell style="text-align:left;">Original Frankfurter grüne Soße</asp:TableCell>
        <asp:TableCell style="text-align:left;">12</asp:TableCell>
        <asp:TableCell style="text-align:left;">2</asp:TableCell>
        <asp:TableCell style="text-align:left;">12 boxes</asp:TableCell>
        <asp:TableCell style="text-align:left;">13</asp:TableCell>
        <asp:TableCell style="text-align:left;">32</asp:TableCell>
        <asp:TableCell style="text-align:left;">0</asp:TableCell>
        <asp:TableCell style="text-align:left;">15</asp:TableCell>
        <asp:TableCell style="text-align:left;">False</asp:TableCell>
    </asp:TableRow>
    </asp:Table>
</div>
```

```
  </form>
 </body>
</html>
```

Just try creating that code by hand — it is 1114 lines. Might take you a week by hand. Why would you want to when you can create it in seconds?
Here's the output:

ProductID	ProductName	SupplierID	CategoryID	QuantityPerUnit	UnitPrice	UnitsInStock	UnitsOnOrder	ReorderLevel	Discontinued
1	Chai	1	1	10 boxes x 20 bags	18	39	0	10	False
2	Chang	1	1	24 - 12 oz bottles	19	17	40	25	False
3	Aniseed Syrup	1	2	12 - 550 ml bottles	10	13	70	25	False
4	Chef Anton's Cajun Seasoning	2	2	48 - 6 oz jars	22	53	0	0	False
5	Chef Anton's Gumbo Mix	2	2	36 boxes	21.35	0	0	0	True
6	Grandma's Boysenberry Spread	3	2	12 - 8 oz jars	25	120	0	25	False
7	Uncle Bob's Organic Dried Pears	3	7	12 - 1 lb pkgs.	30	15	0	10	False
8	Northwoods Cranberry Sauce	3	2	12 - 12 oz jars	40	6	0	0	False
9	Mishi Kobe Niku	4	6	18 - 500 g pkgs.	97	29	0	0	True
10	Ikura	4	8	12 - 200 ml jars	31	31	0	0	False
11	Queso Cabrales	5	4	1 kg pkg.	21	22	30	30	False
12	Queso Manchego La Pastora	5	4	10 - 500 g pkgs.	38	86	0	0	False
13	Konbu	6	8	2 kg box	6	24	0	5	False
14	Tofu	6	7	40 - 100 g pkgs.	23.25	35	0	0	False
15	Genen Shouyu	6	2	24 - 250 ml bottles	15.5	39	0	5	False
16	Pavlova	7	3	32 - 500 g boxes	17.45	29	0	10	False
17	Alice Mutton	7	6	20 - 1 kg tins	39	0	0	0	True
18	Carnarvon Tigers	7	8	16 kg pkg.	62.5	42	0	0	False
19	Teatime Chocolate Biscuits	8	3	10 boxes x 12 pieces	9.2	25	0	5	False
20	Sir Rodney's Marmalade	8	3	30 gift boxes	81	40	0	0	False
21	Sir Rodney's Scones	8	3	24 pkgs. x 4 pieces	10	3	40	5	False
22	Gustaf's Knäckebröd	9	5	24 - 500 g pkgs.	21	104	0	25	False
23	Tunnbröd	9	5	12 - 250 g pkgs.	9	61	0	25	False
24	Guaraná Fantástica	10	1	12 - 355 ml cans	4.5	20	0	0	True
25	NuNuCa Nuß-Nougat-Creme	11	3	20 - 450 g glasses	14	76	0	30	False
26	Gumbär Gummibärchen	11	3	100 - 250 g bags	31.23	15	0	0	False
27	Schoggi Schokolade	11	3	100 - 100 g pieces	43.9	49	0	30	False
28	Rössle Sauerkraut	12	7	25 - 825 g cans	45.6	26	0	0	True
29	Thüringer Rostbratwurst	12	6	50 bags x 30 sausgs.	123.79	0	0	0	True
30	Nord-Ost Matjeshering	13	8	10 - 200 g glasses	25.89	10	0	15	False
31	Gorgonzola Telino	14	4	12 - 100 g pkgs.	12.5	0	70	20	False

The other way to do this is to dynamically force feed the normal html into the form and it looks like this:

```
<html xmlns="http://www.w3.org/1999/xhtml">
<head id="Head1" runat="server">
<title>Products</title>
<style type='text/css'>
body
{
    BORDER-TOP: navy 1px solid;
    BORDER-LEFT: navy 1px solid;
    BORDER-RIGHT: navy 1px solid;
    BORDER-BOTTOM: navy 1px solid;
    PADDING-RIGHT: 1px;
    PADDING-LEFT: 1px;
    FONT-WEIGHT: Normal;
    PADDING-BOTTOM: 1px;
```

```
    COLOR: black;
    PADDING-TOP: 1px;
    BORDER-BOTTOM: #999 1px solid;
    BACKGROUND-COLOR: ButtonFace;
    FONT-FAMILY: Cambria, serif;
    FONT-SIZE: 12px;
    text-align: left;
    display: table-cell;
    white-Space: nowrap;
    width: auto;
    height: auto;
}
Table
{
    BORDER-TOP: navy 1px solid;
    BORDER-LEFT: navy 1px solid;
    BORDER-RIGHT: navy 1px solid;
    BORDER-BOTTOM: navy 1px solid;
    PADDING-RIGHT: 1px;
    PADDING-LEFT: 1px;
    FONT-WEIGHT: Normal;
    PADDING-BOTTOM: 1px;
    COLOR: black;
    PADDING-TOP: 1px;
    BORDER-BOTTOM: #999 1px solid;
    BACKGROUND-COLOR: ButtonFace;
    FONT-FAMILY: Cambria, serif;
    FONT-SIZE: 12px;
    text-align: left;
    display: table-cell;
    white-Space: nowrap;
    width: auto;
    height: auto;
}
th
{
    BORDER-RIGHT: #999999 2px solid;
    PADDING-RIGHT: 6px;
    PADDING-LEFT: 6px;
    FONT-WEIGHT: Bold;
    PADDING-BOTTOM: 6px;
    COLOR: #600000;
    PADDING-TOP: 6px;
    BORDER-BOTTOM: #999 2px solid;
    BACKGROUND-COLOR: #eeeeee;
    FONT-FAMILY: Cambria, serif;
    FONT-SIZE: 16px;
    text-align: right;
    white-Space: nowrap;
}
td
{
    BORDER-RIGHT: #999999 3px solid;
    PADDING-RIGHT: 6px;
    PADDING-LEFT: 6px;
    FONT-WEIGHT: Normal;
    PADDING-BOTTOM: 6px;
    COLOR: navy;
    LINE-HEIGHT: 14px;
    PADDING-TOP: 6px;
    BORDER-BOTTOM: #999 1px solid;
    BACKGROUND-COLOR: #eeeeee;
    FONT-FAMILY: Cambria, serif;
    FONT-SIZE: 12px;
    text-align: left;
    white-Space: nowrap;
```

```css
}
.div
{
    BORDER-RIGHT: #999999 3px solid;
    PADDING-RIGHT: 6px;
    PADDING-LEFT: 6px;
    FONT-WEIGHT: Normal;
    PADDING-BOTTOM: 6px;
    COLOR: white;
    PADDING-TOP: 6px;
    BORDER-BOTTOM: #999 1px solid;
    BACKGROUND-COLOR: navy;
    FONT-FAMILY: Cambria, serif;
    FONT-SIZE: 10px;
    text-align: left;
    white-Space: nowrap;
}
.span
{
    BORDER-RIGHT: #999999 3px solid;
    PADDING-RIGHT: 3px;
    PADDING-LEFT: 3px;
    FONT-WEIGHT: Normal;
    PADDING-BOTTOM: 3px;
    COLOR: white;
    PADDING-TOP: 3px;
    BORDER-BOTTOM: #999 1px solid;
    BACKGROUND-COLOR: navy;
    FONT-FAMILY: Cambria, serif;
    FONT-SIZE: 10px;
    text-align: left;
    white-Space: nowrap;
    display: inline-block;
    width: 100%;
}
.textarea
{
    BORDER-RIGHT: #999999 3px solid;
    PADDING-RIGHT: 3px;
    PADDING-LEFT: 3px;
    FONT-WEIGHT: Normal;
    PADDING-BOTTOM: 3px;
    COLOR: white;
    PADDING-TOP: 3px;
    BORDER-BOTTOM: #999 1px solid;
    BACKGROUND-COLOR: navy;
    FONT-FAMILY: Cambria, serif;
    FONT-SIZE: 10px;
    text-align: left;
    white-Space: nowrap;
    width: 100%;
}
.Select
{
    BORDER-RIGHT: #999999 3px solid;
    PADDING-RIGHT: 6px;
    PADDING-LEFT: 6px;
    FONT-WEIGHT: Normal;
    PADDING-BOTTOM: 6px;
    COLOR: white;
    PADDING-TOP: 6px;
    BORDER-BOTTOM: #999 1px solid;
    BACKGROUND-COLOR: navy;
    FONT-FAMILY: Cambria, serif;
    FONT-SIZE: 10px;
    text-align: left;
```

```
    white-Space: nowrap;
    width: 100%;
}
input
{
    BORDER-RIGHT: #999999 1px solid;
    PADDING-RIGHT: 1px;
    PADDING-LEFT: 1px;
    FONT-WEIGHT: Normal;
    PADDING-BOTTOM: 1px;
    COLOR: White;
    PADDING-TOP: 1px;
    BORDER-BOTTOM: #999 1px solid;
    BACKGROUND-COLOR: navy;
    FONT-FAMILY: Cambria, serif;
    FONT-SIZE: 12px;
    text-align: left;
    display: table-cell;
    white-Space: nowrap;
    width: auto;
}
</style>
</head>
<body>
    <form id="form1" runat="server">
        <div>
<%
    Dim cnstr As String = "Provider=Microsoft.Jet.OLEDB.4.0;Data Source=C:\nwind.mdb;"
    Dim strQuery As String = "Select * From Products"
    Dim cn As System.Data.OleDb.OleDbConnection = New System.Data.OleDb.OleDbConnection()
    cn.ConnectionString = cnstr
    cn.Open()

    Dim cmd As System.Data.OleDb.OleDbCommand = New System.Data.OleDb.OleDbCommand()
    cmd.Connection = cn
    cmd.CommandType = System.Data.CommandType.Text
    cmd.CommandText = strQuery
    cmd.ExecuteNonQuery()

    Dim da As System.Data.OleDb.OleDbDataAdapter = New System.Data.OleDb.OleDbDataAdapter(cmd)
    Dim ds As System.Data.DataSet = New System.Data.DataSet()
    da.Fill(ds)

    Response.Write("        <table cellspacing='2' cellpadding= '2'>" & vbCrLf)
    Response.Write("            <tr>" & vbCrLf)
    For x As Integer = 0 To ds.Tables(0).Columns.Count - 1
        Response.Write("            <th style=""text-align:left;"">" + ds.Tables(0).Columns(x).Caption + "</th>"
& vbCrLf)
    Next
    Response.Write("            </tr>" & vbCrLf)
    For y As Integer = 0 To ds.Tables(0).Rows.Count - 1
        Response.Write("            <tr>" & vbCrLf)
        For x As Integer = 0 To ds.Tables(0).Columns.Count - 1
            Try
                Response.Write("            <td style=""text-align:left;"">" +
ds.Tables(0).Rows(y).Item(ds.Tables(0).Columns(x).Caption).ToString() + "</td>" & vbCrLf)
            Catch ex As Exception
                Response.Write("            <td style=""text-align:left;""></td>" & vbCrLf)
            End Try

        Next
        Response.Write("            </tr>" & vbCrLf)
    Next
    Response.Write("        </table>" & vbCrLf)
%>
        </div>
```

```
</form>
</body>
</html>
```

And, of course, it comes out looking exactly the same.

ProductID	ProductName	SupplierID	CategoryID	QuantityPerUnit	UnitPrice	UnitsInStock	UnitsOnOrder	ReorderLevel	Discontinued
1	Chai	1	1	10 boxes x 20 bags	18	39	0	10	False
2	Chang	1	1	24 - 12 oz bottles	19	17	40	25	False
3	Aniseed Syrup	1	2	12 - 550 ml bottles	10	13	70	25	False
4	Chef Anton's Cajun Seasoning	2	2	48 - 6 oz jars	22	53	0	0	False
5	Chef Anton's Gumbo Mix	2	2	36 boxes	21.35	0	0	0	True
6	Grandma's Boysenberry Spread	3	2	12 - 8 oz jars	25	120	0	25	False
7	Uncle Bob's Organic Dried Pears	3	7	12 - 1 lb pkgs.	30	15	0	10	False
8	Northwoods Cranberry Sauce	3	2	12 - 12 oz jars	40	6	0	0	False
9	Mishi Kobe Niku	4	6	18 - 500 g pkgs.	97	29	0	0	True
10	Ikura	4	8	12 - 200 ml jars	31	31	0	0	False
11	Queso Cabrales	5	4	1 kg pkg.	21	22	30	30	False
12	Queso Manchego La Pastora	5	4	10 - 500 g pkgs.	38	86	0	0	False
13	Konbu	6	8	2 kg box	6	24	0	5	False
14	Tofu	6	7	40 - 100 g pkgs.	23.25	35	0	0	False
15	Genen Shouyu	6	2	24 - 250 ml bottles	15.5	39	0	5	False
16	Pavlova	7	3	32 - 500 g boxes	17.45	29	0	10	False
17	Alice Mutton	7	6	20 - 1 kg tins	39	0	0	0	True
18	Carnarvon Tigers	7	8	16 kg pkg.	62.5	42	0	0	False
19	Teatime Chocolate Biscuits	8	3	10 boxes x 12 pieces	9.2	25	0	5	False
20	Sir Rodney's Marmalade	8	3	30 gift boxes	81	40	0	0	False
21	Sir Rodney's Scones	8	3	24 pkgs. x 4 pieces	10	3	40	5	False
22	Gustaf's Knäckebröd	9	5	24 - 500 g pkgs.	21	104	0	25	False
23	Tunnbröd	9	5	12 - 250 g pkgs.	9	61	0	25	False
24	Guaraná Fantástica	10	1	12 - 355 ml cans	4.5	20	0	0	True
25	NuNuCa Nuß-Nougat-Creme	11	3	20 - 450 g glasses	14	76	0	30	False
26	Gumbär Gummibärchen	11	3	100 - 250 g bags	31.23	15	0	0	False
27	Schoggi Schokolade	11	3	100 - 100 g pieces	43.9	49	0	30	False
28	Rössle Sauerkraut	12	7	25 - 825 g cans	45.6	26	0	0	True
29	Thüringer Rostbratwurst	12	6	50 bags x 30 sausgs.	123.79	0	0	0	True
30	Nord-Ost Matjeshering	13	8	10 - 200 g glasses	25.89	10	0	15	False
31	Gorgonzola Telino	14	4	12 - 100 g pkgs	12.5	0	70	20	False

All well and good but what happens when you want to change the look and feel?

Here's the external code including additional tags and controls:

```
Public Class Form1

    Private Sub Form1_Load(ByVal sender As System.Object, ByVal e As System.EventArgs) Handles MyBase.Load

        Dim fso As Object = CreateObject("Scripting.FileSystemObject")
        Dim txtstream As Object = fso.OpenTextFile(Application.StartupPath & "\Products.aspx", 2, True, -2)
        txtstream.WriteLine("<html xmlns=""http://www.w3.org/1999/xhtml"">")
        txtstream.WriteLine("<head runat=""server"">")
        txtstream.WriteLine("    <title>Products</title>")
        txtstream.WriteLine("<style type='text/css'>")
        txtstream.WriteLine("body")
        txtstream.WriteLine("{")
        txtstream.WriteLine("    BORDER-TOP: navy 1px solid;")
        txtstream.WriteLine("    BORDER-LEFT: navy 1px solid;")
        txtstream.WriteLine("    BORDER-RIGHT: navy 1px solid;")
        txtstream.WriteLine("    BORDER-BOTTOM: navy 1px solid;")
        txtstream.WriteLine("    PADDING-RIGHT: 1px;")
```

```
txtstream.WriteLine("   PADDING-LEFT: 1px;")
txtstream.WriteLine("   FONT-WEIGHT: Normal;")
txtstream.WriteLine("   PADDING-BOTTOM: 1px;")
txtstream.WriteLine("   COLOR: black;")
txtstream.WriteLine("   PADDING-TOP: 1px;")
txtstream.WriteLine("   BORDER-BOTTOM: #999 1px solid;")
txtstream.WriteLine("   BACKGROUND-COLOR: ButtonFace;")
txtstream.WriteLine("   FONT-FAMILY: Cambria, serif;")
txtstream.WriteLine("   FONT-SIZE: 12px;")
txtstream.WriteLine("   text-align: left;")
txtstream.WriteLine("   display: table-cell;")
txtstream.WriteLine("   white-Space: nowrap;")
txtstream.WriteLine("   width: auto;")
txtstream.WriteLine("   height: auto;")
txtstream.WriteLine("}")
txtstream.WriteLine("Table")
txtstream.WriteLine("{")
txtstream.WriteLine("   BORDER-TOP: navy 1px solid;")
txtstream.WriteLine("   BORDER-LEFT: navy 1px solid;")
txtstream.WriteLine("   BORDER-RIGHT: navy 1px solid;")
txtstream.WriteLine("   BORDER-BOTTOM: navy 1px solid;")
txtstream.WriteLine("   PADDING-RIGHT: 1px;")
txtstream.WriteLine("   PADDING-LEFT: 1px;")
txtstream.WriteLine("   FONT-WEIGHT: Normal;")
txtstream.WriteLine("   PADDING-BOTTOM: 1px;")
txtstream.WriteLine("   COLOR: black;")
txtstream.WriteLine("   PADDING-TOP: 1px;")
txtstream.WriteLine("   BORDER-BOTTOM: #999 1px solid;")
txtstream.WriteLine("   BACKGROUND-COLOR: ButtonFace;")
txtstream.WriteLine("   FONT-FAMILY: Cambria, serif;")
txtstream.WriteLine("   FONT-SIZE: 12px;")
txtstream.WriteLine("   text-align: left;")
txtstream.WriteLine("   display: table-cell;")
txtstream.WriteLine("   white-Space: nowrap;")
txtstream.WriteLine("   width: auto;")
txtstream.WriteLine("   height: auto;")
txtstream.WriteLine("}")
txtstream.WriteLine("th")
txtstream.WriteLine("{")
txtstream.WriteLine("   BORDER-RIGHT: #999999 2px solid;")
txtstream.WriteLine("   PADDING-RIGHT: 6px;")
txtstream.WriteLine("   PADDING-LEFT: 6px;")
txtstream.WriteLine("   FONT-WEIGHT: Bold;")
txtstream.WriteLine("   PADDING-BOTTOM: 6px;")
txtstream.WriteLine("   COLOR: #600000;")
txtstream.WriteLine("   PADDING-TOP: 6px;")
txtstream.WriteLine("   BORDER-BOTTOM: #999 2px solid;")
txtstream.WriteLine("   BACKGROUND-COLOR: #eeeeee;")
txtstream.WriteLine("   FONT-FAMILY: Cambria, serif;")
txtstream.WriteLine("   FONT-SIZE: 16px;")
txtstream.WriteLine("   text-align: right;")
txtstream.WriteLine("   white-Space: nowrap;")
txtstream.WriteLine("}")
txtstream.WriteLine("td")
txtstream.WriteLine("{")
txtstream.WriteLine("   BORDER-RIGHT: #999999 3px solid;")
txtstream.WriteLine("   PADDING-RIGHT: 6px;")
txtstream.WriteLine("   PADDING-LEFT: 6px;")
txtstream.WriteLine("   FONT-WEIGHT: Normal;")
txtstream.WriteLine("   PADDING-BOTTOM: 6px;")
txtstream.WriteLine("   COLOR: navy;")
txtstream.WriteLine("   LINE-HEIGHT: 14px;")
txtstream.WriteLine("   PADDING-TOP: 6px;")
txtstream.WriteLine("   BORDER-BOTTOM: #999 1px solid;")
txtstream.WriteLine("   BACKGROUND-COLOR: #eeeeee;")
txtstream.WriteLine("   FONT-FAMILY: Cambria, serif;")
```

```
txtstream.WriteLine("    FONT-SIZE: 12px;")
txtstream.WriteLine("    text-align: left;")
txtstream.WriteLine("    white-Space: nowrap;")
txtstream.WriteLine("}")
txtstream.WriteLine(".div")
txtstream.WriteLine("{")
txtstream.WriteLine("    BORDER-RIGHT: #999999 3px solid;")
txtstream.WriteLine("    PADDING-RIGHT: 6px;")
txtstream.WriteLine("    PADDING-LEFT: 6px;")
txtstream.WriteLine("    FONT-WEIGHT: Normal;")
txtstream.WriteLine("    PADDING-BOTTOM: 6px;")
txtstream.WriteLine("    COLOR: white;")
txtstream.WriteLine("    PADDING-TOP: 6px;")
txtstream.WriteLine("    BORDER-BOTTOM: #999 1px solid;")
txtstream.WriteLine("    BACKGROUND-COLOR: navy;")
txtstream.WriteLine("    FONT-FAMILY: Cambria, serif;")
txtstream.WriteLine("    FONT-SIZE: 10px;")
txtstream.WriteLine("    text-align: left;")
txtstream.WriteLine("    white-Space: nowrap;")
txtstream.WriteLine("}")
txtstream.WriteLine(".span")
txtstream.WriteLine("{")
txtstream.WriteLine("    BORDER-RIGHT: #999999 3px solid;")
txtstream.WriteLine("    PADDING-RIGHT: 3px;")
txtstream.WriteLine("    PADDING-LEFT: 3px;")
txtstream.WriteLine("    FONT-WEIGHT: Normal;")
txtstream.WriteLine("    PADDING-BOTTOM: 3px;")
txtstream.WriteLine("    COLOR: white;")
txtstream.WriteLine("    PADDING-TOP: 3px;")
txtstream.WriteLine("    BORDER-BOTTOM: #999 1px solid;")
txtstream.WriteLine("    BACKGROUND-COLOR: navy;")
txtstream.WriteLine("    FONT-FAMILY: Cambria, serif;")
txtstream.WriteLine("    FONT-SIZE: 10px;")
txtstream.WriteLine("    text-align: left;")
txtstream.WriteLine("    white-Space: nowrap;")
txtstream.WriteLine("    display: inline-block;")
txtstream.WriteLine("    width: 100%;")
txtstream.WriteLine("}")
txtstream.WriteLine(".textarea")
txtstream.WriteLine("{")
txtstream.WriteLine("    BORDER-RIGHT: #999999 3px solid;")
txtstream.WriteLine("    PADDING-RIGHT: 3px;")
txtstream.WriteLine("    PADDING-LEFT: 3px;")
txtstream.WriteLine("    FONT-WEIGHT: Normal;")
txtstream.WriteLine("    PADDING-BOTTOM: 3px;")
txtstream.WriteLine("    COLOR: white;")
txtstream.WriteLine("    PADDING-TOP: 3px;")
txtstream.WriteLine("    BORDER-BOTTOM: #999 1px solid;")
txtstream.WriteLine("    BACKGROUND-COLOR: navy;")
txtstream.WriteLine("    FONT-FAMILY: Cambria, serif;")
txtstream.WriteLine("    FONT-SIZE: 10px;")
txtstream.WriteLine("    text-align: left;")
txtstream.WriteLine("    white-Space: nowrap;")
txtstream.WriteLine("    width: 100%;")
txtstream.WriteLine("}")
txtstream.WriteLine(".Select")
txtstream.WriteLine("{")
txtstream.WriteLine("    BORDER-RIGHT: #999999 3px solid;")
txtstream.WriteLine("    PADDING-RIGHT: 6px;")
txtstream.WriteLine("    PADDING-LEFT: 6px;")
txtstream.WriteLine("    FONT-WEIGHT: Normal;")
txtstream.WriteLine("    PADDING-BOTTOM: 6px;")
txtstream.WriteLine("    COLOR: white;")
txtstream.WriteLine("    PADDING-TOP: 6px;")
txtstream.WriteLine("    BORDER-BOTTOM: #999 1px solid;")
txtstream.WriteLine("    BACKGROUND-COLOR: navy;")
```

```vb
        txtstream.WriteLine("      FONT-FAMILY: Cambria, serif;")
        txtstream.WriteLine("      FONT-SIZE: 10px;")
        txtstream.WriteLine("      text-align: left;")
        txtstream.WriteLine("      white-Space: nowrap;")
        txtstream.WriteLine("      width: 100%;")
        txtstream.WriteLine("}")
        txtstream.WriteLine("input")
        txtstream.WriteLine("{")
        txtstream.WriteLine("      BORDER-RIGHT: #999999 1px solid;")
        txtstream.WriteLine("      PADDING-RIGHT: 1px;")
        txtstream.WriteLine("      PADDING-LEFT: 1px;")
        txtstream.WriteLine("      FONT-WEIGHT: Normal;")
        txtstream.WriteLine("      PADDING-BOTTOM: 1px;")
        txtstream.WriteLine("      COLOR: White;")
        txtstream.WriteLine("      PADDING-TOP: 1px;")
        txtstream.WriteLine("      BORDER-BOTTOM: #999 1px solid;")
        txtstream.WriteLine("      BACKGROUND-COLOR: navy;")
        txtstream.WriteLine("      FONT-FAMILY: Cambria, serif;")
        txtstream.WriteLine("      FONT-SIZE: 12px;")
        txtstream.WriteLine("      text-align: left;")
        txtstream.WriteLine("      display: table-cell;")
        txtstream.WriteLine("      white-Space: nowrap;")
        txtstream.WriteLine("      width: auto;")
        txtstream.WriteLine("}")
        txtstream.WriteLine("</style>")
        txtstream.WriteLine("</head>")
        txtstream.WriteLine("<body>")
        txtstream.WriteLine("   <form id=""form1"" runat=""server"">")
        txtstream.WriteLine("      <div>")
        txtstream.WriteLine("         <asp:Table ID=""Table1"" runat=""Server"">")


        Dim cnstr As String = "Provider=Microsoft.Jet.OLEDB.4.0;Data Source=C:\nwind.mdb;"
        Dim strQuery As String = "Select * From Products"
        Dim cn As System.Data.OleDb.OleDbConnection = New System.Data.OleDb.OleDbConnection()
        cn.ConnectionString = cnstr
        cn.Open()


        Dim cmd As System.Data.OleDb.OleDbCommand = New System.Data.OleDb.OleDbCommand()
        cmd.Connection = cn
        cmd.CommandType = CommandType.Text
        cmd.CommandText = strQuery
        cmd.ExecuteNonQuery()


        Dim da As System.Data.OleDb.OleDbDataAdapter = New System.Data.OleDb.OleDbDataAdapter(cmd)
        Dim ds As System.Data.DataSet = New System.Data.DataSet()
        da.Fill(ds)

        txtstream.WriteLine("            <asp:TableHeaderRow>")
        For x As Integer = 0 To ds.Tables(0).Columns.Count - 1
            txtstream.WriteLine("               <asp:TableHeaderCell style=""text-align:left;"">" +
ds.Tables(0).Columns(x).Caption + "</asp:TableHeaderCell>")
        Next
        txtstream.WriteLine("            </asp:TableHeaderRow>")
        For y As Integer = 0 To ds.Tables(0).Rows.Count - 1
            txtstream.WriteLine("            <asp:TableRow>")
            For x As Integer = 0 To ds.Tables(0).Columns.Count - 1
                Try
                    txtstream.WriteLine("               <asp:TableCell style=""text-align:left;"">" +
Do_Unbound_Controls("Combobox", ds.Tables(0).Rows(y).Item(ds.Tables(0).Columns(x).Caption).ToString()) +
"</asp:TableCell>")
                Catch ex As Exception
                    txtstream.WriteLine("               <asp:TableCell style=""text-align:left;"">" +
Do_Unbound_Controls("Combobox", "") + "</asp:TableCell>")
                End Try
```

```vb
    Next
        txtstream.WriteLine("            </asp:TableRow>")
    Next
    txtstream.WriteLine("          </asp:Table>")
    txtstream.WriteLine("        </div>")
    txtstream.WriteLine("      </form>")
    txtstream.WriteLine("</body>")
    txtstream.WriteLine("</html>")
    txtstream.Close()

End Sub

Function Do_Unbound_Controls(ByVal ControlType As String, ByVal Value As String) As String

    Dim mystr

    Select Case ControlType

        Case "None"

            mystr = Value

        Case "Button"

            mystr = "<button value='" + Value + "' style='Width:100%'></button>"

        Case "Checkbox"

            mystr = "<label><input type='checkbox' value='" + Value + "'></input>" + Value + "</label>"

        Case "Combobox"

            mystr = mystr + "<select style='width:100%;'><option Value='" + Value + "'>" + Value + "</option></select>"

        Case "Div"

            mystr = "<div>" + Value + "</div>"

        Case "Input Button"

            mystr = "<input type='button' value='" + Value + "' style='Width:100%'></input>"

        Case "Label"

            mystr = "<Label>" + Value + "<Label>"

        Case "Listbox"

            mystr = "<select multiple=""true"" style='width:100%;'><option Value='" + Value + "'>" + Value + "</option></select>"

        Case "Radio Button"

            mystr = "<label><input type='radio' value='" + Value + "'></input>" + Value + "</label>"

        Case "Span"

            mystr = "<span>" + Value + "</span>"

        Case "Textbox"

            mystr = "<input type='text' Value='" + Value + "'></input>"

        Case "Textarea"
```

```
            mystr = "<textarea>" + Value + "</textarea>"

        End Select

        Return mystr

    End Function

End Class
```

Combobox example:

ProductID	ProductName		SupplierID	CategoryID	QuantityPerUnit	UnitPrice	UnitsInStock	UnitsOnOrder	ReorderLevel	Discontinued
1	Chai		1	1	10 boxes x 20 bags	18	39	0	10	False
2	Chang		1	1	24 - 12 oz bottles	19	17	40	25	False
3	Aniseed Syrup		1	2	12 - 550 ml bottles	10	13	70	25	False
4	Chef Anton's Cajun Seasoning		2	2	48 - 6 oz jars	22	53	0	0	False
5	Chef Anton's Gumbo Mix		2	2	36 boxes	21.35	0	0	0	True
6	Grandma's Boysenberry Spread		3	2	12 - 8 oz jars	25	120	0	25	False
7	Uncle Bob's Organic Dried Pears		3	7	12 - 1 lb pkgs	30	15	0	10	False
8	Northwoods Cranberry Sauce		3	2	12 - 12 oz jars	40	6	0	0	False
9	Mishi Kobe Niku		4	6	18 - 500 g pkgs	97	29	0	0	True
10	Ikura		4	8	12 - 200 ml jars	31	31	0	0	False
11	Queso Cabrales		5	4	1 kg pkg	21	22	30	30	False
12	Queso Manchego La Pastora		5	4	10 - 500 g pkgs	38	86	0	0	False
13	Konbu		6	8	2 kg box	6	24	0	5	False
14	Tofu		6	7	40 - 100 g pkgs	23.25	35	0	0	False

The Internal Code:

```
<%@ Page Language="VB" AutoEventWireup="false" CodeFile="Default.aspx.vb" Inherits="_Default" %>

<!DOCTYPE html PUBLIC "-//W3C//DTD XHTML 1.0 Transitional//EN"
"http://www.w3.org/TR/xhtml1/DTD/xhtml1-transitional.dtd">

<html xmlns="http://www.w3.org/1999/xhtml">
<head id="Head1" runat="server">
<title>Products</title>
<style type='text/css'>
body
{
    BORDER-TOP: navy 1px solid;
    BORDER-LEFT: navy 1px solid;
    BORDER-RIGHT: navy 1px solid;
    BORDER-BOTTOM: navy 1px solid;
    PADDING-RIGHT: 1px;
    PADDING-LEFT: 1px;
    FONT-WEIGHT: Normal;
    PADDING-BOTTOM: 1px;
    COLOR: black;
    PADDING-TOP: 1px;
    BORDER-BOTTOM: #999 1px solid;
    BACKGROUND-COLOR: ButtonFace;
    FONT-FAMILY: Cambria, serif;
    FONT-SIZE: 12px;
    text-align: left;
    display: table-cell;
```

```css
    white-Space: nowrap;
    width: auto;
    height: auto;
}
Table
{
    BORDER-TOP: navy 1px solid;
    BORDER-LEFT: navy 1px solid;
    BORDER-RIGHT: navy 1px solid;
    BORDER-BOTTOM: navy 1px solid;
    PADDING-RIGHT: 1px;
    PADDING-LEFT: 1px;
    FONT-WEIGHT: Normal;
    PADDING-BOTTOM: 1px;
    COLOR: black;
    PADDING-TOP: 1px;
    BORDER-BOTTOM: #999 1px solid;
    BACKGROUND-COLOR: ButtonFace;
    FONT-FAMILY: Cambria, serif;
    FONT-SIZE: 12px;
    text-align: left;
    display: table-cell;
    white-Space: nowrap;
    width: auto;
    height: auto;
}
th
{
    BORDER-RIGHT: #999999 2px solid;
    PADDING-RIGHT: 6px;
    PADDING-LEFT: 6px;
    FONT-WEIGHT: Bold;
    PADDING-BOTTOM: 6px;
    COLOR: #600000;
    PADDING-TOP: 6px;
    BORDER-BOTTOM: #999 2px solid;
    BACKGROUND-COLOR: #eeeeee;
    FONT-FAMILY: Cambria, serif;
    FONT-SIZE: 16px;
    text-align: right;
    white-Space: nowrap;
}
td
{
    BORDER-RIGHT: #999999 3px solid;
    PADDING-RIGHT: 6px;
    PADDING-LEFT: 6px;
    FONT-WEIGHT: Normal;
    PADDING-BOTTOM: 6px;
    COLOR: navy;
    LINE-HEIGHT: 14px;
    PADDING-TOP: 6px;
    BORDER-BOTTOM: #999 1px solid;
    BACKGROUND-COLOR: #eeeeee;
    FONT-FAMILY: Cambria, serif;
    FONT-SIZE: 12px;
    text-align: left;
    white-Space: nowrap;
}
.div
{
    BORDER-RIGHT: #999999 3px solid;
    PADDING-RIGHT: 6px;
    PADDING-LEFT: 6px;
    FONT-WEIGHT: Normal;
    PADDING-BOTTOM: 6px;
```

```css
    COLOR: white;
    PADDING-TOP: 6px;
    BORDER-BOTTOM: #999 1px solid;
    BACKGROUND-COLOR: navy;
    FONT-FAMILY: Cambria, serif;
    FONT-SIZE: 10px;
    text-align: left;
    white-Space: nowrap;
}
.span
{
    BORDER-RIGHT: #999999 3px solid;
    PADDING-RIGHT: 3px;
    PADDING-LEFT: 3px;
    FONT-WEIGHT: Normal;
    PADDING-BOTTOM: 3px;
    COLOR: white;
    PADDING-TOP: 3px;
    BORDER-BOTTOM: #999 1px solid;
    BACKGROUND-COLOR: navy;
    FONT-FAMILY: Cambria, serif;
    FONT-SIZE: 10px;
    text-align: left;
    white-Space: nowrap;
    display: inline-block;
    width: 100%;
}
.textarea
{
    BORDER-RIGHT: #999999 3px solid;
    PADDING-RIGHT: 3px;
    PADDING-LEFT: 3px;
    FONT-WEIGHT: Normal;
    PADDING-BOTTOM: 3px;
    COLOR: white;
    PADDING-TOP: 3px;
    BORDER-BOTTOM: #999 1px solid;
    BACKGROUND-COLOR: navy;
    FONT-FAMILY: Cambria, serif;
    FONT-SIZE: 10px;
    text-align: left;
    white-Space: nowrap;
    width: 100%;
}
.Select
{
    BORDER-RIGHT: #999999 3px solid;
    PADDING-RIGHT: 6px;
    PADDING-LEFT: 6px;
    FONT-WEIGHT: Normal;
    PADDING-BOTTOM: 6px;
    COLOR: white;
    PADDING-TOP: 6px;
    BORDER-BOTTOM: #999 1px solid;
    BACKGROUND-COLOR: navy;
    FONT-FAMILY: Cambria, serif;
    FONT-SIZE: 10px;
    text-align: left;
    white-Space: nowrap;
    width: 100%;
}
input
{
    BORDER-RIGHT: #999999 1px solid;
    PADDING-RIGHT: 1px;
    PADDING-LEFT: 1px;
```

```
                FONT-WEIGHT: Normal;
                PADDING-BOTTOM: 1px;
                COLOR: White;
                PADDING-TOP: 1px;
                BORDER-BOTTOM: #999 1px solid;
                BACKGROUND-COLOR: navy;
                FONT-FAMILY: Cambria, serif;
                FONT-SIZE: 12px;
                text-align: left;
                display: table-cell;
                white-Space: nowrap;
                width: auto;
        }
        </style>
        </head>
        <body>
            <form id="form1" runat="server">
                <div>
        <%
            Write_The_Code()
        %>
                </div>
            </form>
        </body>
        </html>
```

And the code behind:

```
Partial Class _Default
    Inherits System.Web.UI.Page

    Public Sub Write_The_Code()

        Dim cnstr As String = "Provider=Microsoft.Jet.OLEDB.4.0;Data Source=C:\nwind.mdb;"
        Dim strQuery As String = "Select * From Products"
        Dim cn As System.Data.OleDb.OleDbConnection = New System.Data.OleDb.OleDbConnection()
        cn.ConnectionString = cnstr
        cn.Open()

        Dim cmd As System.Data.OleDb.OleDbCommand = New System.Data.OleDb.OleDbCommand()
        cmd.Connection = cn
        cmd.CommandType = System.Data.CommandType.Text
        cmd.CommandText = strQuery
        cmd.ExecuteNonQuery()

        Dim da As System.Data.OleDb.OleDbDataAdapter = New System.Data.OleDb.OleDbDataAdapter(cmd)
        Dim ds As System.Data.DataSet = New System.Data.DataSet()
        da.Fill(ds)

        Response.Write("          <table cellspacing='2' cellpadding= '2'>" & vbCrLf)
        Response.Write("            <tr>" & vbCrLf)
        For x As Integer = 0 To ds.Tables(0).Columns.Count - 1
            Response.Write("            <th style=""text-align:left;"">" + ds.Tables(0).Columns(x).Caption +
"</th>" & vbCrLf)
        Next
        Response.Write("            </tr>" & vbCrLf)
        For y As Integer = 0 To ds.Tables(0).Rows.Count - 1
            Response.Write("            <tr>" & vbCrLf)
            For x As Integer = 0 To ds.Tables(0).Columns.Count - 1
            Try
                Response.Write("            <td style=""text-align:left;"">" + Do_Unbound_Controls("Combobox",
ds.Tables(0).Rows(y).Item(ds.Tables(0).Columns(x).Caption).ToString()) + "</td>" & vbCrLf)
            Catch ex As Exception
                Response.Write("            <td style=""text-align:left;"">" + Do_Unbound_Controls("Combobox",
"") + "</td>" & vbCrLf)
```

```vb
            End Try

        Next
            Response.Write("            </tr>" & vbCrLf)
        Next
        Response.Write("            </table>" & vbCrLf)


    End Sub

    Function Do_Unbound_Controls(ByVal ControlType As String, ByVal Value As String) As String

        Dim mystr As String = ""

        Select Case ControlType


            Case "None"

                mystr = Value

            Case "Button"

                mystr = "<button value='" + Value + "' style='Width:100%'></button>"

            Case "Checkbox"

                mystr = "<label><input type='checkbox' value='" + Value + "'></input>" + Value + "</label>"

            Case "Combobox"

                mystr = mystr + "<select style='width:100%;'><option Value='" + Value + "'>" + Value +
"</option></select>"

            Case "Div"

                mystr = "<div>" + Value + "</div>"

            Case "Input Button"

                mystr = "<input type='button' value='" + Value + "' style='Width:100%'></input>"

            Case "Label"

                mystr = "<Label>" + Value + "<Label>"

            Case "Listbox"

                mystr = "<select multiple=""true"" style='width:100%;'><option Value='" + Value + "'>" + Value +
"</option></select>"

            Case "Radio Button"

                mystr = "<label><input type='radio' value='" + Value + "'></input>" + Value + "</label>"

            Case "Span"

                mystr = "<span>" + Value + "</span>"

            Case "Textbox"

                mystr = "<input type='text' Value='" + Value + "'></input>"

            Case "Textarea"

                mystr = "<textarea>" + Value + "</textarea>"
```

End Select

Return mystr

End Function

End Class

This gives us a lot more flexibility. Can we do the same for verticals?

Here's the external code:

Public Class Form1

```vbnet
Private Sub Form1_Load(ByVal sender As System.Object, ByVal e As System.EventArgs) Handles MyBase.Load

    Dim fso As Object = CreateObject("Scripting.FileSystemObject")
    Dim txtstream As Object = fso.OpenTextFile(Application.StartupPath & "\Products.aspx", 2, True, -2)
    txtstream.WriteLine("<html xmlns=""http://www.w3.org/1999/xhtml"">")
    txtstream.WriteLine("<head runat=""server"">")
    txtstream.WriteLine("  <title>Products</title>")
    txtstream.WriteLine("<style type='text/css'>")
    txtstream.WriteLine("body")
    txtstream.WriteLine("{")
    txtstream.WriteLine("    BORDER-TOP: navy 1px solid;")
    txtstream.WriteLine("    BORDER-LEFT: navy 1px solid;")
    txtstream.WriteLine("    BORDER-RIGHT: navy 1px solid;")
    txtstream.WriteLine("    BORDER-BOTTOM: navy 1px solid;")
    txtstream.WriteLine("    PADDING-RIGHT: 1px;")
    txtstream.WriteLine("    PADDING-LEFT: 1px;")
    txtstream.WriteLine("    FONT-WEIGHT: Normal;")
    txtstream.WriteLine("    PADDING-BOTTOM: 1px;")
    txtstream.WriteLine("    COLOR: black;")
    txtstream.WriteLine("    PADDING-TOP: 1px;")
    txtstream.WriteLine("    BORDER-BOTTOM: #999 1px solid;")
    txtstream.WriteLine("    BACKGROUND-COLOR: ButtonFace;")
    txtstream.WriteLine("    FONT-FAMILY: Cambria, serif;")
    txtstream.WriteLine("    FONT-SIZE: 12px;")
    txtstream.WriteLine("    text-align: left;")
    txtstream.WriteLine("    display: table-cell;")
    txtstream.WriteLine("    white-Space: nowrap;")
    txtstream.WriteLine("    width: auto;")
    txtstream.WriteLine("    height: auto;")
    txtstream.WriteLine("}")
    txtstream.WriteLine("Table")
    txtstream.WriteLine("{")
    txtstream.WriteLine("    BORDER-TOP: navy 1px solid;")
    txtstream.WriteLine("    BORDER-LEFT: navy 1px solid;")
    txtstream.WriteLine("    BORDER-RIGHT: navy 1px solid;")
    txtstream.WriteLine("    BORDER-BOTTOM: navy 1px solid;")
    txtstream.WriteLine("    PADDING-RIGHT: 1px;")
    txtstream.WriteLine("    PADDING-LEFT: 1px;")
    txtstream.WriteLine("    FONT-WEIGHT: Normal;")
    txtstream.WriteLine("    PADDING-BOTTOM: 1px;")
    txtstream.WriteLine("    COLOR: black;")
    txtstream.WriteLine("    PADDING-TOP: 1px;")
    txtstream.WriteLine("    BORDER-BOTTOM: #999 1px solid;")
    txtstream.WriteLine("    BACKGROUND-COLOR: ButtonFace;")
    txtstream.WriteLine("    FONT-FAMILY: Cambria, serif;")
    txtstream.WriteLine("    FONT-SIZE: 12px;")
    txtstream.WriteLine("    text-align: left;")
    txtstream.WriteLine("    display: table-cell;")
    txtstream.WriteLine("    white-Space: nowrap;")
    txtstream.WriteLine("    width: auto;")
    txtstream.WriteLine("    height: auto;")
```

```
txtstream.WriteLine("}")
txtstream.WriteLine("th")
txtstream.WriteLine("{")
txtstream.WriteLine("    BORDER-RIGHT: #999999 2px solid;")
txtstream.WriteLine("    PADDING-RIGHT: 6px;")
txtstream.WriteLine("    PADDING-LEFT: 6px;")
txtstream.WriteLine("    FONT-WEIGHT: Bold;")
txtstream.WriteLine("    PADDING-BOTTOM: 6px;")
txtstream.WriteLine("    COLOR: #600000;")
txtstream.WriteLine("    PADDING-TOP: 6px;")
txtstream.WriteLine("    BORDER-BOTTOM: #999 2px solid;")
txtstream.WriteLine("    BACKGROUND-COLOR: #eeeeee;")
txtstream.WriteLine("    FONT-FAMILY: Cambria, serif;")
txtstream.WriteLine("    FONT-SIZE: 16px;")
txtstream.WriteLine("    text-align: right;")
txtstream.WriteLine("    white-Space: nowrap;")
txtstream.WriteLine("}")
txtstream.WriteLine("td")
txtstream.WriteLine("{")
txtstream.WriteLine("    BORDER-RIGHT: #999999 3px solid;")
txtstream.WriteLine("    PADDING-RIGHT: 6px;")
txtstream.WriteLine("    PADDING-LEFT: 6px;")
txtstream.WriteLine("    FONT-WEIGHT: Normal;")
txtstream.WriteLine("    PADDING-BOTTOM: 6px;")
txtstream.WriteLine("    COLOR: navy;")
txtstream.WriteLine("    LINE-HEIGHT: 14px;")
txtstream.WriteLine("    PADDING-TOP: 6px;")
txtstream.WriteLine("    BORDER-BOTTOM: #999 1px solid;")
txtstream.WriteLine("    BACKGROUND-COLOR: #eeeeee;")
txtstream.WriteLine("    FONT-FAMILY: Cambria, serif;")
txtstream.WriteLine("    FONT-SIZE: 12px;")
txtstream.WriteLine("    text-align: left;")
txtstream.WriteLine("    white-Space: nowrap;")
txtstream.WriteLine("}")
txtstream.WriteLine(".div")
txtstream.WriteLine("{")
txtstream.WriteLine("    BORDER-RIGHT: #999999 3px solid;")
txtstream.WriteLine("    PADDING-RIGHT: 6px;")
txtstream.WriteLine("    PADDING-LEFT: 6px;")
txtstream.WriteLine("    FONT-WEIGHT: Normal;")
txtstream.WriteLine("    PADDING-BOTTOM: 6px;")
txtstream.WriteLine("    COLOR: white;")
txtstream.WriteLine("    PADDING-TOP: 6px;")
txtstream.WriteLine("    BORDER-BOTTOM: #999 1px solid;")
txtstream.WriteLine("    BACKGROUND-COLOR: navy;")
txtstream.WriteLine("    FONT-FAMILY: Cambria, serif;")
txtstream.WriteLine("    FONT-SIZE: 10px;")
txtstream.WriteLine("    text-align: left;")
txtstream.WriteLine("    white-Space: nowrap;")
txtstream.WriteLine("}")
txtstream.WriteLine(".span")
txtstream.WriteLine("{")
txtstream.WriteLine("    BORDER-RIGHT: #999999 3px solid;")
txtstream.WriteLine("    PADDING-RIGHT: 3px;")
txtstream.WriteLine("    PADDING-LEFT: 3px;")
txtstream.WriteLine("    FONT-WEIGHT: Normal;")
txtstream.WriteLine("    PADDING-BOTTOM: 3px;")
txtstream.WriteLine("    COLOR: white;")
txtstream.WriteLine("    PADDING-TOP: 3px;")
txtstream.WriteLine("    BORDER-BOTTOM: #999 1px solid;")
txtstream.WriteLine("    BACKGROUND-COLOR: navy;")
txtstream.WriteLine("    FONT-FAMILY: Cambria, serif;")
txtstream.WriteLine("    FONT-SIZE: 10px;")
txtstream.WriteLine("    text-align: left;")
txtstream.WriteLine("    white-Space: nowrap;")
txtstream.WriteLine("    display: inline-block;")
```

```vb
txtstream.WriteLine("    width: 100%;")
txtstream.WriteLine("}")
txtstream.WriteLine(".textarea")
txtstream.WriteLine("{")
txtstream.WriteLine("    BORDER-RIGHT: #999999 3px solid;")
txtstream.WriteLine("    PADDING-RIGHT: 3px;")
txtstream.WriteLine("    PADDING-LEFT: 3px;")
txtstream.WriteLine("    FONT-WEIGHT: Normal;")
txtstream.WriteLine("    PADDING-BOTTOM: 3px;")
txtstream.WriteLine("    COLOR: white;")
txtstream.WriteLine("    PADDING-TOP: 3px;")
txtstream.WriteLine("    BORDER-BOTTOM: #999 1px solid;")
txtstream.WriteLine("    BACKGROUND-COLOR: navy;")
txtstream.WriteLine("    FONT-FAMILY: Cambria, serif;")
txtstream.WriteLine("    FONT-SIZE: 10px;")
txtstream.WriteLine("    text-align: left;")
txtstream.WriteLine("    white-Space: nowrap;")
txtstream.WriteLine("    width: 100%;")
txtstream.WriteLine("}")
txtstream.WriteLine(".Select")
txtstream.WriteLine("{")
txtstream.WriteLine("    BORDER-RIGHT: #999999 3px solid;")
txtstream.WriteLine("    PADDING-RIGHT: 6px;")
txtstream.WriteLine("    PADDING-LEFT: 6px;")
txtstream.WriteLine("    FONT-WEIGHT: Normal;")
txtstream.WriteLine("    PADDING-BOTTOM: 6px;")
txtstream.WriteLine("    COLOR: white;")
txtstream.WriteLine("    PADDING-TOP: 6px;")
txtstream.WriteLine("    BORDER-BOTTOM: #999 1px solid;")
txtstream.WriteLine("    BACKGROUND-COLOR: navy;")
txtstream.WriteLine("    FONT-FAMILY: Cambria, serif;")
txtstream.WriteLine("    FONT-SIZE: 10px;")
txtstream.WriteLine("    text-align: left;")
txtstream.WriteLine("    white-Space: nowrap;")
txtstream.WriteLine("    width: 100%;")
txtstream.WriteLine("}")
txtstream.WriteLine("input")
txtstream.WriteLine("{")
txtstream.WriteLine("    BORDER-RIGHT: #999999 1px solid;")
txtstream.WriteLine("    PADDING-RIGHT: 1px;")
txtstream.WriteLine("    PADDING-LEFT: 1px;")
txtstream.WriteLine("    FONT-WEIGHT: Normal;")
txtstream.WriteLine("    PADDING-BOTTOM: 1px;")
txtstream.WriteLine("    COLOR: White;")
txtstream.WriteLine("    PADDING-TOP: 1px;")
txtstream.WriteLine("    BORDER-BOTTOM: #999 1px solid;")
txtstream.WriteLine("    BACKGROUND-COLOR: navy;")
txtstream.WriteLine("    FONT-FAMILY: Cambria, serif;")
txtstream.WriteLine("    FONT-SIZE: 12px;")
txtstream.WriteLine("    text-align: left;")
txtstream.WriteLine("    display: table-cell;")
txtstream.WriteLine("    white-Space: nowrap;")
txtstream.WriteLine("    width: auto;")
txtstream.WriteLine("}")
txtstream.WriteLine("</style>")
txtstream.WriteLine("</head>")
txtstream.WriteLine("<body>")
txtstream.WriteLine("    <form id=""form1"" runat=""server"">")
txtstream.WriteLine("        <div>")
txtstream.WriteLine("            <asp:Table ID=""Table1"" runat=""Server"">")


Dim cnstr As String = "Provider=Microsoft.Jet.OLEDB.4.0;Data Source=C:\nwind.mdb;"
Dim strQuery As String = "Select * From Products"
Dim cn As System.Data.OleDb.OleDbConnection = New System.Data.OleDb.OleDbConnection()
cn.ConnectionString = cnstr
```

```vb
cn.Open()

Dim cmd As System.Data.OleDb.OleDbCommand = New System.Data.OleDb.OleDbCommand()
cmd.Connection = cn
cmd.CommandType = CommandType.Text
cmd.CommandText = strQuery
cmd.ExecuteNonQuery()

Dim da As System.Data.OleDb.OleDbDataAdapter = New System.Data.OleDb.OleDbDataAdapter(cmd)
Dim ds As System.Data.DataSet = New System.Data.DataSet()
da.Fill(ds)

txtstream.WriteLine("            <asp:TableHeaderRow>")
txtstream.WriteLine("                <asp:TableHeaderCell style=""text-align:left;"">Property
Name</asp:TableHeaderCell>")
    For y As Integer = 0 To ds.Tables(0).Rows.Count - 1
        txtstream.WriteLine("                <asp:TableHeaderCell style=""text-align:left;"">Row" + y.ToString() +
"</asp:TableHeaderCell>")
    Next
txtstream.WriteLine("            </asp:TableHeaderRow>")

    For x As Integer = 0 To ds.Tables(0).Columns.Count - 1
        txtstream.WriteLine("            <asp:TableRow><asp:TableCell style=""text-align:left;"">" +
ds.Tables(0).Columns(x).Caption + "</asp:TableCell>")
        For y As Integer = 0 To ds.Tables(0).Rows.Count - 1
            Try
                txtstream.WriteLine("                <asp:TableCell style=""text-align:left;"">" +
Do_Unbound_Controls("Textbox", ds.Tables(0).Rows(y).Item(ds.Tables(0).Columns(x).Caption).ToString()) +
"</asp:TableCell>")
            Catch ex As Exception
                txtstream.WriteLine("                <asp:TableCell style=""text-align:left;"">" +
Do_Unbound_Controls("Textbox", "") + "</asp:TableCell>")
            End Try
        Next
        txtstream.WriteLine("            </asp:TableRow>")
    Next
txtstream.WriteLine("            </asp:Table>")
txtstream.WriteLine("        </div>")
txtstream.WriteLine("    </form>")
txtstream.WriteLine("</body>")
txtstream.WriteLine("</html>")
txtstream.Close()

End Sub

Function Do_Unbound_Controls(ByVal ControlType As String, ByVal Value As String) As String

    Dim mystr

    Select Case ControlType

        Case "None"

            mystr = Value

        Case "Button"

            mystr = "<button value='" + Value + "' style='Width:100%'></button>"

        Case "Checkbox"

            mystr = "<label><input type='checkbox' value='" + Value + "'></input>" + Value + "</label>"

        Case "Combobox"
```

```vb
        mystr = mystr + "<select style='width:100%;'><option Value='" + Value + "'>" + Value +
"</option></select>"

        Case "Div"

            mystr = "<div>" + Value + "</div>"

        Case "Input Button"

            mystr = "<input type='button' value='" + Value + "' style='Width:100%'></input>"

        Case "Label"

            mystr = "<Label>" + Value + "<Label>"

        Case "Listbox"

            mystr = "<select multiple=""true"" style='width:100%;'><option Value='" + Value + "'>" + Value +
"</option></select>"

        Case "Radio Button"

            mystr = "<label><input type='radio' value='" + Value + "'></input>" + Value + "</label>"

        Case "Span"

            mystr = "<span>" + Value + "</span>"

        Case "Textbox"

            mystr = "<input type='text' Value='" + Value + "'></input>"

        Case "Textarea"

            mystr = "<textarea>" + Value + "</textarea>"

    End Select

    Return mystr

  End Function

End Class
```

The Code it produces:

```html
<html xmlns="http://www.w3.org/1999/xhtml">
<head id="Head1" runat="server">
  <title>Products</title>
<style type='text/css'>
body
{
  BORDER-TOP: navy 1px solid;
  BORDER-LEFT: navy 1px solid;
  BORDER-RIGHT: navy 1px solid;
  BORDER-BOTTOM: navy 1px solid;
  PADDING-RIGHT: 1px;
  PADDING-LEFT: 1px;
  FONT-WEIGHT: Normal;
  PADDING-BOTTOM: 1px;
  COLOR: black;
  PADDING-TOP: 1px;
  BORDER-BOTTOM: #999 1px solid;
  BACKGROUND-COLOR: ButtonFace;
  FONT-FAMILY: Cambria, serif;
```

```
    FONT-SIZE: 12px;
    text-align: left;
    display: table-cell;
    white-Space: nowrap;
    width: auto;
    height: auto;
}
Table
{
    BORDER-TOP: navy 1px solid;
    BORDER-LEFT: navy 1px solid;
    BORDER-RIGHT: navy 1px solid;
    BORDER-BOTTOM: navy 1px solid;
    PADDING-RIGHT: 1px;
    PADDING-LEFT: 1px;
    FONT-WEIGHT: Normal;
    PADDING-BOTTOM: 1px;
    COLOR: black;
    PADDING-TOP: 1px;
    BORDER-BOTTOM: #999 1px solid;
    BACKGROUND-COLOR: ButtonFace;
    FONT-FAMILY: Cambria, serif;
    FONT-SIZE: 12px;
    text-align: left;
    display: table-cell;
    white-Space: nowrap;
    width: auto;
    height: auto;
}
th
{
    BORDER-RIGHT: #999999 2px solid;
    PADDING-RIGHT: 6px;
    PADDING-LEFT: 6px;
    FONT-WEIGHT: Bold;
    PADDING-BOTTOM: 6px;
    COLOR: #600000;
    PADDING-TOP: 6px;
    BORDER-BOTTOM: #999 2px solid;
    BACKGROUND-COLOR: #eeeeee;
    FONT-FAMILY: Cambria, serif;
    FONT-SIZE: 16px;
    text-align: right;
    white-Space: nowrap;
}
td
{
    BORDER-RIGHT: #999999 3px solid;
    PADDING-RIGHT: 6px;
    PADDING-LEFT: 6px;
    FONT-WEIGHT: Normal;
    PADDING-BOTTOM: 6px;
    COLOR: navy;
    LINE-HEIGHT: 14px;
    PADDING-TOP: 6px;
    BORDER-BOTTOM: #999 1px solid;
    BACKGROUND-COLOR: #eeeeee;
    FONT-FAMILY: Cambria, serif;
    FONT-SIZE: 12px;
    text-align: left;
    white-Space: nowrap;
}
.div
{
    BORDER-RIGHT: #999999 3px solid;
    PADDING-RIGHT: 6px;
```

```css
    PADDING-LEFT: 6px;
    FONT-WEIGHT: Normal;
    PADDING-BOTTOM: 6px;
    COLOR: white;
    PADDING-TOP: 6px;
    BORDER-BOTTOM: #999 1px solid;
    BACKGROUND-COLOR: navy;
    FONT-FAMILY: Cambria, serif;
    FONT-SIZE: 10px;
    text-align: left;
    white-Space: nowrap;
}
.span
{
    BORDER-RIGHT: #999999 3px solid;
    PADDING-RIGHT: 3px;
    PADDING-LEFT: 3px;
    FONT-WEIGHT: Normal;
    PADDING-BOTTOM: 3px;
    COLOR: white;
    PADDING-TOP: 3px;
    BORDER-BOTTOM: #999 1px solid;
    BACKGROUND-COLOR: navy;
    FONT-FAMILY: Cambria, serif;
    FONT-SIZE: 10px;
    text-align: left;
    white-Space: nowrap;
    display: inline-block;
    width: 100%;
}
.textarea
{
    BORDER-RIGHT: #999999 3px solid;
    PADDING-RIGHT: 3px;
    PADDING-LEFT: 3px;
    FONT-WEIGHT: Normal;
    PADDING-BOTTOM: 3px;
    COLOR: white;
    PADDING-TOP: 3px;
    BORDER-BOTTOM: #999 1px solid;
    BACKGROUND-COLOR: navy;
    FONT-FAMILY: Cambria, serif;
    FONT-SIZE: 10px;
    text-align: left;
    white-Space: nowrap;
    width: 100%;
}
.Select
{
    BORDER-RIGHT: #999999 3px solid;
    PADDING-RIGHT: 6px;
    PADDING-LEFT: 6px;
    FONT-WEIGHT: Normal;
    PADDING-BOTTOM: 6px;
    COLOR: white;
    PADDING-TOP: 6px;
    BORDER-BOTTOM: #999 1px solid;
    BACKGROUND-COLOR: navy;
    FONT-FAMILY: Cambria, serif;
    FONT-SIZE: 10px;
    text-align: left;
    white-Space: nowrap;
    width: 100%;
}
input
{
```

```
    BORDER-RIGHT: #999999 1px solid;
    PADDING-RIGHT: 1px;
    PADDING-LEFT: 1px;
    FONT-WEIGHT: Normal;
    PADDING-BOTTOM: 1px;
    COLOR: White;
    PADDING-TOP: 1px;
    BORDER-BOTTOM: #999 1px solid;
    BACKGROUND-COLOR: navy;
    FONT-FAMILY: Cambria, serif;
    FONT-SIZE: 12px;
    text-align: left;
    display: table-cell;
    white-Space: nowrap;
    width: auto;
}
</style>
</head>
<body>
    <form id="form1" runat="server">
        <div>
            <asp:Table ID="Table1" runat="Server">
                <asp:TableHeaderRow>
                    <asp:TableHeaderCell style="text-align:left;">Property Name</asp:TableHeaderCell>
                    <asp:TableHeaderCell style="text-align:left;">Row0</asp:TableHeaderCell>
                    <asp:TableHeaderCell style="text-align:left;">Row1</asp:TableHeaderCell>
                    <asp:TableHeaderCell style="text-align:left;">Row2</asp:TableHeaderCell>
                    <asp:TableHeaderCell style="text-align:left;">Row3</asp:TableHeaderCell>
                    <asp:TableHeaderCell style="text-align:left;">Row4</asp:TableHeaderCell>
                    <asp:TableHeaderCell style="text-align:left;">Row5</asp:TableHeaderCell>
                    <asp:TableHeaderCell style="text-align:left;">Row6</asp:TableHeaderCell>
                    <asp:TableHeaderCell style="text-align:left;">Row7</asp:TableHeaderCell>
                    <asp:TableHeaderCell style="text-align:left;">Row8</asp:TableHeaderCell>
                    <asp:TableHeaderCell style="text-align:left;">Row9</asp:TableHeaderCell>
                    <asp:TableHeaderCell style="text-align:left;">Row10</asp:TableHeaderCell>
                    <asp:TableHeaderCell style="text-align:left;">Row11</asp:TableHeaderCell>
                    <asp:TableHeaderCell style="text-align:left;">Row12</asp:TableHeaderCell>
                    <asp:TableHeaderCell style="text-align:left;">Row13</asp:TableHeaderCell>
                    <asp:TableHeaderCell style="text-align:left;">Row14</asp:TableHeaderCell>
                    <asp:TableHeaderCell style="text-align:left;">Row15</asp:TableHeaderCell>
                    <asp:TableHeaderCell style="text-align:left;">Row16</asp:TableHeaderCell>
                    <asp:TableHeaderCell style="text-align:left;">Row17</asp:TableHeaderCell>
                    <asp:TableHeaderCell style="text-align:left;">Row18</asp:TableHeaderCell>
                    <asp:TableHeaderCell style="text-align:left;">Row19</asp:TableHeaderCell>
                    <asp:TableHeaderCell style="text-align:left;">Row20</asp:TableHeaderCell>
                    <asp:TableHeaderCell style="text-align:left;">Row21</asp:TableHeaderCell>
                    <asp:TableHeaderCell style="text-align:left;">Row22</asp:TableHeaderCell>
                    <asp:TableHeaderCell style="text-align:left;">Row23</asp:TableHeaderCell>
                    <asp:TableHeaderCell style="text-align:left;">Row24</asp:TableHeaderCell>
                    <asp:TableHeaderCell style="text-align:left;">Row25</asp:TableHeaderCell>
                    <asp:TableHeaderCell style="text-align:left;">Row26</asp:TableHeaderCell>
                    <asp:TableHeaderCell style="text-align:left;">Row27</asp:TableHeaderCell>
                    <asp:TableHeaderCell style="text-align:left;">Row28</asp:TableHeaderCell>
                    <asp:TableHeaderCell style="text-align:left;">Row29</asp:TableHeaderCell>
                    <asp:TableHeaderCell style="text-align:left;">Row30</asp:TableHeaderCell>
                    <asp:TableHeaderCell style="text-align:left;">Row31</asp:TableHeaderCell>
                    <asp:TableHeaderCell style="text-align:left;">Row32</asp:TableHeaderCell>
                    <asp:TableHeaderCell style="text-align:left;">Row33</asp:TableHeaderCell>
                    <asp:TableHeaderCell style="text-align:left;">Row34</asp:TableHeaderCell>
                    <asp:TableHeaderCell style="text-align:left;">Row35</asp:TableHeaderCell>
                    <asp:TableHeaderCell style="text-align:left;">Row36</asp:TableHeaderCell>
                    <asp:TableHeaderCell style="text-align:left;">Row37</asp:TableHeaderCell>
                    <asp:TableHeaderCell style="text-align:left;">Row38</asp:TableHeaderCell>
                    <asp:TableHeaderCell style="text-align:left;">Row39</asp:TableHeaderCell>
                    <asp:TableHeaderCell style="text-align:left;">Row40</asp:TableHeaderCell>
                    <asp:TableHeaderCell style="text-align:left;">Row41</asp:TableHeaderCell>
```

```
    <asp:TableHeaderCell style="text-align:left;">Row42</asp:TableHeaderCell>
    <asp:TableHeaderCell style="text-align:left;">Row43</asp:TableHeaderCell>
    <asp:TableHeaderCell style="text-align:left;">Row44</asp:TableHeaderCell>
    <asp:TableHeaderCell style="text-align:left;">Row45</asp:TableHeaderCell>
    <asp:TableHeaderCell style="text-align:left;">Row46</asp:TableHeaderCell>
    <asp:TableHeaderCell style="text-align:left;">Row47</asp:TableHeaderCell>
    <asp:TableHeaderCell style="text-align:left;">Row48</asp:TableHeaderCell>
    <asp:TableHeaderCell style="text-align:left;">Row49</asp:TableHeaderCell>
    <asp:TableHeaderCell style="text-align:left;">Row50</asp:TableHeaderCell>
    <asp:TableHeaderCell style="text-align:left;">Row51</asp:TableHeaderCell>
    <asp:TableHeaderCell style="text-align:left;">Row52</asp:TableHeaderCell>
    <asp:TableHeaderCell style="text-align:left;">Row53</asp:TableHeaderCell>
    <asp:TableHeaderCell style="text-align:left;">Row54</asp:TableHeaderCell>
    <asp:TableHeaderCell style="text-align:left;">Row55</asp:TableHeaderCell>
    <asp:TableHeaderCell style="text-align:left;">Row56</asp:TableHeaderCell>
    <asp:TableHeaderCell style="text-align:left;">Row57</asp:TableHeaderCell>
    <asp:TableHeaderCell style="text-align:left;">Row58</asp:TableHeaderCell>
    <asp:TableHeaderCell style="text-align:left;">Row59</asp:TableHeaderCell>
    <asp:TableHeaderCell style="text-align:left;">Row60</asp:TableHeaderCell>
    <asp:TableHeaderCell style="text-align:left;">Row61</asp:TableHeaderCell>
    <asp:TableHeaderCell style="text-align:left;">Row62</asp:TableHeaderCell>
    <asp:TableHeaderCell style="text-align:left;">Row63</asp:TableHeaderCell>
    <asp:TableHeaderCell style="text-align:left;">Row64</asp:TableHeaderCell>
    <asp:TableHeaderCell style="text-align:left;">Row65</asp:TableHeaderCell>
    <asp:TableHeaderCell style="text-align:left;">Row66</asp:TableHeaderCell>
    <asp:TableHeaderCell style="text-align:left;">Row67</asp:TableHeaderCell>
    <asp:TableHeaderCell style="text-align:left;">Row68</asp:TableHeaderCell>
    <asp:TableHeaderCell style="text-align:left;">Row69</asp:TableHeaderCell>
    <asp:TableHeaderCell style="text-align:left;">Row70</asp:TableHeaderCell>
    <asp:TableHeaderCell style="text-align:left;">Row71</asp:TableHeaderCell>
    <asp:TableHeaderCell style="text-align:left;">Row72</asp:TableHeaderCell>
    <asp:TableHeaderCell style="text-align:left;">Row73</asp:TableHeaderCell>
    <asp:TableHeaderCell style="text-align:left;">Row74</asp:TableHeaderCell>
    <asp:TableHeaderCell style="text-align:left;">Row75</asp:TableHeaderCell>
    <asp:TableHeaderCell style="text-align:left;">Row76</asp:TableHeaderCell>
</asp:TableHeaderRow>
    <asp:TableRow><asp:TableCell style="text-align:left;">ProductID</asp:TableCell>
    <asp:TableCell style="text-align:left;"><input type='text' Value='1'></input></asp:TableCell>
    <asp:TableCell style="text-align:left;"><input type='text' Value='2'></input></asp:TableCell>
    <asp:TableCell style="text-align:left;"><input type='text' Value='3'></input></asp:TableCell>
    <asp:TableCell style="text-align:left;"><input type='text' Value='4'></input></asp:TableCell>
    <asp:TableCell style="text-align:left;"><input type='text' Value='5'></input></asp:TableCell>
    <asp:TableCell style="text-align:left;"><input type='text' Value='6'></input></asp:TableCell>
    <asp:TableCell style="text-align:left;"><input type='text' Value='7'></input></asp:TableCell>
    <asp:TableCell style="text-align:left;"><input type='text' Value='8'></input></asp:TableCell>
    <asp:TableCell style="text-align:left;"><input type='text' Value='9'></input></asp:TableCell>
    <asp:TableCell style="text-align:left;"><input type='text' Value='10'></input></asp:TableCell>
    <asp:TableCell style="text-align:left;"><input type='text' Value='11'></input></asp:TableCell>
    <asp:TableCell style="text-align:left;"><input type='text' Value='12'></input></asp:TableCell>
    <asp:TableCell style="text-align:left;"><input type='text' Value='13'></input></asp:TableCell>
    <asp:TableCell style="text-align:left;"><input type='text' Value='14'></input></asp:TableCell>
    <asp:TableCell style="text-align:left;"><input type='text' Value='15'></input></asp:TableCell>
    <asp:TableCell style="text-align:left;"><input type='text' Value='16'></input></asp:TableCell>
    <asp:TableCell style="text-align:left;"><input type='text' Value='17'></input></asp:TableCell>
    <asp:TableCell style="text-align:left;"><input type='text' Value='18'></input></asp:TableCell>
    <asp:TableCell style="text-align:left;"><input type='text' Value='19'></input></asp:TableCell>
    <asp:TableCell style="text-align:left;"><input type='text' Value='20'></input></asp:TableCell>
    <asp:TableCell style="text-align:left;"><input type='text' Value='21'></input></asp:TableCell>
    <asp:TableCell style="text-align:left;"><input type='text' Value='22'></input></asp:TableCell>
    <asp:TableCell style="text-align:left;"><input type='text' Value='23'></input></asp:TableCell>
    <asp:TableCell style="text-align:left;"><input type='text' Value='24'></input></asp:TableCell>
    <asp:TableCell style="text-align:left;"><input type='text' Value='25'></input></asp:TableCell>
    <asp:TableCell style="text-align:left;"><input type='text' Value='26'></input></asp:TableCell>
    <asp:TableCell style="text-align:left;"><input type='text' Value='27'></input></asp:TableCell>
    <asp:TableCell style="text-align:left;"><input type='text' Value='28'></input></asp:TableCell>
    <asp:TableCell style="text-align:left;"><input type='text' Value='29'></input></asp:TableCell>
```

```
            <asp:TableCell style="text-align:left;"><input type='text' Value='30'></input></asp:TableCell>
            <asp:TableCell style="text-align:left;"><input type='text' Value='31'></input></asp:TableCell>
            <asp:TableCell style="text-align:left;"><input type='text' Value='32'></input></asp:TableCell>
            <asp:TableCell style="text-align:left;"><input type='text' Value='33'></input></asp:TableCell>
            <asp:TableCell style="text-align:left;"><input type='text' Value='34'></input></asp:TableCell>
            <asp:TableCell style="text-align:left;"><input type='text' Value='35'></input></asp:TableCell>
            <asp:TableCell style="text-align:left;"><input type='text' Value='36'></input></asp:TableCell>
            <asp:TableCell style="text-align:left;"><input type='text' Value='37'></input></asp:TableCell>
            <asp:TableCell style="text-align:left;"><input type='text' Value='38'></input></asp:TableCell>
            <asp:TableCell style="text-align:left;"><input type='text' Value='39'></input></asp:TableCell>
            <asp:TableCell style="text-align:left;"><input type='text' Value='40'></input></asp:TableCell>
            <asp:TableCell style="text-align:left;"><input type='text' Value='41'></input></asp:TableCell>
            <asp:TableCell style="text-align:left;"><input type='text' Value='42'></input></asp:TableCell>
            <asp:TableCell style="text-align:left;"><input type='text' Value='43'></input></asp:TableCell>
            <asp:TableCell style="text-align:left;"><input type='text' Value='44'></input></asp:TableCell>
            <asp:TableCell style="text-align:left;"><input type='text' Value='45'></input></asp:TableCell>
            <asp:TableCell style="text-align:left;"><input type='text' Value='46'></input></asp:TableCell>
            <asp:TableCell style="text-align:left;"><input type='text' Value='47'></input></asp:TableCell>
            <asp:TableCell style="text-align:left;"><input type='text' Value='48'></input></asp:TableCell>
            <asp:TableCell style="text-align:left;"><input type='text' Value='49'></input></asp:TableCell>
            <asp:TableCell style="text-align:left;"><input type='text' Value='50'></input></asp:TableCell>
            <asp:TableCell style="text-align:left;"><input type='text' Value='51'></input></asp:TableCell>
            <asp:TableCell style="text-align:left;"><input type='text' Value='52'></input></asp:TableCell>
            <asp:TableCell style="text-align:left;"><input type='text' Value='53'></input></asp:TableCell>
            <asp:TableCell style="text-align:left;"><input type='text' Value='54'></input></asp:TableCell>
            <asp:TableCell style="text-align:left;"><input type='text' Value='55'></input></asp:TableCell>
            <asp:TableCell style="text-align:left;"><input type='text' Value='56'></input></asp:TableCell>
            <asp:TableCell style="text-align:left;"><input type='text' Value='57'></input></asp:TableCell>
            <asp:TableCell style="text-align:left;"><input type='text' Value='58'></input></asp:TableCell>
            <asp:TableCell style="text-align:left;"><input type='text' Value='59'></input></asp:TableCell>
            <asp:TableCell style="text-align:left;"><input type='text' Value='60'></input></asp:TableCell>
            <asp:TableCell style="text-align:left;"><input type='text' Value='61'></input></asp:TableCell>
            <asp:TableCell style="text-align:left;"><input type='text' Value='62'></input></asp:TableCell>
            <asp:TableCell style="text-align:left;"><input type='text' Value='63'></input></asp:TableCell>
            <asp:TableCell style="text-align:left;"><input type='text' Value='64'></input></asp:TableCell>
            <asp:TableCell style="text-align:left;"><input type='text' Value='65'></input></asp:TableCell>
            <asp:TableCell style="text-align:left;"><input type='text' Value='66'></input></asp:TableCell>
            <asp:TableCell style="text-align:left;"><input type='text' Value='67'></input></asp:TableCell>
            <asp:TableCell style="text-align:left;"><input type='text' Value='68'></input></asp:TableCell>
            <asp:TableCell style="text-align:left;"><input type='text' Value='69'></input></asp:TableCell>
            <asp:TableCell style="text-align:left;"><input type='text' Value='70'></input></asp:TableCell>
            <asp:TableCell style="text-align:left;"><input type='text' Value='71'></input></asp:TableCell>
            <asp:TableCell style="text-align:left;"><input type='text' Value='72'></input></asp:TableCell>
            <asp:TableCell style="text-align:left;"><input type='text' Value='73'></input></asp:TableCell>
            <asp:TableCell style="text-align:left;"><input type='text' Value='74'></input></asp:TableCell>
            <asp:TableCell style="text-align:left;"><input type='text' Value='75'></input></asp:TableCell>
            <asp:TableCell style="text-align:left;"><input type='text' Value='76'></input></asp:TableCell>
            <asp:TableCell style="text-align:left;"><input type='text' Value='77'></input></asp:TableCell>
        </asp:TableRow>
            <asp:TableRow><asp:TableCell style="text-align:left;">ProductName</asp:TableCell>
            <asp:TableCell style="text-align:left;"><input type='text' Value='Chai'></input></asp:TableCell>
            <asp:TableCell style="text-align:left;"><input type='text' Value='Chang'></input></asp:TableCell>
            <asp:TableCell style="text-align:left;"><input type='text' Value='Aniseed
Syrup'></input></asp:TableCell>
            <asp:TableCell style="text-align:left;"><input type='text' Value='Chef Anton's Cajun
Seasoning'></input></asp:TableCell>
            <asp:TableCell style="text-align:left;"><input type='text' Value='Chef Anton's Gumbo
Mix'></input></asp:TableCell>
            <asp:TableCell style="text-align:left;"><input type='text' Value='Grandma's Boysenberry
Spread'></input></asp:TableCell>
            <asp:TableCell style="text-align:left;"><input type='text' Value='Uncle Bob's Organic Dried
Pears'></input></asp:TableCell>
            <asp:TableCell style="text-align:left;"><input type='text' Value='Northwoods Cranberry
Sauce'></input></asp:TableCell>
            <asp:TableCell style="text-align:left;"><input type='text' Value='Mishi Kobe
Niku'></input></asp:TableCell>
```

```
        <asp:TableCell style="text-align:left;"><input type='text' Value='Ikura'></input></asp:TableCell>
        <asp:TableCell style="text-align:left;"><input type='text' Value='Queso
Cabrales'></input></asp:TableCell>
        <asp:TableCell style="text-align:left;"><input type='text' Value='Queso Manchego La
Pastora'></input></asp:TableCell>
        <asp:TableCell style="text-align:left;"><input type='text' Value='Konbu'></input></asp:TableCell>
        <asp:TableCell style="text-align:left;"><input type='text' Value='Tofu'></input></asp:TableCell>
        <asp:TableCell style="text-align:left;"><input type='text' Value='Genen
Shouyu'></input></asp:TableCell>
        <asp:TableCell style="text-align:left;"><input type='text' Value='Pavlova'></input></asp:TableCell>
        <asp:TableCell style="text-align:left;"><input type='text' Value='Alice
Mutton'></input></asp:TableCell>
        <asp:TableCell style="text-align:left;"><input type='text' Value='Carnarvon
Tigers'></input></asp:TableCell>
        <asp:TableCell style="text-align:left;"><input type='text' Value='Teatime Chocolate
Biscuits'></input></asp:TableCell>
        <asp:TableCell style="text-align:left;"><input type='text' Value='Sir Rodney's
Marmalade'></input></asp:TableCell>
        <asp:TableCell style="text-align:left;"><input type='text' Value='Sir Rodney's
Scones'></input></asp:TableCell>
        <asp:TableCell style="text-align:left;"><input type='text' Value='Gustaf's
Knäckebröd'></input></asp:TableCell>
        <asp:TableCell style="text-align:left;"><input type='text' Value='Tunnbröd'></input></asp:TableCell>
        <asp:TableCell style="text-align:left;"><input type='text' Value='Guaraná
Fantástica'></input></asp:TableCell>
        <asp:TableCell style="text-align:left;"><input type='text' Value='NuNuCa Nuß-Nougat-
Creme'></input></asp:TableCell>
        <asp:TableCell style="text-align:left;"><input type='text' Value='Gumbär
Gummibärchen'></input></asp:TableCell>
        <asp:TableCell style="text-align:left;"><input type='text' Value='Schoggi
Schokolade'></input></asp:TableCell>
        <asp:TableCell style="text-align:left;"><input type='text' Value='Rössle
Sauerkraut'></input></asp:TableCell>
        <asp:TableCell style="text-align:left;"><input type='text' Value='Thüringer
Rostbratwurst'></input></asp:TableCell>
        <asp:TableCell style="text-align:left;"><input type='text' Value='Nord-Ost
Matjeshering'></input></asp:TableCell>
        <asp:TableCell style="text-align:left;"><input type='text' Value='Gorgonzola
Telino'></input></asp:TableCell>
        <asp:TableCell style="text-align:left;"><input type='text' Value='Mascarpone
Fabioli'></input></asp:TableCell>
        <asp:TableCell style="text-align:left;"><input type='text' Value='Geitost'></input></asp:TableCell>
        <asp:TableCell style="text-align:left;"><input type='text' Value='Sasquatch
Ale'></input></asp:TableCell>
        <asp:TableCell style="text-align:left;"><input type='text' Value='Steeleye
Stout'></input></asp:TableCell>
        <asp:TableCell style="text-align:left;"><input type='text' Value='Inlagd Sill'></input></asp:TableCell>
        <asp:TableCell style="text-align:left;"><input type='text' Value='Gravad
lax'></input></asp:TableCell>
        <asp:TableCell style="text-align:left;"><input type='text' Value='Côte de
Blaye'></input></asp:TableCell>
        <asp:TableCell style="text-align:left;"><input type='text' Value='Chartreuse
verte'></input></asp:TableCell>
        <asp:TableCell style="text-align:left;"><input type='text' Value='Boston Crab
Meat'></input></asp:TableCell>
        <asp:TableCell style="text-align:left;"><input type='text' Value='Jack's New England Clam
Chowder'></input></asp:TableCell>
        <asp:TableCell style="text-align:left;"><input type='text' Value='Singaporean Hokkien Fried
Mee'></input></asp:TableCell>
        <asp:TableCell style="text-align:left;"><input type='text' Value='Ipoh
Coffee'></input></asp:TableCell>
        <asp:TableCell style="text-align:left;"><input type='text' Value='Gula
Malacca'></input></asp:TableCell>
        <asp:TableCell style="text-align:left;"><input type='text' Value='Røgede
sild'></input></asp:TableCell>
        <asp:TableCell style="text-align:left;"><input type='text' Value='Spegesild'></input></asp:TableCell>
```

```
                <asp:TableCell style="text-align:left;"><input type='text' Value='Zaanse
koeken'></input></asp:TableCell>
                    <asp:TableCell style="text-align:left;"><input type='text' Value='Chocolade'></input></asp:TableCell>
                    <asp:TableCell style="text-align:left;"><input type='text' Value='Maxilaku'></input></asp:TableCell>
                    <asp:TableCell style="text-align:left;"><input type='text' Value='Valkoinen
suklaa'></input></asp:TableCell>
                    <asp:TableCell style="text-align:left;"><input type='text' Value='Manjimup Dried
Apples'></input></asp:TableCell>
                    <asp:TableCell style="text-align:left;"><input type='text' Value='Filo Mix'></input></asp:TableCell>
                    <asp:TableCell style="text-align:left;"><input type='text' Value='Perth
Pasties'></input></asp:TableCell>
                    <asp:TableCell style="text-align:left;"><input type='text' Value='Tourtière'></input></asp:TableCell>
                    <asp:TableCell style="text-align:left;"><input type='text' Value='Pâté
chinois'></input></asp:TableCell>
                    <asp:TableCell style="text-align:left;"><input type='text' Value='Gnocchi di nonna
Alice'></input></asp:TableCell>
                    <asp:TableCell style="text-align:left;"><input type='text' Value='Ravioli
Angelo'></input></asp:TableCell>
                    <asp:TableCell style="text-align:left;"><input type='text' Value='Escargots de
Bourgogne'></input></asp:TableCell>
                    <asp:TableCell style="text-align:left;"><input type='text' Value='Raclette
Courdavault'></input></asp:TableCell>
                    <asp:TableCell style="text-align:left;"><input type='text' Value='Camembert
Pierrot'></input></asp:TableCell>
                    <asp:TableCell style="text-align:left;"><input type='text' Value='Sirop
d'érable'></input></asp:TableCell>
                    <asp:TableCell style="text-align:left;"><input type='text' Value='Tarte au
sucre'></input></asp:TableCell>
                    <asp:TableCell style="text-align:left;"><input type='text' Value='Vegie-
spread'></input></asp:TableCell>
                    <asp:TableCell style="text-align:left;"><input type='text' Value='Wimmers gute
Semmelknödel'></input></asp:TableCell>
                    <asp:TableCell style="text-align:left;"><input type='text' Value='Louisiana Fiery Hot Pepper
Sauce'></input></asp:TableCell>
                    <asp:TableCell style="text-align:left;"><input type='text' Value='Louisiana Hot Spiced
Okra'></input></asp:TableCell>
                    <asp:TableCell style="text-align:left;"><input type='text' Value='Laughing Lumberjack
Lager'></input></asp:TableCell>
                    <asp:TableCell style="text-align:left;"><input type='text' Value='Scottish
Longbreads'></input></asp:TableCell>
                    <asp:TableCell style="text-align:left;"><input type='text'
Value='Gudbrandsdalsost'></input></asp:TableCell>
                    <asp:TableCell style="text-align:left;"><input type='text' Value='Outback
Lager'></input></asp:TableCell>
                    <asp:TableCell style="text-align:left;"><input type='text'
Value='Fløtemysost'></input></asp:TableCell>
                    <asp:TableCell style="text-align:left;"><input type='text' Value='Mozzarella di
Giovanni'></input></asp:TableCell>
                    <asp:TableCell style="text-align:left;"><input type='text' Value='Röd
Kaviar'></input></asp:TableCell>
                    <asp:TableCell style="text-align:left;"><input type='text' Value='Longlife
Tofu'></input></asp:TableCell>
                    <asp:TableCell style="text-align:left;"><input type='text' Value='Rhönbräu
Klosterbier'></input></asp:TableCell>
                    <asp:TableCell style="text-align:left;"><input type='text'
Value='Lakkalikööri'></input></asp:TableCell>
                    <asp:TableCell style="text-align:left;"><input type='text' Value='Original Frankfurter grüne
Soße'></input></asp:TableCell>
            </asp:TableRow>
                <asp:TableRow><asp:TableCell style="text-align:left;">SupplierID</asp:TableCell>
                    <asp:TableCell style="text-align:left;"><input type='text' Value='1'></input></asp:TableCell>
                    <asp:TableCell style="text-align:left;"><input type='text' Value='1'></input></asp:TableCell>
                    <asp:TableCell style="text-align:left;"><input type='text' Value='1'></input></asp:TableCell>
                    <asp:TableCell style="text-align:left;"><input type='text' Value='2'></input></asp:TableCell>
                    <asp:TableCell style="text-align:left;"><input type='text' Value='2'></input></asp:TableCell>
                    <asp:TableCell style="text-align:left;"><input type='text' Value='3'></input></asp:TableCell>
```

```
<asp:TableCell style="text-align:left;"><input type='text' Value='3'></input></asp:TableCell>
<asp:TableCell style="text-align:left;"><input type='text' Value='3'></input></asp:TableCell>
<asp:TableCell style="text-align:left;"><input type='text' Value='4'></input></asp:TableCell>
<asp:TableCell style="text-align:left;"><input type='text' Value='4'></input></asp:TableCell>
<asp:TableCell style="text-align:left;"><input type='text' Value='5'></input></asp:TableCell>
<asp:TableCell style="text-align:left;"><input type='text' Value='5'></input></asp:TableCell>
<asp:TableCell style="text-align:left;"><input type='text' Value='6'></input></asp:TableCell>
<asp:TableCell style="text-align:left;"><input type='text' Value='6'></input></asp:TableCell>
<asp:TableCell style="text-align:left;"><input type='text' Value='6'></input></asp:TableCell>
<asp:TableCell style="text-align:left;"><input type='text' Value='7'></input></asp:TableCell>
<asp:TableCell style="text-align:left;"><input type='text' Value='7'></input></asp:TableCell>
<asp:TableCell style="text-align:left;"><input type='text' Value='7'></input></asp:TableCell>
<asp:TableCell style="text-align:left;"><input type='text' Value='8'></input></asp:TableCell>
<asp:TableCell style="text-align:left;"><input type='text' Value='8'></input></asp:TableCell>
<asp:TableCell style="text-align:left;"><input type='text' Value='8'></input></asp:TableCell>
<asp:TableCell style="text-align:left;"><input type='text' Value='9'></input></asp:TableCell>
<asp:TableCell style="text-align:left;"><input type='text' Value='9'></input></asp:TableCell>
<asp:TableCell style="text-align:left;"><input type='text' Value='10'></input></asp:TableCell>
<asp:TableCell style="text-align:left;"><input type='text' Value='11'></input></asp:TableCell>
<asp:TableCell style="text-align:left;"><input type='text' Value='11'></input></asp:TableCell>
<asp:TableCell style="text-align:left;"><input type='text' Value='11'></input></asp:TableCell>
<asp:TableCell style="text-align:left;"><input type='text' Value='12'></input></asp:TableCell>
<asp:TableCell style="text-align:left;"><input type='text' Value='12'></input></asp:TableCell>
<asp:TableCell style="text-align:left;"><input type='text' Value='13'></input></asp:TableCell>
<asp:TableCell style="text-align:left;"><input type='text' Value='14'></input></asp:TableCell>
<asp:TableCell style="text-align:left;"><input type='text' Value='14'></input></asp:TableCell>
<asp:TableCell style="text-align:left;"><input type='text' Value='15'></input></asp:TableCell>
<asp:TableCell style="text-align:left;"><input type='text' Value='16'></input></asp:TableCell>
<asp:TableCell style="text-align:left;"><input type='text' Value='16'></input></asp:TableCell>
<asp:TableCell style="text-align:left;"><input type='text' Value='17'></input></asp:TableCell>
<asp:TableCell style="text-align:left;"><input type='text' Value='17'></input></asp:TableCell>
<asp:TableCell style="text-align:left;"><input type='text' Value='18'></input></asp:TableCell>
<asp:TableCell style="text-align:left;"><input type='text' Value='18'></input></asp:TableCell>
<asp:TableCell style="text-align:left;"><input type='text' Value='19'></input></asp:TableCell>
<asp:TableCell style="text-align:left;"><input type='text' Value='19'></input></asp:TableCell>
<asp:TableCell style="text-align:left;"><input type='text' Value='20'></input></asp:TableCell>
<asp:TableCell style="text-align:left;"><input type='text' Value='20'></input></asp:TableCell>
<asp:TableCell style="text-align:left;"><input type='text' Value='20'></input></asp:TableCell>
<asp:TableCell style="text-align:left;"><input type='text' Value='21'></input></asp:TableCell>
<asp:TableCell style="text-align:left;"><input type='text' Value='21'></input></asp:TableCell>
<asp:TableCell style="text-align:left;"><input type='text' Value='22'></input></asp:TableCell>
<asp:TableCell style="text-align:left;"><input type='text' Value='22'></input></asp:TableCell>
<asp:TableCell style="text-align:left;"><input type='text' Value='23'></input></asp:TableCell>
<asp:TableCell style="text-align:left;"><input type='text' Value='23'></input></asp:TableCell>
<asp:TableCell style="text-align:left;"><input type='text' Value='24'></input></asp:TableCell>
<asp:TableCell style="text-align:left;"><input type='text' Value='24'></input></asp:TableCell>
<asp:TableCell style="text-align:left;"><input type='text' Value='24'></input></asp:TableCell>
<asp:TableCell style="text-align:left;"><input type='text' Value='25'></input></asp:TableCell>
<asp:TableCell style="text-align:left;"><input type='text' Value='25'></input></asp:TableCell>
<asp:TableCell style="text-align:left;"><input type='text' Value='26'></input></asp:TableCell>
<asp:TableCell style="text-align:left;"><input type='text' Value='26'></input></asp:TableCell>
<asp:TableCell style="text-align:left;"><input type='text' Value='27'></input></asp:TableCell>
<asp:TableCell style="text-align:left;"><input type='text' Value='28'></input></asp:TableCell>
<asp:TableCell style="text-align:left;"><input type='text' Value='28'></input></asp:TableCell>
<asp:TableCell style="text-align:left;"><input type='text' Value='29'></input></asp:TableCell>
<asp:TableCell style="text-align:left;"><input type='text' Value='29'></input></asp:TableCell>
<asp:TableCell style="text-align:left;"><input type='text' Value='7'></input></asp:TableCell>
<asp:TableCell style="text-align:left;"><input type='text' Value='12'></input></asp:TableCell>
<asp:TableCell style="text-align:left;"><input type='text' Value='2'></input></asp:TableCell>
<asp:TableCell style="text-align:left;"><input type='text' Value='2'></input></asp:TableCell>
<asp:TableCell style="text-align:left;"><input type='text' Value='16'></input></asp:TableCell>
<asp:TableCell style="text-align:left;"><input type='text' Value='8'></input></asp:TableCell>
<asp:TableCell style="text-align:left;"><input type='text' Value='15'></input></asp:TableCell>
<asp:TableCell style="text-align:left;"><input type='text' Value='7'></input></asp:TableCell>
<asp:TableCell style="text-align:left;"><input type='text' Value='15'></input></asp:TableCell>
<asp:TableCell style="text-align:left;"><input type='text' Value='14'></input></asp:TableCell>
```

```
<asp:TableCell style="text-align:left;"><input type='text' Value='17'></input></asp:TableCell>
<asp:TableCell style="text-align:left;"><input type='text' Value='4'></input></asp:TableCell>
<asp:TableCell style="text-align:left;"><input type='text' Value='12'></input></asp:TableCell>
<asp:TableCell style="text-align:left;"><input type='text' Value='23'></input></asp:TableCell>
<asp:TableCell style="text-align:left;"><input type='text' Value='12'></input></asp:TableCell>
</asp:TableRow>
    <asp:TableRow><asp:TableCell style="text-align:left;">CategoryID</asp:TableCell>
<asp:TableCell style="text-align:left;"><input type='text' Value='1'></input></asp:TableCell>
<asp:TableCell style="text-align:left;"><input type='text' Value='1'></input></asp:TableCell>
<asp:TableCell style="text-align:left;"><input type='text' Value='2'></input></asp:TableCell>
<asp:TableCell style="text-align:left;"><input type='text' Value='2'></input></asp:TableCell>
<asp:TableCell style="text-align:left;"><input type='text' Value='2'></input></asp:TableCell>
<asp:TableCell style="text-align:left;"><input type='text' Value='2'></input></asp:TableCell>
<asp:TableCell style="text-align:left;"><input type='text' Value='7'></input></asp:TableCell>
<asp:TableCell style="text-align:left;"><input type='text' Value='2'></input></asp:TableCell>
<asp:TableCell style="text-align:left;"><input type='text' Value='6'></input></asp:TableCell>
<asp:TableCell style="text-align:left;"><input type='text' Value='8'></input></asp:TableCell>
<asp:TableCell style="text-align:left;"><input type='text' Value='4'></input></asp:TableCell>
<asp:TableCell style="text-align:left;"><input type='text' Value='4'></input></asp:TableCell>
<asp:TableCell style="text-align:left;"><input type='text' Value='8'></input></asp:TableCell>
<asp:TableCell style="text-align:left;"><input type='text' Value='7'></input></asp:TableCell>
<asp:TableCell style="text-align:left;"><input type='text' Value='2'></input></asp:TableCell>
<asp:TableCell style="text-align:left;"><input type='text' Value='3'></input></asp:TableCell>
<asp:TableCell style="text-align:left;"><input type='text' Value='6'></input></asp:TableCell>
<asp:TableCell style="text-align:left;"><input type='text' Value='8'></input></asp:TableCell>
<asp:TableCell style="text-align:left;"><input type='text' Value='3'></input></asp:TableCell>
<asp:TableCell style="text-align:left;"><input type='text' Value='3'></input></asp:TableCell>
<asp:TableCell style="text-align:left;"><input type='text' Value='3'></input></asp:TableCell>
<asp:TableCell style="text-align:left;"><input type='text' Value='5'></input></asp:TableCell>
<asp:TableCell style="text-align:left;"><input type='text' Value='5'></input></asp:TableCell>
<asp:TableCell style="text-align:left;"><input type='text' Value='1'></input></asp:TableCell>
<asp:TableCell style="text-align:left;"><input type='text' Value='3'></input></asp:TableCell>
<asp:TableCell style="text-align:left;"><input type='text' Value='3'></input></asp:TableCell>
<asp:TableCell style="text-align:left;"><input type='text' Value='3'></input></asp:TableCell>
<asp:TableCell style="text-align:left;"><input type='text' Value='7'></input></asp:TableCell>
<asp:TableCell style="text-align:left;"><input type='text' Value='6'></input></asp:TableCell>
<asp:TableCell style="text-align:left;"><input type='text' Value='8'></input></asp:TableCell>
<asp:TableCell style="text-align:left;"><input type='text' Value='4'></input></asp:TableCell>
<asp:TableCell style="text-align:left;"><input type='text' Value='4'></input></asp:TableCell>
<asp:TableCell style="text-align:left;"><input type='text' Value='4'></input></asp:TableCell>
<asp:TableCell style="text-align:left;"><input type='text' Value='1'></input></asp:TableCell>
<asp:TableCell style="text-align:left;"><input type='text' Value='1'></input></asp:TableCell>
<asp:TableCell style="text-align:left;"><input type='text' Value='8'></input></asp:TableCell>
<asp:TableCell style="text-align:left;"><input type='text' Value='8'></input></asp:TableCell>
<asp:TableCell style="text-align:left;"><input type='text' Value='1'></input></asp:TableCell>
<asp:TableCell style="text-align:left;"><input type='text' Value='1'></input></asp:TableCell>
<asp:TableCell style="text-align:left;"><input type='text' Value='8'></input></asp:TableCell>
<asp:TableCell style="text-align:left;"><input type='text' Value='8'></input></asp:TableCell>
<asp:TableCell style="text-align:left;"><input type='text' Value='5'></input></asp:TableCell>
<asp:TableCell style="text-align:left;"><input type='text' Value='1'></input></asp:TableCell>
<asp:TableCell style="text-align:left;"><input type='text' Value='2'></input></asp:TableCell>
<asp:TableCell style="text-align:left;"><input type='text' Value='8'></input></asp:TableCell>
<asp:TableCell style="text-align:left;"><input type='text' Value='8'></input></asp:TableCell>
<asp:TableCell style="text-align:left;"><input type='text' Value='3'></input></asp:TableCell>
<asp:TableCell style="text-align:left;"><input type='text' Value='3'></input></asp:TableCell>
<asp:TableCell style="text-align:left;"><input type='text' Value='3'></input></asp:TableCell>
<asp:TableCell style="text-align:left;"><input type='text' Value='3'></input></asp:TableCell>
<asp:TableCell style="text-align:left;"><input type='text' Value='7'></input></asp:TableCell>
<asp:TableCell style="text-align:left;"><input type='text' Value='5'></input></asp:TableCell>
<asp:TableCell style="text-align:left;"><input type='text' Value='6'></input></asp:TableCell>
<asp:TableCell style="text-align:left;"><input type='text' Value='6'></input></asp:TableCell>
<asp:TableCell style="text-align:left;"><input type='text' Value='6'></input></asp:TableCell>
<asp:TableCell style="text-align:left;"><input type='text' Value='5'></input></asp:TableCell>
<asp:TableCell style="text-align:left;"><input type='text' Value='5'></input></asp:TableCell>
<asp:TableCell style="text-align:left;"><input type='text' Value='8'></input></asp:TableCell>
<asp:TableCell style="text-align:left;"><input type='text' Value='4'></input></asp:TableCell>
```

```
<asp:TableCell style="text-align:left;"><input type='text' Value='4'></input></asp:TableCell>
<asp:TableCell style="text-align:left;"><input type='text' Value='2'></input></asp:TableCell>
<asp:TableCell style="text-align:left;"><input type='text' Value='3'></input></asp:TableCell>
<asp:TableCell style="text-align:left;"><input type='text' Value='2'></input></asp:TableCell>
<asp:TableCell style="text-align:left;"><input type='text' Value='5'></input></asp:TableCell>
<asp:TableCell style="text-align:left;"><input type='text' Value='2'></input></asp:TableCell>
<asp:TableCell style="text-align:left;"><input type='text' Value='2'></input></asp:TableCell>
<asp:TableCell style="text-align:left;"><input type='text' Value='1'></input></asp:TableCell>
<asp:TableCell style="text-align:left;"><input type='text' Value='3'></input></asp:TableCell>
<asp:TableCell style="text-align:left;"><input type='text' Value='4'></input></asp:TableCell>
<asp:TableCell style="text-align:left;"><input type='text' Value='1'></input></asp:TableCell>
<asp:TableCell style="text-align:left;"><input type='text' Value='4'></input></asp:TableCell>
<asp:TableCell style="text-align:left;"><input type='text' Value='4'></input></asp:TableCell>
<asp:TableCell style="text-align:left;"><input type='text' Value='8'></input></asp:TableCell>
<asp:TableCell style="text-align:left;"><input type='text' Value='7'></input></asp:TableCell>
<asp:TableCell style="text-align:left;"><input type='text' Value='1'></input></asp:TableCell>
<asp:TableCell style="text-align:left;"><input type='text' Value='1'></input></asp:TableCell>
<asp:TableCell style="text-align:left;"><input type='text' Value='2'></input></asp:TableCell>
</asp:TableRow>
        <asp:TableRow><asp:TableCell style="text-align:left;">QuantityPerUnit</asp:TableCell>
        <asp:TableCell style="text-align:left;"><input type='text' Value='10 boxes x 20
bags'></input></asp:TableCell>
        <asp:TableCell style="text-align:left;"><input type='text' Value='24 - 12 oz
bottles'></input></asp:TableCell>
        <asp:TableCell style="text-align:left;"><input type='text' Value='12 - 550 ml
bottles'></input></asp:TableCell>
        <asp:TableCell style="text-align:left;"><input type='text' Value='48 - 6 oz
jars'></input></asp:TableCell>
        <asp:TableCell style="text-align:left;"><input type='text' Value='36 boxes'></input></asp:TableCell>
        <asp:TableCell style="text-align:left;"><input type='text' Value='12 - 8 oz
jars'></input></asp:TableCell>
        <asp:TableCell style="text-align:left;"><input type='text' Value='12 - 1 lb
pkgs.'></input></asp:TableCell>
        <asp:TableCell style="text-align:left;"><input type='text' Value='12 - 12 oz
jars'></input></asp:TableCell>
        <asp:TableCell style="text-align:left;"><input type='text' Value='18 - 500 g
pkgs.'></input></asp:TableCell>
        <asp:TableCell style="text-align:left;"><input type='text' Value='12 - 200 ml
jars'></input></asp:TableCell>
        <asp:TableCell style="text-align:left;"><input type='text' Value='1 kg pkg.'></input></asp:TableCell>
        <asp:TableCell style="text-align:left;"><input type='text' Value='10 - 500 g
pkgs.'></input></asp:TableCell>
        <asp:TableCell style="text-align:left;"><input type='text' Value='2 kg box'></input></asp:TableCell>
        <asp:TableCell style="text-align:left;"><input type='text' Value='40 - 100 g
pkgs.'></input></asp:TableCell>
        <asp:TableCell style="text-align:left;"><input type='text' Value='24 - 250 ml
bottles'></input></asp:TableCell>
        <asp:TableCell style="text-align:left;"><input type='text' Value='32 - 500 g
boxes'></input></asp:TableCell>
        <asp:TableCell style="text-align:left;"><input type='text' Value='20 - 1 kg
tins'></input></asp:TableCell>
        <asp:TableCell style="text-align:left;"><input type='text' Value='16 kg pkg.'></input></asp:TableCell>
        <asp:TableCell style="text-align:left;"><input type='text' Value='10 boxes x 12
pieces'></input></asp:TableCell>
        <asp:TableCell style="text-align:left;"><input type='text' Value='30 gift
boxes'></input></asp:TableCell>
        <asp:TableCell style="text-align:left;"><input type='text' Value='24 pkgs. x 4
pieces'></input></asp:TableCell>
        <asp:TableCell style="text-align:left;"><input type='text' Value='24 - 500 g
pkgs.'></input></asp:TableCell>
        <asp:TableCell style="text-align:left;"><input type='text' Value='12 - 250 g
pkgs.'></input></asp:TableCell>
        <asp:TableCell style="text-align:left;"><input type='text' Value='12 - 355 ml
cans'></input></asp:TableCell>
        <asp:TableCell style="text-align:left;"><input type='text' Value='20 - 450 g
glasses'></input></asp:TableCell>
```

```
            <asp:TableCell style="text-align:left;"><input type='text' Value='100 – 250 g
bags'></input></asp:TableCell>
            <asp:TableCell style="text-align:left;"><input type='text' Value='100 - 100 g
pieces'></input></asp:TableCell>
            <asp:TableCell style="text-align:left;"><input type='text' Value='25 – 825 g
cans'></input></asp:TableCell>
            <asp:TableCell style="text-align:left;"><input type='text' Value='50 bags x 30
sausgs.'></input></asp:TableCell>
            <asp:TableCell style="text-align:left;"><input type='text' Value='10 – 200 g
glasses'></input></asp:TableCell>
            <asp:TableCell style="text-align:left;"><input type='text' Value='12 - 100 g
pkgs'></input></asp:TableCell>
            <asp:TableCell style="text-align:left;"><input type='text' Value='24 - 200 g
pkgs.'></input></asp:TableCell>
            <asp:TableCell style="text-align:left;"><input type='text' Value='500 g'></input></asp:TableCell>
            <asp:TableCell style="text-align:left;"><input type='text' Value='24 - 12 oz
bottles'></input></asp:TableCell>
            <asp:TableCell style="text-align:left;"><input type='text' Value='24 - 12 oz
bottles'></input></asp:TableCell>
            <asp:TableCell style="text-align:left;"><input type='text' Value='24 - 250 g
jars'></input></asp:TableCell>
            <asp:TableCell style="text-align:left;"><input type='text' Value='12 – 500 g
pkgs.'></input></asp:TableCell>
            <asp:TableCell style="text-align:left;"><input type='text' Value='12 - 75 cl
bottles'></input></asp:TableCell>
            <asp:TableCell style="text-align:left;"><input type='text' Value='750 cc per
bottle'></input></asp:TableCell>
            <asp:TableCell style="text-align:left;"><input type='text' Value='24 - 4 oz
tins'></input></asp:TableCell>
            <asp:TableCell style="text-align:left;"><input type='text' Value='12 - 12 oz
cans'></input></asp:TableCell>
            <asp:TableCell style="text-align:left;"><input type='text' Value='32 - 1 kg
pkgs.'></input></asp:TableCell>
            <asp:TableCell style="text-align:left;"><input type='text' Value='16 – 500 g
tins'></input></asp:TableCell>
            <asp:TableCell style="text-align:left;"><input type='text' Value='20 - 2 kg
bags'></input></asp:TableCell>
            <asp:TableCell style="text-align:left;"><input type='text' Value='1k pkg.'></input></asp:TableCell>
            <asp:TableCell style="text-align:left;"><input type='text' Value='4 - 450 g
glasses'></input></asp:TableCell>
            <asp:TableCell style="text-align:left;"><input type='text' Value='10 - 4 oz
boxes'></input></asp:TableCell>
            <asp:TableCell style="text-align:left;"><input type='text' Value='10 pkgs.'></input></asp:TableCell>
            <asp:TableCell style="text-align:left;"><input type='text' Value='24 - 50 g
pkgs.'></input></asp:TableCell>
            <asp:TableCell style="text-align:left;"><input type='text' Value='12 - 100 g
bars'></input></asp:TableCell>
            <asp:TableCell style="text-align:left;"><input type='text' Value='50 - 300 g
pkgs.'></input></asp:TableCell>
            <asp:TableCell style="text-align:left;"><input type='text' Value='16 - 2 kg
boxes'></input></asp:TableCell>
            <asp:TableCell style="text-align:left;"><input type='text' Value='48 pieces'></input></asp:TableCell>
            <asp:TableCell style="text-align:left;"><input type='text' Value='16 pies'></input></asp:TableCell>
            <asp:TableCell style="text-align:left;"><input type='text' Value='24 boxes x 2
pies'></input></asp:TableCell>
            <asp:TableCell style="text-align:left;"><input type='text' Value='24 - 250 g
pkgs.'></input></asp:TableCell>
            <asp:TableCell style="text-align:left;"><input type='text' Value='24 - 250 g
pkgs.'></input></asp:TableCell>
            <asp:TableCell style="text-align:left;"><input type='text' Value='24 pieces'></input></asp:TableCell>
            <asp:TableCell style="text-align:left;"><input type='text' Value='5 kg pkg.'></input></asp:TableCell>
            <asp:TableCell style="text-align:left;"><input type='text' Value='15 - 300 g
rounds'></input></asp:TableCell>
            <asp:TableCell style="text-align:left;"><input type='text' Value='24 - 500 ml
bottles'></input></asp:TableCell>
            <asp:TableCell style="text-align:left;"><input type='text' Value='48 pies'></input></asp:TableCell>
```

```
            <asp:TableCell style="text-align:left;"><input type='text' Value='15 - 625 g
jars'></input></asp:TableCell>
            <asp:TableCell style="text-align:left;"><input type='text' Value='20 bags x 4
pieces'></input></asp:TableCell>
            <asp:TableCell style="text-align:left;"><input type='text' Value='32 - 8 oz
bottles'></input></asp:TableCell>
            <asp:TableCell style="text-align:left;"><input type='text' Value='24 - 8 oz
jars'></input></asp:TableCell>
            <asp:TableCell style="text-align:left;"><input type='text' Value='24 - 12 oz
bottles'></input></asp:TableCell>
            <asp:TableCell style="text-align:left;"><input type='text' Value='10 boxes x 8
pieces'></input></asp:TableCell>
            <asp:TableCell style="text-align:left;"><input type='text' Value='10 kg pkg.'></input></asp:TableCell>
            <asp:TableCell style="text-align:left;"><input type='text' Value='24 - 355 ml
bottles'></input></asp:TableCell>
            <asp:TableCell style="text-align:left;"><input type='text' Value='10 - 500 g
pkgs.'></input></asp:TableCell>
            <asp:TableCell style="text-align:left;"><input type='text' Value='24 - 200 g
pkgs.'></input></asp:TableCell>
            <asp:TableCell style="text-align:left;"><input type='text' Value='24 - 150 g
jars'></input></asp:TableCell>
            <asp:TableCell style="text-align:left;"><input type='text' Value='5 kg pkg.'></input></asp:TableCell>
            <asp:TableCell style="text-align:left;"><input type='text' Value='24 - 0.5 l
bottles'></input></asp:TableCell>
            <asp:TableCell style="text-align:left;"><input type='text' Value='500 ml'></input></asp:TableCell>
            <asp:TableCell style="text-align:left;"><input type='text' Value='12 boxes'></input></asp:TableCell>
        </asp:TableRow>
            <asp:TableRow><asp:TableCell style="text-align:left;">UnitPrice</asp:TableCell>
            <asp:TableCell style="text-align:left;"><input type='text' Value='18'></input></asp:TableCell>
            <asp:TableCell style="text-align:left;"><input type='text' Value='19'></input></asp:TableCell>
            <asp:TableCell style="text-align:left;"><input type='text' Value='10'></input></asp:TableCell>
            <asp:TableCell style="text-align:left;"><input type='text' Value='22'></input></asp:TableCell>
            <asp:TableCell style="text-align:left;"><input type='text' Value='21.35'></input></asp:TableCell>
            <asp:TableCell style="text-align:left;"><input type='text' Value='25'></input></asp:TableCell>
            <asp:TableCell style="text-align:left;"><input type='text' Value='30'></input></asp:TableCell>
            <asp:TableCell style="text-align:left;"><input type='text' Value='40'></input></asp:TableCell>
            <asp:TableCell style="text-align:left;"><input type='text' Value='97'></input></asp:TableCell>
            <asp:TableCell style="text-align:left;"><input type='text' Value='31'></input></asp:TableCell>
            <asp:TableCell style="text-align:left;"><input type='text' Value='21'></input></asp:TableCell>
            <asp:TableCell style="text-align:left;"><input type='text' Value='38'></input></asp:TableCell>
            <asp:TableCell style="text-align:left;"><input type='text' Value='6'></input></asp:TableCell>
            <asp:TableCell style="text-align:left;"><input type='text' Value='23.25'></input></asp:TableCell>
            <asp:TableCell style="text-align:left;"><input type='text' Value='15.5'></input></asp:TableCell>
            <asp:TableCell style="text-align:left;"><input type='text' Value='17.45'></input></asp:TableCell>
            <asp:TableCell style="text-align:left;"><input type='text' Value='39'></input></asp:TableCell>
            <asp:TableCell style="text-align:left;"><input type='text' Value='62.5'></input></asp:TableCell>
            <asp:TableCell style="text-align:left;"><input type='text' Value='9.2'></input></asp:TableCell>
            <asp:TableCell style="text-align:left;"><input type='text' Value='81'></input></asp:TableCell>
            <asp:TableCell style="text-align:left;"><input type='text' Value='10'></input></asp:TableCell>
            <asp:TableCell style="text-align:left;"><input type='text' Value='21'></input></asp:TableCell>
            <asp:TableCell style="text-align:left;"><input type='text' Value='9'></input></asp:TableCell>
            <asp:TableCell style="text-align:left;"><input type='text' Value='4.5'></input></asp:TableCell>
            <asp:TableCell style="text-align:left;"><input type='text' Value='14'></input></asp:TableCell>
            <asp:TableCell style="text-align:left;"><input type='text' Value='31.23'></input></asp:TableCell>
            <asp:TableCell style="text-align:left;"><input type='text' Value='43.9'></input></asp:TableCell>
            <asp:TableCell style="text-align:left;"><input type='text' Value='45.6'></input></asp:TableCell>
            <asp:TableCell style="text-align:left;"><input type='text' Value='123.79'></input></asp:TableCell>
            <asp:TableCell style="text-align:left;"><input type='text' Value='25.89'></input></asp:TableCell>
            <asp:TableCell style="text-align:left;"><input type='text' Value='12.5'></input></asp:TableCell>
            <asp:TableCell style="text-align:left;"><input type='text' Value='32'></input></asp:TableCell>
            <asp:TableCell style="text-align:left;"><input type='text' Value='2.5'></input></asp:TableCell>
            <asp:TableCell style="text-align:left;"><input type='text' Value='14'></input></asp:TableCell>
            <asp:TableCell style="text-align:left;"><input type='text' Value='18'></input></asp:TableCell>
            <asp:TableCell style="text-align:left;"><input type='text' Value='19'></input></asp:TableCell>
            <asp:TableCell style="text-align:left;"><input type='text' Value='26'></input></asp:TableCell>
            <asp:TableCell style="text-align:left;"><input type='text' Value='263.5'></input></asp:TableCell>
```

```
<asp:TableCell style="text-align:left;"><input type='text' Value='18'></input></asp:TableCell>
<asp:TableCell style="text-align:left;"><input type='text' Value='18.4'></input></asp:TableCell>
<asp:TableCell style="text-align:left;"><input type='text' Value='9.65'></input></asp:TableCell>
<asp:TableCell style="text-align:left;"><input type='text' Value='14'></input></asp:TableCell>
<asp:TableCell style="text-align:left;"><input type='text' Value='46'></input></asp:TableCell>
<asp:TableCell style="text-align:left;"><input type='text' Value='19.45'></input></asp:TableCell>
<asp:TableCell style="text-align:left;"><input type='text' Value='9.5'></input></asp:TableCell>
<asp:TableCell style="text-align:left;"><input type='text' Value='12'></input></asp:TableCell>
<asp:TableCell style="text-align:left;"><input type='text' Value='9.5'></input></asp:TableCell>
<asp:TableCell style="text-align:left;"><input type='text' Value='12.75'></input></asp:TableCell>
<asp:TableCell style="text-align:left;"><input type='text' Value='20'></input></asp:TableCell>
<asp:TableCell style="text-align:left;"><input type='text' Value='16.25'></input></asp:TableCell>
<asp:TableCell style="text-align:left;"><input type='text' Value='53'></input></asp:TableCell>
<asp:TableCell style="text-align:left;"><input type='text' Value='7'></input></asp:TableCell>
<asp:TableCell style="text-align:left;"><input type='text' Value='32.8'></input></asp:TableCell>
<asp:TableCell style="text-align:left;"><input type='text' Value='7.45'></input></asp:TableCell>
<asp:TableCell style="text-align:left;"><input type='text' Value='24'></input></asp:TableCell>
<asp:TableCell style="text-align:left;"><input type='text' Value='38'></input></asp:TableCell>
<asp:TableCell style="text-align:left;"><input type='text' Value='19.5'></input></asp:TableCell>
<asp:TableCell style="text-align:left;"><input type='text' Value='13.25'></input></asp:TableCell>
<asp:TableCell style="text-align:left;"><input type='text' Value='55'></input></asp:TableCell>
<asp:TableCell style="text-align:left;"><input type='text' Value='34'></input></asp:TableCell>
<asp:TableCell style="text-align:left;"><input type='text' Value='28.5'></input></asp:TableCell>
<asp:TableCell style="text-align:left;"><input type='text' Value='49.3'></input></asp:TableCell>
<asp:TableCell style="text-align:left;"><input type='text' Value='43.9'></input></asp:TableCell>
<asp:TableCell style="text-align:left;"><input type='text' Value='33.25'></input></asp:TableCell>
<asp:TableCell style="text-align:left;"><input type='text' Value='21.05'></input></asp:TableCell>
<asp:TableCell style="text-align:left;"><input type='text' Value='17'></input></asp:TableCell>
<asp:TableCell style="text-align:left;"><input type='text' Value='14'></input></asp:TableCell>
<asp:TableCell style="text-align:left;"><input type='text' Value='12.5'></input></asp:TableCell>
<asp:TableCell style="text-align:left;"><input type='text' Value='36'></input></asp:TableCell>
<asp:TableCell style="text-align:left;"><input type='text' Value='15'></input></asp:TableCell>
<asp:TableCell style="text-align:left;"><input type='text' Value='21.5'></input></asp:TableCell>
<asp:TableCell style="text-align:left;"><input type='text' Value='34.8'></input></asp:TableCell>
<asp:TableCell style="text-align:left;"><input type='text' Value='15'></input></asp:TableCell>
<asp:TableCell style="text-align:left;"><input type='text' Value='10'></input></asp:TableCell>
<asp:TableCell style="text-align:left;"><input type='text' Value='7.75'></input></asp:TableCell>
<asp:TableCell style="text-align:left;"><input type='text' Value='18'></input></asp:TableCell>
<asp:TableCell style="text-align:left;"><input type='text' Value='13'></input></asp:TableCell>
</asp:TableRow>
    <asp:TableRow><asp:TableCell style="text-align:left;">UnitsInStock</asp:TableCell>
<asp:TableCell style="text-align:left;"><input type='text' Value='39'></input></asp:TableCell>
<asp:TableCell style="text-align:left;"><input type='text' Value='17'></input></asp:TableCell>
<asp:TableCell style="text-align:left;"><input type='text' Value='13'></input></asp:TableCell>
<asp:TableCell style="text-align:left;"><input type='text' Value='53'></input></asp:TableCell>
<asp:TableCell style="text-align:left;"><input type='text' Value='0'></input></asp:TableCell>
<asp:TableCell style="text-align:left;"><input type='text' Value='120'></input></asp:TableCell>
<asp:TableCell style="text-align:left;"><input type='text' Value='15'></input></asp:TableCell>
<asp:TableCell style="text-align:left;"><input type='text' Value='6'></input></asp:TableCell>
<asp:TableCell style="text-align:left;"><input type='text' Value='29'></input></asp:TableCell>
<asp:TableCell style="text-align:left;"><input type='text' Value='31'></input></asp:TableCell>
<asp:TableCell style="text-align:left;"><input type='text' Value='22'></input></asp:TableCell>
<asp:TableCell style="text-align:left;"><input type='text' Value='86'></input></asp:TableCell>
<asp:TableCell style="text-align:left;"><input type='text' Value='24'></input></asp:TableCell>
<asp:TableCell style="text-align:left;"><input type='text' Value='35'></input></asp:TableCell>
<asp:TableCell style="text-align:left;"><input type='text' Value='39'></input></asp:TableCell>
<asp:TableCell style="text-align:left;"><input type='text' Value='29'></input></asp:TableCell>
<asp:TableCell style="text-align:left;"><input type='text' Value='0'></input></asp:TableCell>
<asp:TableCell style="text-align:left;"><input type='text' Value='42'></input></asp:TableCell>
<asp:TableCell style="text-align:left;"><input type='text' Value='25'></input></asp:TableCell>
<asp:TableCell style="text-align:left;"><input type='text' Value='40'></input></asp:TableCell>
<asp:TableCell style="text-align:left;"><input type='text' Value='3'></input></asp:TableCell>
<asp:TableCell style="text-align:left;"><input type='text' Value='104'></input></asp:TableCell>
<asp:TableCell style="text-align:left;"><input type='text' Value='61'></input></asp:TableCell>
<asp:TableCell style="text-align:left;"><input type='text' Value='20'></input></asp:TableCell>
<asp:TableCell style="text-align:left;"><input type='text' Value='76'></input></asp:TableCell>
```

```
<asp:TableCell style="text-align:left;"><input type='text' Value='15'></input></asp:TableCell>
<asp:TableCell style="text-align:left;"><input type='text' Value='49'></input></asp:TableCell>
<asp:TableCell style="text-align:left;"><input type='text' Value='26'></input></asp:TableCell>
<asp:TableCell style="text-align:left;"><input type='text' Value='0'></input></asp:TableCell>
<asp:TableCell style="text-align:left;"><input type='text' Value='10'></input></asp:TableCell>
<asp:TableCell style="text-align:left;"><input type='text' Value='0'></input></asp:TableCell>
<asp:TableCell style="text-align:left;"><input type='text' Value='9'></input></asp:TableCell>
<asp:TableCell style="text-align:left;"><input type='text' Value='112'></input></asp:TableCell>
<asp:TableCell style="text-align:left;"><input type='text' Value='111'></input></asp:TableCell>
<asp:TableCell style="text-align:left;"><input type='text' Value='20'></input></asp:TableCell>
<asp:TableCell style="text-align:left;"><input type='text' Value='112'></input></asp:TableCell>
<asp:TableCell style="text-align:left;"><input type='text' Value='11'></input></asp:TableCell>
<asp:TableCell style="text-align:left;"><input type='text' Value='17'></input></asp:TableCell>
<asp:TableCell style="text-align:left;"><input type='text' Value='69'></input></asp:TableCell>
<asp:TableCell style="text-align:left;"><input type='text' Value='123'></input></asp:TableCell>
<asp:TableCell style="text-align:left;"><input type='text' Value='85'></input></asp:TableCell>
<asp:TableCell style="text-align:left;"><input type='text' Value='26'></input></asp:TableCell>
<asp:TableCell style="text-align:left;"><input type='text' Value='17'></input></asp:TableCell>
<asp:TableCell style="text-align:left;"><input type='text' Value='27'></input></asp:TableCell>
<asp:TableCell style="text-align:left;"><input type='text' Value='5'></input></asp:TableCell>
<asp:TableCell style="text-align:left;"><input type='text' Value='95'></input></asp:TableCell>
<asp:TableCell style="text-align:left;"><input type='text' Value='36'></input></asp:TableCell>
<asp:TableCell style="text-align:left;"><input type='text' Value='15'></input></asp:TableCell>
<asp:TableCell style="text-align:left;"><input type='text' Value='10'></input></asp:TableCell>
<asp:TableCell style="text-align:left;"><input type='text' Value='65'></input></asp:TableCell>
<asp:TableCell style="text-align:left;"><input type='text' Value='20'></input></asp:TableCell>
<asp:TableCell style="text-align:left;"><input type='text' Value='38'></input></asp:TableCell>
<asp:TableCell style="text-align:left;"><input type='text' Value='0'></input></asp:TableCell>
<asp:TableCell style="text-align:left;"><input type='text' Value='21'></input></asp:TableCell>
<asp:TableCell style="text-align:left;"><input type='text' Value='115'></input></asp:TableCell>
<asp:TableCell style="text-align:left;"><input type='text' Value='21'></input></asp:TableCell>
<asp:TableCell style="text-align:left;"><input type='text' Value='36'></input></asp:TableCell>
<asp:TableCell style="text-align:left;"><input type='text' Value='62'></input></asp:TableCell>
<asp:TableCell style="text-align:left;"><input type='text' Value='79'></input></asp:TableCell>
<asp:TableCell style="text-align:left;"><input type='text' Value='19'></input></asp:TableCell>
<asp:TableCell style="text-align:left;"><input type='text' Value='113'></input></asp:TableCell>
<asp:TableCell style="text-align:left;"><input type='text' Value='17'></input></asp:TableCell>
<asp:TableCell style="text-align:left;"><input type='text' Value='24'></input></asp:TableCell>
<asp:TableCell style="text-align:left;"><input type='text' Value='22'></input></asp:TableCell>
<asp:TableCell style="text-align:left;"><input type='text' Value='76'></input></asp:TableCell>
<asp:TableCell style="text-align:left;"><input type='text' Value='4'></input></asp:TableCell>
<asp:TableCell style="text-align:left;"><input type='text' Value='52'></input></asp:TableCell>
<asp:TableCell style="text-align:left;"><input type='text' Value='6'></input></asp:TableCell>
<asp:TableCell style="text-align:left;"><input type='text' Value='26'></input></asp:TableCell>
<asp:TableCell style="text-align:left;"><input type='text' Value='15'></input></asp:TableCell>
<asp:TableCell style="text-align:left;"><input type='text' Value='26'></input></asp:TableCell>
<asp:TableCell style="text-align:left;"><input type='text' Value='14'></input></asp:TableCell>
<asp:TableCell style="text-align:left;"><input type='text' Value='101'></input></asp:TableCell>
<asp:TableCell style="text-align:left;"><input type='text' Value='4'></input></asp:TableCell>
<asp:TableCell style="text-align:left;"><input type='text' Value='125'></input></asp:TableCell>
<asp:TableCell style="text-align:left;"><input type='text' Value='57'></input></asp:TableCell>
<asp:TableCell style="text-align:left;"><input type='text' Value='32'></input></asp:TableCell>
</asp:TableRow>
    <asp:TableRow><asp:TableCell style="text-align:left;">UnitsOnOrder</asp:TableCell>
<asp:TableCell style="text-align:left;"><input type='text' Value='0'></input></asp:TableCell>
<asp:TableCell style="text-align:left;"><input type='text' Value='40'></input></asp:TableCell>
<asp:TableCell style="text-align:left;"><input type='text' Value='70'></input></asp:TableCell>
<asp:TableCell style="text-align:left;"><input type='text' Value='0'></input></asp:TableCell>
<asp:TableCell style="text-align:left;"><input type='text' Value='0'></input></asp:TableCell>
<asp:TableCell style="text-align:left;"><input type='text' Value='0'></input></asp:TableCell>
<asp:TableCell style="text-align:left;"><input type='text' Value='0'></input></asp:TableCell>
<asp:TableCell style="text-align:left;"><input type='text' Value='0'></input></asp:TableCell>
<asp:TableCell style="text-align:left;"><input type='text' Value='0'></input></asp:TableCell>
<asp:TableCell style="text-align:left;"><input type='text' Value='30'></input></asp:TableCell>
<asp:TableCell style="text-align:left;"><input type='text' Value='0'></input></asp:TableCell>
```

```
<asp:TableCell style="text-align:left;"><input type='text' Value='0'></input></asp:TableCell>
<asp:TableCell style="text-align:left;"><input type='text' Value='0'></input></asp:TableCell>
<asp:TableCell style="text-align:left;"><input type='text' Value='0'></input></asp:TableCell>
<asp:TableCell style="text-align:left;"><input type='text' Value='0'></input></asp:TableCell>
<asp:TableCell style="text-align:left;"><input type='text' Value='0'></input></asp:TableCell>
<asp:TableCell style="text-align:left;"><input type='text' Value='0'></input></asp:TableCell>
<asp:TableCell style="text-align:left;"><input type='text' Value='0'></input></asp:TableCell>
<asp:TableCell style="text-align:left;"><input type='text' Value='0'></input></asp:TableCell>
<asp:TableCell style="text-align:left;"><input type='text' Value='40'></input></asp:TableCell>
<asp:TableCell style="text-align:left;"><input type='text' Value='0'></input></asp:TableCell>
<asp:TableCell style="text-align:left;"><input type='text' Value='0'></input></asp:TableCell>
<asp:TableCell style="text-align:left;"><input type='text' Value='0'></input></asp:TableCell>
<asp:TableCell style="text-align:left;"><input type='text' Value='0'></input></asp:TableCell>
<asp:TableCell style="text-align:left;"><input type='text' Value='0'></input></asp:TableCell>
<asp:TableCell style="text-align:left;"><input type='text' Value='0'></input></asp:TableCell>
<asp:TableCell style="text-align:left;"><input type='text' Value='0'></input></asp:TableCell>
<asp:TableCell style="text-align:left;"><input type='text' Value='70'></input></asp:TableCell>
<asp:TableCell style="text-align:left;"><input type='text' Value='40'></input></asp:TableCell>
<asp:TableCell style="text-align:left;"><input type='text' Value='0'></input></asp:TableCell>
<asp:TableCell style="text-align:left;"><input type='text' Value='0'></input></asp:TableCell>
<asp:TableCell style="text-align:left;"><input type='text' Value='0'></input></asp:TableCell>
<asp:TableCell style="text-align:left;"><input type='text' Value='50'></input></asp:TableCell>
<asp:TableCell style="text-align:left;"><input type='text' Value='0'></input></asp:TableCell>
<asp:TableCell style="text-align:left;"><input type='text' Value='0'></input></asp:TableCell>
<asp:TableCell style="text-align:left;"><input type='text' Value='0'></input></asp:TableCell>
<asp:TableCell style="text-align:left;"><input type='text' Value='0'></input></asp:TableCell>
<asp:TableCell style="text-align:left;"><input type='text' Value='10'></input></asp:TableCell>
<asp:TableCell style="text-align:left;"><input type='text' Value='0'></input></asp:TableCell>
<asp:TableCell style="text-align:left;"><input type='text' Value='70'></input></asp:TableCell>
<asp:TableCell style="text-align:left;"><input type='text' Value='0'></input></asp:TableCell>
<asp:TableCell style="text-align:left;"><input type='text' Value='0'></input></asp:TableCell>
<asp:TableCell style="text-align:left;"><input type='text' Value='70'></input></asp:TableCell>
<asp:TableCell style="text-align:left;"><input type='text' Value='60'></input></asp:TableCell>
<asp:TableCell style="text-align:left;"><input type='text' Value='0'></input></asp:TableCell>
<asp:TableCell style="text-align:left;"><input type='text' Value='0'></input></asp:TableCell>
<asp:TableCell style="text-align:left;"><input type='text' Value='0'></input></asp:TableCell>
<asp:TableCell style="text-align:left;"><input type='text' Value='0'></input></asp:TableCell>
<asp:TableCell style="text-align:left;"><input type='text' Value='10'></input></asp:TableCell>
<asp:TableCell style="text-align:left;"><input type='text' Value='0'></input></asp:TableCell>
<asp:TableCell style="text-align:left;"><input type='text' Value='0'></input></asp:TableCell>
<asp:TableCell style="text-align:left;"><input type='text' Value='0'></input></asp:TableCell>
<asp:TableCell style="text-align:left;"><input type='text' Value='0'></input></asp:TableCell>
<asp:TableCell style="text-align:left;"><input type='text' Value='0'></input></asp:TableCell>
<asp:TableCell style="text-align:left;"><input type='text' Value='80'></input></asp:TableCell>
<asp:TableCell style="text-align:left;"><input type='text' Value='0'></input></asp:TableCell>
<asp:TableCell style="text-align:left;"><input type='text' Value='100'></input></asp:TableCell>
<asp:TableCell style="text-align:left;"><input type='text' Value='0'></input></asp:TableCell>
<asp:TableCell style="text-align:left;"><input type='text' Value='10'></input></asp:TableCell>
<asp:TableCell style="text-align:left;"><input type='text' Value='0'></input></asp:TableCell>
<asp:TableCell style="text-align:left;"><input type='text' Value='10'></input></asp:TableCell>
<asp:TableCell style="text-align:left;"><input type='text' Value='0'></input></asp:TableCell>
<asp:TableCell style="text-align:left;"><input type='text' Value='0'></input></asp:TableCell>
<asp:TableCell style="text-align:left;"><input type='text' Value='0'></input></asp:TableCell>
<asp:TableCell style="text-align:left;"><input type='text' Value='20'></input></asp:TableCell>
<asp:TableCell style="text-align:left;"><input type='text' Value='0'></input></asp:TableCell>
<asp:TableCell style="text-align:left;"><input type='text' Value='0'></input></asp:TableCell>
<asp:TableCell style="text-align:left;"><input type='text' Value='0'></input></asp:TableCell>
</asp:TableRow>
```

```
<asp:TableRow><asp:TableCell style="text-align:left;">ReorderLevel</asp:TableCell>
<asp:TableCell style="text-align:left;"><input type='text' Value='10'></input></asp:TableCell>
<asp:TableCell style="text-align:left;"><input type='text' Value='25'></input></asp:TableCell>
<asp:TableCell style="text-align:left;"><input type='text' Value='25'></input></asp:TableCell>
<asp:TableCell style="text-align:left;"><input type='text' Value='0'></input></asp:TableCell>
<asp:TableCell style="text-align:left;"><input type='text' Value='0'></input></asp:TableCell>
<asp:TableCell style="text-align:left;"><input type='text' Value='25'></input></asp:TableCell>
<asp:TableCell style="text-align:left;"><input type='text' Value='10'></input></asp:TableCell>
<asp:TableCell style="text-align:left;"><input type='text' Value='0'></input></asp:TableCell>
<asp:TableCell style="text-align:left;"><input type='text' Value='0'></input></asp:TableCell>
<asp:TableCell style="text-align:left;"><input type='text' Value='0'></input></asp:TableCell>
<asp:TableCell style="text-align:left;"><input type='text' Value='30'></input></asp:TableCell>
<asp:TableCell style="text-align:left;"><input type='text' Value='0'></input></asp:TableCell>
<asp:TableCell style="text-align:left;"><input type='text' Value='5'></input></asp:TableCell>
<asp:TableCell style="text-align:left;"><input type='text' Value='0'></input></asp:TableCell>
<asp:TableCell style="text-align:left;"><input type='text' Value='5'></input></asp:TableCell>
<asp:TableCell style="text-align:left;"><input type='text' Value='10'></input></asp:TableCell>
<asp:TableCell style="text-align:left;"><input type='text' Value='0'></input></asp:TableCell>
<asp:TableCell style="text-align:left;"><input type='text' Value='0'></input></asp:TableCell>
<asp:TableCell style="text-align:left;"><input type='text' Value='5'></input></asp:TableCell>
<asp:TableCell style="text-align:left;"><input type='text' Value='0'></input></asp:TableCell>
<asp:TableCell style="text-align:left;"><input type='text' Value='5'></input></asp:TableCell>
<asp:TableCell style="text-align:left;"><input type='text' Value='25'></input></asp:TableCell>
<asp:TableCell style="text-align:left;"><input type='text' Value='25'></input></asp:TableCell>
<asp:TableCell style="text-align:left;"><input type='text' Value='0'></input></asp:TableCell>
<asp:TableCell style="text-align:left;"><input type='text' Value='30'></input></asp:TableCell>
<asp:TableCell style="text-align:left;"><input type='text' Value='0'></input></asp:TableCell>
<asp:TableCell style="text-align:left;"><input type='text' Value='30'></input></asp:TableCell>
<asp:TableCell style="text-align:left;"><input type='text' Value='0'></input></asp:TableCell>
<asp:TableCell style="text-align:left;"><input type='text' Value='0'></input></asp:TableCell>
<asp:TableCell style="text-align:left;"><input type='text' Value='15'></input></asp:TableCell>
<asp:TableCell style="text-align:left;"><input type='text' Value='20'></input></asp:TableCell>
<asp:TableCell style="text-align:left;"><input type='text' Value='25'></input></asp:TableCell>
<asp:TableCell style="text-align:left;"><input type='text' Value='20'></input></asp:TableCell>
<asp:TableCell style="text-align:left;"><input type='text' Value='15'></input></asp:TableCell>
<asp:TableCell style="text-align:left;"><input type='text' Value='15'></input></asp:TableCell>
<asp:TableCell style="text-align:left;"><input type='text' Value='20'></input></asp:TableCell>
<asp:TableCell style="text-align:left;"><input type='text' Value='25'></input></asp:TableCell>
<asp:TableCell style="text-align:left;"><input type='text' Value='15'></input></asp:TableCell>
<asp:TableCell style="text-align:left;"><input type='text' Value='5'></input></asp:TableCell>
<asp:TableCell style="text-align:left;"><input type='text' Value='30'></input></asp:TableCell>
<asp:TableCell style="text-align:left;"><input type='text' Value='10'></input></asp:TableCell>
<asp:TableCell style="text-align:left;"><input type='text' Value='0'></input></asp:TableCell>
<asp:TableCell style="text-align:left;"><input type='text' Value='25'></input></asp:TableCell>
<asp:TableCell style="text-align:left;"><input type='text' Value='15'></input></asp:TableCell>
<asp:TableCell style="text-align:left;"><input type='text' Value='15'></input></asp:TableCell>
<asp:TableCell style="text-align:left;"><input type='text' Value='0'></input></asp:TableCell>
<asp:TableCell style="text-align:left;"><input type='text' Value='0'></input></asp:TableCell>
<asp:TableCell style="text-align:left;"><input type='text' Value='25'></input></asp:TableCell>
<asp:TableCell style="text-align:left;"><input type='text' Value='15'></input></asp:TableCell>
<asp:TableCell style="text-align:left;"><input type='text' Value='30'></input></asp:TableCell>
<asp:TableCell style="text-align:left;"><input type='text' Value='10'></input></asp:TableCell>
<asp:TableCell style="text-align:left;"><input type='text' Value='25'></input></asp:TableCell>
<asp:TableCell style="text-align:left;"><input type='text' Value='0'></input></asp:TableCell>
<asp:TableCell style="text-align:left;"><input type='text' Value='10'></input></asp:TableCell>
<asp:TableCell style="text-align:left;"><input type='text' Value='20'></input></asp:TableCell>
<asp:TableCell style="text-align:left;"><input type='text' Value='30'></input></asp:TableCell>
<asp:TableCell style="text-align:left;"><input type='text' Value='20'></input></asp:TableCell>
<asp:TableCell style="text-align:left;"><input type='text' Value='20'></input></asp:TableCell>
<asp:TableCell style="text-align:left;"><input type='text' Value='0'></input></asp:TableCell>
<asp:TableCell style="text-align:left;"><input type='text' Value='0'></input></asp:TableCell>
<asp:TableCell style="text-align:left;"><input type='text' Value='25'></input></asp:TableCell>
<asp:TableCell style="text-align:left;"><input type='text' Value='5'></input></asp:TableCell>
<asp:TableCell style="text-align:left;"><input type='text' Value='30'></input></asp:TableCell>
<asp:TableCell style="text-align:left;"><input type='text' Value='0'></input></asp:TableCell>
```

```
<asp:TableCell style="text-align:left;"><input type='text' Value='20'></input></asp:TableCell>
<asp:TableCell style="text-align:left;"><input type='text' Value='10'></input></asp:TableCell>
<asp:TableCell style="text-align:left;"><input type='text' Value='15'></input></asp:TableCell>
<asp:TableCell style="text-align:left;"><input type='text' Value='15'></input></asp:TableCell>
<asp:TableCell style="text-align:left;"><input type='text' Value='30'></input></asp:TableCell>
<asp:TableCell style="text-align:left;"><input type='text' Value='0'></input></asp:TableCell>
<asp:TableCell style="text-align:left;"><input type='text' Value='0'></input></asp:TableCell>
<asp:TableCell style="text-align:left;"><input type='text' Value='5'></input></asp:TableCell>
<asp:TableCell style="text-align:left;"><input type='text' Value='5'></input></asp:TableCell>
<asp:TableCell style="text-align:left;"><input type='text' Value='25'></input></asp:TableCell>
<asp:TableCell style="text-align:left;"><input type='text' Value='20'></input></asp:TableCell>
<asp:TableCell style="text-align:left;"><input type='text' Value='15'></input></asp:TableCell>
</asp:TableRow>
    <asp:TableRow><asp:TableCell style="text-align:left;">Discontinued</asp:TableCell>
<asp:TableCell style="text-align:left;"><input type='text' Value='False'></input></asp:TableCell>
<asp:TableCell style="text-align:left;"><input type='text' Value='False'></input></asp:TableCell>
<asp:TableCell style="text-align:left;"><input type='text' Value='False'></input></asp:TableCell>
<asp:TableCell style="text-align:left;"><input type='text' Value='False'></input></asp:TableCell>
<asp:TableCell style="text-align:left;"><input type='text' Value='True'></input></asp:TableCell>
<asp:TableCell style="text-align:left;"><input type='text' Value='False'></input></asp:TableCell>
<asp:TableCell style="text-align:left;"><input type='text' Value='False'></input></asp:TableCell>
<asp:TableCell style="text-align:left;"><input type='text' Value='False'></input></asp:TableCell>
<asp:TableCell style="text-align:left;"><input type='text' Value='True'></input></asp:TableCell>
<asp:TableCell style="text-align:left;"><input type='text' Value='False'></input></asp:TableCell>
<asp:TableCell style="text-align:left;"><input type='text' Value='False'></input></asp:TableCell>
<asp:TableCell style="text-align:left;"><input type='text' Value='False'></input></asp:TableCell>
<asp:TableCell style="text-align:left;"><input type='text' Value='False'></input></asp:TableCell>
<asp:TableCell style="text-align:left;"><input type='text' Value='False'></input></asp:TableCell>
<asp:TableCell style="text-align:left;"><input type='text' Value='True'></input></asp:TableCell>
<asp:TableCell style="text-align:left;"><input type='text' Value='False'></input></asp:TableCell>
<asp:TableCell style="text-align:left;"><input type='text' Value='False'></input></asp:TableCell>
<asp:TableCell style="text-align:left;"><input type='text' Value='False'></input></asp:TableCell>
<asp:TableCell style="text-align:left;"><input type='text' Value='False'></input></asp:TableCell>
<asp:TableCell style="text-align:left;"><input type='text' Value='False'></input></asp:TableCell>
<asp:TableCell style="text-align:left;"><input type='text' Value='True'></input></asp:TableCell>
<asp:TableCell style="text-align:left;"><input type='text' Value='False'></input></asp:TableCell>
<asp:TableCell style="text-align:left;"><input type='text' Value='False'></input></asp:TableCell>
<asp:TableCell style="text-align:left;"><input type='text' Value='True'></input></asp:TableCell>
<asp:TableCell style="text-align:left;"><input type='text' Value='True'></input></asp:TableCell>
<asp:TableCell style="text-align:left;"><input type='text' Value='False'></input></asp:TableCell>
<asp:TableCell style="text-align:left;"><input type='text' Value='False'></input></asp:TableCell>
<asp:TableCell style="text-align:left;"><input type='text' Value='False'></input></asp:TableCell>
<asp:TableCell style="text-align:left;"><input type='text' Value='False'></input></asp:TableCell>
<asp:TableCell style="text-align:left;"><input type='text' Value='False'></input></asp:TableCell>
<asp:TableCell style="text-align:left;"><input type='text' Value='False'></input></asp:TableCell>
<asp:TableCell style="text-align:left;"><input type='text' Value='False'></input></asp:TableCell>
<asp:TableCell style="text-align:left;"><input type='text' Value='False'></input></asp:TableCell>
<asp:TableCell style="text-align:left;"><input type='text' Value='False'></input></asp:TableCell>
<asp:TableCell style="text-align:left;"><input type='text' Value='True'></input></asp:TableCell>
<asp:TableCell style="text-align:left;"><input type='text' Value='False'></input></asp:TableCell>
<asp:TableCell style="text-align:left;"><input type='text' Value='False'></input></asp:TableCell>
<asp:TableCell style="text-align:left;"><input type='text' Value='False'></input></asp:TableCell>
<asp:TableCell style="text-align:left;"><input type='text' Value='False'></input></asp:TableCell>
<asp:TableCell style="text-align:left;"><input type='text' Value='False'></input></asp:TableCell>
<asp:TableCell style="text-align:left;"><input type='text' Value='False'></input></asp:TableCell>
<asp:TableCell style="text-align:left;"><input type='text' Value='False'></input></asp:TableCell>
<asp:TableCell style="text-align:left;"><input type='text' Value='False'></input></asp:TableCell>
```

```
            <asp:TableCell style="text-align:left;"><input type='text' Value='True'></input></asp:TableCell>
            <asp:TableCell style="text-align:left;"><input type='text' Value='False'></input></asp:TableCell>
            <asp:TableCell style="text-align:left;"><input type='text' Value='False'></input></asp:TableCell>
            <asp:TableCell style="text-align:left;"><input type='text' Value='False'></input></asp:TableCell>
            <asp:TableCell style="text-align:left;"><input type='text' Value='False'></input></asp:TableCell>
            <asp:TableCell style="text-align:left;"><input type='text' Value='False'></input></asp:TableCell>
            <asp:TableCell style="text-align:left;"><input type='text' Value='False'></input></asp:TableCell>
            <asp:TableCell style="text-align:left;"><input type='text' Value='False'></input></asp:TableCell>
            <asp:TableCell style="text-align:left;"><input type='text' Value='False'></input></asp:TableCell>
            <asp:TableCell style="text-align:left;"><input type='text' Value='False'></input></asp:TableCell>
            <asp:TableCell style="text-align:left;"><input type='text' Value='False'></input></asp:TableCell>
            <asp:TableCell style="text-align:left;"><input type='text' Value='False'></input></asp:TableCell>
            <asp:TableCell style="text-align:left;"><input type='text' Value='False'></input></asp:TableCell>
            <asp:TableCell style="text-align:left;"><input type='text' Value='False'></input></asp:TableCell>
            <asp:TableCell style="text-align:left;"><input type='text' Value='False'></input></asp:TableCell>
            <asp:TableCell style="text-align:left;"><input type='text' Value='False'></input></asp:TableCell>
            <asp:TableCell style="text-align:left;"><input type='text' Value='False'></input></asp:TableCell>
            <asp:TableCell style="text-align:left;"><input type='text' Value='False'></input></asp:TableCell>
            <asp:TableCell style="text-align:left;"><input type='text' Value='False'></input></asp:TableCell>
            <asp:TableCell style="text-align:left;"><input type='text' Value='False'></input></asp:TableCell>
        </asp:TableRow>
    </asp:Table>
  </div>
  </form>
</body>
</html>
```

The output it creates:

Property Name	Row0	Row1	Row2	Row3	Row4	Row5	Row6
ProductID	1	2	3	4	5	6	7
ProductName	Chai	Chang	Aniseed Syrup	Chef Anton	Chef Anton	Grandma	Uncle Bob
SupplierID	1	1	1	2	2	3	3
CategoryID	1	1	2	2	2	2	7
QuantityPerUnit	10 boxes x 20 bags	24 - 12 oz bottles	12 - 550 ml bottles	48 - 6 oz jars	36 boxes	12 - 8 oz jars	12 - 1 lb pkgs.
UnitPrice	18	19	10	22	21.35	25	30
UnitsInStock	39	17	13	53	0	120	15
UnitsOnOrder	0	40	70	0	0	0	0
ReorderLevel	10	25	25	0	0	25	10
Discontinued	False	False	False	False	True	False	False

Now, the Form code:

```
<%@ Page Language="VB" AutoEventWireup="false" CodeFile="Default.aspx.vb" Inherits="_Default" %>

<!DOCTYPE html PUBLIC "-//W3C//DTD XHTML 1.0 Transitional//EN"
"http://www.w3.org/TR/xhtml1/DTD/xhtml1-transitional.dtd">

<html xmlns="http://www.w3.org/1999/xhtml">
<head id="Head1" runat="server">
<title>Products</title>
<style type='text/css'>
body
{
    BORDER-TOP: navy 1px solid;
    BORDER-LEFT: navy 1px solid;
    BORDER-RIGHT: navy 1px solid;
```

```
    BORDER-BOTTOM: navy 1px solid;
    PADDING-RIGHT: 1px;
    PADDING-LEFT: 1px;
    FONT-WEIGHT: Normal;
    PADDING-BOTTOM: 1px;
    COLOR: black;
    PADDING-TOP: 1px;
    BORDER-BOTTOM: #999 1px solid;
    BACKGROUND-COLOR: ButtonFace;
    FONT-FAMILY: Cambria, serif;
    FONT-SIZE: 12px;
    text-align: left;
    display: table-cell;
    white-Space: nowrap;
    width: auto;
    height: auto;
}
Table
{
    BORDER-TOP: navy 1px solid;
    BORDER-LEFT: navy 1px solid;
    BORDER-RIGHT: navy 1px solid;
    BORDER-BOTTOM: navy 1px solid;
    PADDING-RIGHT: 1px;
    PADDING-LEFT: 1px;
    FONT-WEIGHT: Normal;
    PADDING-BOTTOM: 1px;
    COLOR: black;
    PADDING-TOP: 1px;
    BORDER-BOTTOM: #999 1px solid;
    BACKGROUND-COLOR: ButtonFace;
    FONT-FAMILY: Cambria, serif;
    FONT-SIZE: 12px;
    text-align: left;
    display: table-cell;
    white-Space: nowrap;
    width: auto;
    height: auto;
}
th
{
    BORDER-RIGHT: #999999 2px solid;
    PADDING-RIGHT: 6px;
    PADDING-LEFT: 6px;
    FONT-WEIGHT: Bold;
    PADDING-BOTTOM: 6px;
    COLOR: #600000;
    PADDING-TOP: 6px;
    BORDER-BOTTOM: #999 2px solid;
    BACKGROUND-COLOR: #eeeeee;
    FONT-FAMILY: Cambria, serif;
    FONT-SIZE: 16px;
    text-align: right;
    white-Space: nowrap;
}
td
{
    BORDER-RIGHT: #999999 3px solid;
    PADDING-RIGHT: 6px;
    PADDING-LEFT: 6px;
    FONT-WEIGHT: Normal;
    PADDING-BOTTOM: 6px;
    COLOR: navy;
    LINE-HEIGHT: 14px;
    PADDING-TOP: 6px;
    BORDER-BOTTOM: #999 1px solid;
```

```css
    BACKGROUND-COLOR: #eeeeee;
    FONT-FAMILY: Cambria, serif;
    FONT-SIZE: 12px;
    text-align: left;
    white-Space: nowrap;
}
.div
{
    BORDER-RIGHT: #999999 3px solid;
    PADDING-RIGHT: 6px;
    PADDING-LEFT: 6px;
    FONT-WEIGHT: Normal;
    PADDING-BOTTOM: 6px;
    COLOR: white;
    PADDING-TOP: 6px;
    BORDER-BOTTOM: #999 1px solid;
    BACKGROUND-COLOR: navy;
    FONT-FAMILY: Cambria, serif;
    FONT-SIZE: 10px;
    text-align: left;
    white-Space: nowrap;
}
.span
{
    BORDER-RIGHT: #999999 3px solid;
    PADDING-RIGHT: 3px;
    PADDING-LEFT: 3px;
    FONT-WEIGHT: Normal;
    PADDING-BOTTOM: 3px;
    COLOR: white;
    PADDING-TOP: 3px;
    BORDER-BOTTOM: #999 1px solid;
    BACKGROUND-COLOR: navy;
    FONT-FAMILY: Cambria, serif;
    FONT-SIZE: 10px;
    text-align: left;
    white-Space: nowrap;
    display: inline-block;
    width: 100%;
}
.textarea
{
    BORDER-RIGHT: #999999 3px solid;
    PADDING-RIGHT: 3px;
    PADDING-LEFT: 3px;
    FONT-WEIGHT: Normal;
    PADDING-BOTTOM: 3px;
    COLOR: white;
    PADDING-TOP: 3px;
    BORDER-BOTTOM: #999 1px solid;
    BACKGROUND-COLOR: navy;
    FONT-FAMILY: Cambria, serif;
    FONT-SIZE: 10px;
    text-align: left;
    white-Space: nowrap;
    width: 100%;
}
.Select
{
    BORDER-RIGHT: #999999 3px solid;
    PADDING-RIGHT: 6px;
    PADDING-LEFT: 6px;
    FONT-WEIGHT: Normal;
    PADDING-BOTTOM: 6px;
    COLOR: white;
    PADDING-TOP: 6px;
```

```css
      BORDER-BOTTOM: #999 1px solid;
      BACKGROUND-COLOR: navy;
      FONT-FAMILY: Cambria, serif;
      FONT-SIZE: 10px;
      text-align: left;
      white-Space: nowrap;
      width: 100%;
}
input
{
      BORDER-RIGHT: #999999 1px solid;
      PADDING-RIGHT: 1px;
      PADDING-LEFT: 1px;
      FONT-WEIGHT: Normal;
      PADDING-BOTTOM: 1px;
      COLOR: White;
      PADDING-TOP: 1px;
      BORDER-BOTTOM: #999 1px solid;
      BACKGROUND-COLOR: navy;
      FONT-FAMILY: Cambria, serif;
      FONT-SIZE: 12px;
      text-align: left;
      display: table-cell;
      white-Space: nowrap;
      width: auto;
}
</style>
</head>
<body>
    <form id="form1" runat="server">
        <div>
<%
    Write_The_Code()
%>
        </div>
    </form>
</body>
</html>
```

The code Behind:

The Output:

```
<!DOCTYPE html PUBLIC "-//W3C//DTD XHTML 1.0 Transitional//EN"
"http://www.w3.org/TR/xhtml1/DTD/xhtml1-transitional.dtd">

<html xmlns="http://www.w3.org/1999/xhtml">
<head id="Head1"><title>
            Products
</title>
<style type='text/css'>
body
{
      BORDER-TOP: navy 1px solid;
      BORDER-LEFT: navy 1px solid;
      BORDER-RIGHT: navy 1px solid;
      BORDER-BOTTOM: navy 1px solid;
      PADDING-RIGHT: 1px;
      PADDING-LEFT: 1px;
      FONT-WEIGHT: Normal;
```

```
      PADDING-BOTTOM: 1px;
      COLOR: black;
      PADDING-TOP: 1px;
      BORDER-BOTTOM: #999 1px solid;
      BACKGROUND-COLOR: ButtonFace;
      FONT-FAMILY: Cambria, serif;
      FONT-SIZE: 12px;
      text-align: left;
      display: table-cell;
      white-Space: nowrap;
      width: auto;
      height: auto;
}
Table
{
      BORDER-TOP: navy 1px solid;
      BORDER-LEFT: navy 1px solid;
      BORDER-RIGHT: navy 1px solid;
      BORDER-BOTTOM: navy 1px solid;
      PADDING-RIGHT: 1px;
      PADDING-LEFT: 1px;
      FONT-WEIGHT: Normal;
      PADDING-BOTTOM: 1px;
      COLOR: black;
      PADDING-TOP: 1px;
      BORDER-BOTTOM: #999 1px solid;
      BACKGROUND-COLOR: ButtonFace;
      FONT-FAMILY: Cambria, serif;
      FONT-SIZE: 12px;
      text-align: left;
      display: table-cell;
      white-Space: nowrap;
      width: auto;
      height: auto;
}
th
{
      BORDER-RIGHT: #999999 2px solid;
      PADDING-RIGHT: 6px;
      PADDING-LEFT: 6px;
      FONT-WEIGHT: Bold;
      PADDING-BOTTOM: 6px;
      COLOR: #600000;
      PADDING-TOP: 6px;
      BORDER-BOTTOM: #999 2px solid;
      BACKGROUND-COLOR: #eeeeee;
      FONT-FAMILY: Cambria, serif;
      FONT-SIZE: 16px;
      text-align: right;
      white-Space: nowrap;
}
td
{
      BORDER-RIGHT: #999999 3px solid;
      PADDING-RIGHT: 6px;
      PADDING-LEFT: 6px;
      FONT-WEIGHT: Normal;
      PADDING-BOTTOM: 6px;
      COLOR: navy;
      LINE-HEIGHT: 14px;
      PADDING-TOP: 6px;
      BORDER-BOTTOM: #999 1px solid;
      BACKGROUND-COLOR: #eeeeee;
      FONT-FAMILY: Cambria, serif;
      FONT-SIZE: 12px;
      text-align: left;
```

```
    white-Space: nowrap;
}
.div
{
   BORDER-RIGHT: #999999 3px solid;
   PADDING-RIGHT: 6px;
   PADDING-LEFT: 6px;
   FONT-WEIGHT: Normal;
   PADDING-BOTTOM: 6px;
   COLOR: white;
   PADDING-TOP: 6px;
   BORDER-BOTTOM: #999 1px solid;
   BACKGROUND-COLOR: navy;
   FONT-FAMILY: Cambria, serif;
   FONT-SIZE: 10px;
   text-align: left;
   white-Space: nowrap;
}
.span
{
   BORDER-RIGHT: #999999 3px solid;
   PADDING-RIGHT: 3px;
   PADDING-LEFT: 3px;
   FONT-WEIGHT: Normal;
   PADDING-BOTTOM: 3px;
   COLOR: white;
   PADDING-TOP: 3px;
   BORDER-BOTTOM: #999 1px solid;
   BACKGROUND-COLOR: navy;
   FONT-FAMILY: Cambria, serif;
   FONT-SIZE: 10px;
   text-align: left;
   white-Space: nowrap;
   display: inline-block;
   width: 100%;
}
.textarea
{
   BORDER-RIGHT: #999999 3px solid;
   PADDING-RIGHT: 3px;
   PADDING-LEFT: 3px;
   FONT-WEIGHT: Normal;
   PADDING-BOTTOM: 3px;
   COLOR: white;
   PADDING-TOP: 3px;
   BORDER-BOTTOM: #999 1px solid;
   BACKGROUND-COLOR: navy;
   FONT-FAMILY: Cambria, serif;
   FONT-SIZE: 10px;
   text-align: left;
   white-Space: nowrap;
   width: 100%;
}
.Select
{
   BORDER-RIGHT: #999999 3px solid;
   PADDING-RIGHT: 6px;
   PADDING-LEFT: 6px;
   FONT-WEIGHT: Normal;
   PADDING-BOTTOM: 6px;
   COLOR: white;
   PADDING-TOP: 6px;
   BORDER-BOTTOM: #999 1px solid;
   BACKGROUND-COLOR: navy;
   FONT-FAMILY: Cambria, serif;
   FONT-SIZE: 10px;
```

```
    text-align: left;
    white-Space: nowrap;
    width: 100%;
}
input
{
    BORDER-RIGHT: #999999 1px solid;
    PADDING-RIGHT: 1px;
    PADDING-LEFT: 1px;
    FONT-WEIGHT: Normal;
    PADDING-BOTTOM: 1px;
    COLOR: White;
    PADDING-TOP: 1px;
    BORDER-BOTTOM: #999 1px solid;
    BACKGROUND-COLOR: navy;
    FONT-FAMILY: Cambria, serif;
    FONT-SIZE: 12px;
    text-align: left;
    display: table-cell;
    white-Space: nowrap;
    width: auto;
}
</style>
</head>
<body>
    <form id="form1">
        <div>
            <table cellspacing='2' cellpadding= '2'>
                <tr>
                    <th style="text-align:left;">Property Name</th>
                    <th style="text-align:left;">Row0</th>
                    <th style="text-align:left;">Row1</th>
                    <th style="text-align:left;">Row2</th>
                    <th style="text-align:left;">Row3</th>
                    <th style="text-align:left;">Row4</th>
                    <th style="text-align:left;">Row5</th>
                    <th style="text-align:left;">Row6</th>
                    <th style="text-align:left;">Row7</th>
                    <th style="text-align:left;">Row8</th>
                    <th style="text-align:left;">Row9</th>
                    <th style="text-align:left;">Row10</th>
                    <th style="text-align:left;">Row11</th>
                    <th style="text-align:left;">Row12</th>
                    <th style="text-align:left;">Row13</th>
                    <th style="text-align:left;">Row14</th>
                    <th style="text-align:left;">Row15</th>
                    <th style="text-align:left;">Row16</th>
                    <th style="text-align:left;">Row17</th>
                    <th style="text-align:left;">Row18</th>
                    <th style="text-align:left;">Row19</th>
                    <th style="text-align:left;">Row20</th>
                    <th style="text-align:left;">Row21</th>
                    <th style="text-align:left;">Row22</th>
                    <th style="text-align:left;">Row23</th>
                    <th style="text-align:left;">Row24</th>
                    <th style="text-align:left;">Row25</th>
                    <th style="text-align:left;">Row26</th>
                    <th style="text-align:left;">Row27</th>
                    <th style="text-align:left;">Row28</th>
                    <th style="text-align:left;">Row29</th>
                    <th style="text-align:left;">Row30</th>
                    <th style="text-align:left;">Row31</th>
                    <th style="text-align:left;">Row32</th>
                    <th style="text-align:left;">Row33</th>
                    <th style="text-align:left;">Row34</th>
                    <th style="text-align:left;">Row35</th>
```

```html
    <th style="text-align:left;">Row36</th>
    <th style="text-align:left;">Row37</th>
    <th style="text-align:left;">Row38</th>
    <th style="text-align:left;">Row39</th>
    <th style="text-align:left;">Row40</th>
    <th style="text-align:left;">Row41</th>
    <th style="text-align:left;">Row42</th>
    <th style="text-align:left;">Row43</th>
    <th style="text-align:left;">Row44</th>
    <th style="text-align:left;">Row45</th>
    <th style="text-align:left;">Row46</th>
    <th style="text-align:left;">Row47</th>
    <th style="text-align:left;">Row48</th>
    <th style="text-align:left;">Row49</th>
    <th style="text-align:left;">Row50</th>
    <th style="text-align:left;">Row51</th>
    <th style="text-align:left;">Row52</th>
    <th style="text-align:left;">Row53</th>
    <th style="text-align:left;">Row54</th>
    <th style="text-align:left;">Row55</th>
    <th style="text-align:left;">Row56</th>
    <th style="text-align:left;">Row57</th>
    <th style="text-align:left;">Row58</th>
    <th style="text-align:left;">Row59</th>
    <th style="text-align:left;">Row60</th>
    <th style="text-align:left;">Row61</th>
    <th style="text-align:left;">Row62</th>
    <th style="text-align:left;">Row63</th>
    <th style="text-align:left;">Row64</th>
    <th style="text-align:left;">Row65</th>
    <th style="text-align:left;">Row66</th>
    <th style="text-align:left;">Row67</th>
    <th style="text-align:left;">Row68</th>
    <th style="text-align:left;">Row69</th>
    <th style="text-align:left;">Row70</th>
    <th style="text-align:left;">Row71</th>
    <th style="text-align:left;">Row72</th>
    <th style="text-align:left;">Row73</th>
    <th style="text-align:left;">Row74</th>
    <th style="text-align:left;">Row75</th>
    <th style="text-align:left;">Row76</th>
</tr>
    <tr><th style="text-align:left;">ProductID</th>
<td style="text-align:left;"><Label>1<Label></td>
<td style="text-align:left;"><Label>2<Label></td>
<td style="text-align:left;"><Label>3<Label></td>
<td style="text-align:left;"><Label>4<Label></td>
<td style="text-align:left;"><Label>5<Label></td>
<td style="text-align:left;"><Label>6<Label></td>
<td style="text-align:left;"><Label>7<Label></td>
<td style="text-align:left;"><Label>8<Label></td>
<td style="text-align:left;"><Label>9<Label></td>
<td style="text-align:left;"><Label>10<Label></td>
<td style="text-align:left;"><Label>11<Label></td>
<td style="text-align:left;"><Label>12<Label></td>
<td style="text-align:left;"><Label>13<Label></td>
<td style="text-align:left;"><Label>14<Label></td>
<td style="text-align:left;"><Label>15<Label></td>
<td style="text-align:left;"><Label>16<Label></td>
<td style="text-align:left;"><Label>17<Label></td>
<td style="text-align:left;"><Label>18<Label></td>
<td style="text-align:left;"><Label>19<Label></td>
<td style="text-align:left;"><Label>20<Label></td>
<td style="text-align:left;"><Label>21<Label></td>
<td style="text-align:left;"><Label>22<Label></td>
<td style="text-align:left;"><Label>23<Label></td>
```

```
        <td style="text-align:left;"><Label>24<Label></td>
        <td style="text-align:left;"><Label>25<Label></td>
        <td style="text-align:left;"><Label>26<Label></td>
        <td style="text-align:left;"><Label>27<Label></td>
        <td style="text-align:left;"><Label>28<Label></td>
        <td style="text-align:left;"><Label>29<Label></td>
        <td style="text-align:left;"><Label>30<Label></td>
        <td style="text-align:left;"><Label>31<Label></td>
        <td style="text-align:left;"><Label>32<Label></td>
        <td style="text-align:left;"><Label>33<Label></td>
        <td style="text-align:left;"><Label>34<Label></td>
        <td style="text-align:left;"><Label>35<Label></td>
        <td style="text-align:left;"><Label>36<Label></td>
        <td style="text-align:left;"><Label>37<Label></td>
        <td style="text-align:left;"><Label>38<Label></td>
        <td style="text-align:left;"><Label>39<Label></td>
        <td style="text-align:left;"><Label>40<Label></td>
        <td style="text-align:left;"><Label>41<Label></td>
        <td style="text-align:left;"><Label>42<Label></td>
        <td style="text-align:left;"><Label>43<Label></td>
        <td style="text-align:left;"><Label>44<Label></td>
        <td style="text-align:left;"><Label>45<Label></td>
        <td style="text-align:left;"><Label>46<Label></td>
        <td style="text-align:left;"><Label>47<Label></td>
        <td style="text-align:left;"><Label>48<Label></td>
        <td style="text-align:left;"><Label>49<Label></td>
        <td style="text-align:left;"><Label>50<Label></td>
        <td style="text-align:left;"><Label>51<Label></td>
        <td style="text-align:left;"><Label>52<Label></td>
        <td style="text-align:left;"><Label>53<Label></td>
        <td style="text-align:left;"><Label>54<Label></td>
        <td style="text-align:left;"><Label>55<Label></td>
        <td style="text-align:left;"><Label>56<Label></td>
        <td style="text-align:left;"><Label>57<Label></td>
        <td style="text-align:left;"><Label>58<Label></td>
        <td style="text-align:left;"><Label>59<Label></td>
        <td style="text-align:left;"><Label>60<Label></td>
        <td style="text-align:left;"><Label>61<Label></td>
        <td style="text-align:left;"><Label>62<Label></td>
        <td style="text-align:left;"><Label>63<Label></td>
        <td style="text-align:left;"><Label>64<Label></td>
        <td style="text-align:left;"><Label>65<Label></td>
        <td style="text-align:left;"><Label>66<Label></td>
        <td style="text-align:left;"><Label>67<Label></td>
        <td style="text-align:left;"><Label>68<Label></td>
        <td style="text-align:left;"><Label>69<Label></td>
        <td style="text-align:left;"><Label>70<Label></td>
        <td style="text-align:left;"><Label>71<Label></td>
        <td style="text-align:left;"><Label>72<Label></td>
        <td style="text-align:left;"><Label>73<Label></td>
        <td style="text-align:left;"><Label>74<Label></td>
        <td style="text-align:left;"><Label>75<Label></td>
        <td style="text-align:left;"><Label>76<Label></td>
        <td style="text-align:left;"><Label>77<Label></td>
</tr>
    <tr><th style="text-align:left;">ProductName</th>
    <td style="text-align:left;"><Label>Chai<Label></td>
    <td style="text-align:left;"><Label>Chang<Label></td>
    <td style="text-align:left;"><Label>Aniseed Syrup<Label></td>
    <td style="text-align:left;"><Label>Chef Anton's Cajun Seasoning<Label></td>
    <td style="text-align:left;"><Label>Chef Anton's Gumbo Mix<Label></td>
    <td style="text-align:left;"><Label>Grandma's Boysenberry Spread<Label></td>
    <td style="text-align:left;"><Label>Uncle Bob's Organic Dried Pears<Label></td>
    <td style="text-align:left;"><Label>Northwoods Cranberry Sauce<Label></td>
    <td style="text-align:left;"><Label>Mishi Kobe Niku<Label></td>
    <td style="text-align:left;"><Label>Ikura<Label></td>
```

```html
<td style="text-align:left;"><Label>Queso Cabrales<Label></td>
<td style="text-align:left;"><Label>Queso Manchego La Pastora<Label></td>
<td style="text-align:left;"><Label>Konbu<Label></td>
<td style="text-align:left;"><Label>Tofu<Label></td>
<td style="text-align:left;"><Label>Genen Shouyu<Label></td>
<td style="text-align:left;"><Label>Pavlova<Label></td>
<td style="text-align:left;"><Label>Alice Mutton<Label></td>
<td style="text-align:left;"><Label>Carnarvon Tigers<Label></td>
<td style="text-align:left;"><Label>Teatime Chocolate Biscuits<Label></td>
<td style="text-align:left;"><Label>Sir Rodney's Marmalade<Label></td>
<td style="text-align:left;"><Label>Sir Rodney's Scones<Label></td>
<td style="text-align:left;"><Label>Gustaf's Knäckebröd<Label></td>
<td style="text-align:left;"><Label>Tunnbröd<Label></td>
<td style="text-align:left;"><Label>Guaraná Fantástica<Label></td>
<td style="text-align:left;"><Label>NuNuCa Nuß-Nougat-Creme<Label></td>
<td style="text-align:left;"><Label>Gumbär Gummibärchen<Label></td>
<td style="text-align:left;"><Label>Schoggi Schokolade<Label></td>
<td style="text-align:left;"><Label>Rössle Sauerkraut<Label></td>
<td style="text-align:left;"><Label>Thüringer Rostbratwurst<Label></td>
<td style="text-align:left;"><Label>Nord-Ost Matjeshering<Label></td>
<td style="text-align:left;"><Label>Gorgonzola Telino<Label></td>
<td style="text-align:left;"><Label>Mascarpone Fabioli<Label></td>
<td style="text-align:left;"><Label>Geitost<Label></td>
<td style="text-align:left;"><Label>Sasquatch Ale<Label></td>
<td style="text-align:left;"><Label>Steeleye Stout<Label></td>
<td style="text-align:left;"><Label>Inlagd Sill<Label></td>
<td style="text-align:left;"><Label>Gravad lax<Label></td>
<td style="text-align:left;"><Label>Côte de Blaye<Label></td>
<td style="text-align:left;"><Label>Chartreuse verte<Label></td>
<td style="text-align:left;"><Label>Boston Crab Meat<Label></td>
<td style="text-align:left;"><Label>Jack's New England Clam Chowder<Label></td>
<td style="text-align:left;"><Label>Singaporean Hokkien Fried Mee<Label></td>
<td style="text-align:left;"><Label>Ipoh Coffee<Label></td>
<td style="text-align:left;"><Label>Gula Malacca<Label></td>
<td style="text-align:left;"><Label>Røgede sild<Label></td>
<td style="text-align:left;"><Label>Spegesild<Label></td>
<td style="text-align:left;"><Label>Zaanse koeken<Label></td>
<td style="text-align:left;"><Label>Chocolade<Label></td>
<td style="text-align:left;"><Label>Maxilaku<Label></td>
<td style="text-align:left;"><Label>Valkoinen suklaa<Label></td>
<td style="text-align:left;"><Label>Manjimup Dried Apples<Label></td>
<td style="text-align:left;"><Label>Filo Mix<Label></td>
<td style="text-align:left;"><Label>Perth Pasties<Label></td>
<td style="text-align:left;"><Label>Tourtière<Label></td>
<td style="text-align:left;"><Label>Pâté chinois<Label></td>
<td style="text-align:left;"><Label>Gnocchi di nonna Alice<Label></td>
<td style="text-align:left;"><Label>Ravioli Angelo<Label></td>
<td style="text-align:left;"><Label>Escargots de Bourgogne<Label></td>
<td style="text-align:left;"><Label>Raclette Courdavault<Label></td>
<td style="text-align:left;"><Label>Camembert Pierrot<Label></td>
<td style="text-align:left;"><Label>Sirop d'érable<Label></td>
<td style="text-align:left;"><Label>Tarte au sucre<Label></td>
<td style="text-align:left;"><Label>Vegie-spread<Label></td>
<td style="text-align:left;"><Label>Wimmers gute Semmelknödel<Label></td>
<td style="text-align:left;"><Label>Louisiana Fiery Hot Pepper Sauce<Label></td>
<td style="text-align:left;"><Label>Louisiana Hot Spiced Okra<Label></td>
<td style="text-align:left;"><Label>Laughing Lumberjack Lager<Label></td>
<td style="text-align:left;"><Label>Scottish Longbreads<Label></td>
<td style="text-align:left;"><Label>Gudbrandsdalsost<Label></td>
<td style="text-align:left;"><Label>Outback Lager<Label></td>
<td style="text-align:left;"><Label>Fløtemysost<Label></td>
<td style="text-align:left;"><Label>Mozzarella di Giovanni<Label></td>
<td style="text-align:left;"><Label>Röd Kaviar<Label></td>
<td style="text-align:left;"><Label>Longlife Tofu<Label></td>
<td style="text-align:left;"><Label>Rhönbräu Klosterbier<Label></td>
<td style="text-align:left;"><Label>Lakkalikööri<Label></td>
```

```
        <td style="text-align:left;"><Label>Original Frankfurter grüne Soße<Label></td>
</tr>
        <tr><th style="text-align:left;">SupplierID</th>
        <td style="text-align:left;"><Label>1<Label></td>
        <td style="text-align:left;"><Label>1<Label></td>
        <td style="text-align:left;"><Label>1<Label></td>
        <td style="text-align:left;"><Label>2<Label></td>
        <td style="text-align:left;"><Label>2<Label></td>
        <td style="text-align:left;"><Label>3<Label></td>
        <td style="text-align:left;"><Label>3<Label></td>
        <td style="text-align:left;"><Label>3<Label></td>
        <td style="text-align:left;"><Label>4<Label></td>
        <td style="text-align:left;"><Label>4<Label></td>
        <td style="text-align:left;"><Label>5<Label></td>
        <td style="text-align:left;"><Label>5<Label></td>
        <td style="text-align:left;"><Label>6<Label></td>
        <td style="text-align:left;"><Label>6<Label></td>
        <td style="text-align:left;"><Label>6<Label></td>
        <td style="text-align:left;"><Label>7<Label></td>
        <td style="text-align:left;"><Label>7<Label></td>
        <td style="text-align:left;"><Label>7<Label></td>
        <td style="text-align:left;"><Label>8<Label></td>
        <td style="text-align:left;"><Label>8<Label></td>
        <td style="text-align:left;"><Label>8<Label></td>
        <td style="text-align:left;"><Label>9<Label></td>
        <td style="text-align:left;"><Label>9<Label></td>
        <td style="text-align:left;"><Label>10<Label></td>
        <td style="text-align:left;"><Label>11<Label></td>
        <td style="text-align:left;"><Label>11<Label></td>
        <td style="text-align:left;"><Label>11<Label></td>
        <td style="text-align:left;"><Label>12<Label></td>
        <td style="text-align:left;"><Label>12<Label></td>
        <td style="text-align:left;"><Label>13<Label></td>
        <td style="text-align:left;"><Label>14<Label></td>
        <td style="text-align:left;"><Label>14<Label></td>
        <td style="text-align:left;"><Label>15<Label></td>
        <td style="text-align:left;"><Label>16<Label></td>
        <td style="text-align:left;"><Label>16<Label></td>
        <td style="text-align:left;"><Label>17<Label></td>
        <td style="text-align:left;"><Label>17<Label></td>
        <td style="text-align:left;"><Label>18<Label></td>
        <td style="text-align:left;"><Label>18<Label></td>
        <td style="text-align:left;"><Label>19<Label></td>
        <td style="text-align:left;"><Label>19<Label></td>
        <td style="text-align:left;"><Label>20<Label></td>
        <td style="text-align:left;"><Label>20<Label></td>
        <td style="text-align:left;"><Label>20<Label></td>
        <td style="text-align:left;"><Label>21<Label></td>
        <td style="text-align:left;"><Label>21<Label></td>
        <td style="text-align:left;"><Label>22<Label></td>
        <td style="text-align:left;"><Label>22<Label></td>
        <td style="text-align:left;"><Label>23<Label></td>
        <td style="text-align:left;"><Label>23<Label></td>
        <td style="text-align:left;"><Label>24<Label></td>
        <td style="text-align:left;"><Label>24<Label></td>
        <td style="text-align:left;"><Label>24<Label></td>
        <td style="text-align:left;"><Label>25<Label></td>
        <td style="text-align:left;"><Label>25<Label></td>
        <td style="text-align:left;"><Label>26<Label></td>
        <td style="text-align:left;"><Label>26<Label></td>
        <td style="text-align:left;"><Label>27<Label></td>
        <td style="text-align:left;"><Label>28<Label></td>
        <td style="text-align:left;"><Label>28<Label></td>
        <td style="text-align:left;"><Label>29<Label></td>
        <td style="text-align:left;"><Label>29<Label></td>
        <td style="text-align:left;"><Label>7<Label></td>
```

```html
    <td style="text-align:left;"><Label>12<Label></td>
    <td style="text-align:left;"><Label>2<Label></td>
    <td style="text-align:left;"><Label>2<Label></td>
    <td style="text-align:left;"><Label>16<Label></td>
    <td style="text-align:left;"><Label>8<Label></td>
    <td style="text-align:left;"><Label>15<Label></td>
    <td style="text-align:left;"><Label>7<Label></td>
    <td style="text-align:left;"><Label>15<Label></td>
    <td style="text-align:left;"><Label>14<Label></td>
    <td style="text-align:left;"><Label>17<Label></td>
    <td style="text-align:left;"><Label>4<Label></td>
    <td style="text-align:left;"><Label>12<Label></td>
    <td style="text-align:left;"><Label>23<Label></td>
    <td style="text-align:left;"><Label>12<Label></td>
</tr>
    <tr><th style="text-align:left;">CategoryID</th>
    <td style="text-align:left;"><Label>1<Label></td>
    <td style="text-align:left;"><Label>1<Label></td>
    <td style="text-align:left;"><Label>2<Label></td>
    <td style="text-align:left;"><Label>2<Label></td>
    <td style="text-align:left;"><Label>2<Label></td>
    <td style="text-align:left;"><Label>2<Label></td>
    <td style="text-align:left;"><Label>7<Label></td>
    <td style="text-align:left;"><Label>2<Label></td>
    <td style="text-align:left;"><Label>6<Label></td>
    <td style="text-align:left;"><Label>8<Label></td>
    <td style="text-align:left;"><Label>4<Label></td>
    <td style="text-align:left;"><Label>4<Label></td>
    <td style="text-align:left;"><Label>8<Label></td>
    <td style="text-align:left;"><Label>7<Label></td>
    <td style="text-align:left;"><Label>2<Label></td>
    <td style="text-align:left;"><Label>3<Label></td>
    <td style="text-align:left;"><Label>6<Label></td>
    <td style="text-align:left;"><Label>8<Label></td>
    <td style="text-align:left;"><Label>3<Label></td>
    <td style="text-align:left;"><Label>3<Label></td>
    <td style="text-align:left;"><Label>3<Label></td>
    <td style="text-align:left;"><Label>5<Label></td>
    <td style="text-align:left;"><Label>5<Label></td>
    <td style="text-align:left;"><Label>1<Label></td>
    <td style="text-align:left;"><Label>3<Label></td>
    <td style="text-align:left;"><Label>3<Label></td>
    <td style="text-align:left;"><Label>3<Label></td>
    <td style="text-align:left;"><Label>7<Label></td>
    <td style="text-align:left;"><Label>6<Label></td>
    <td style="text-align:left;"><Label>8<Label></td>
    <td style="text-align:left;"><Label>4<Label></td>
    <td style="text-align:left;"><Label>4<Label></td>
    <td style="text-align:left;"><Label>4<Label></td>
    <td style="text-align:left;"><Label>1<Label></td>
    <td style="text-align:left;"><Label>1<Label></td>
    <td style="text-align:left;"><Label>8<Label></td>
    <td style="text-align:left;"><Label>8<Label></td>
    <td style="text-align:left;"><Label>1<Label></td>
    <td style="text-align:left;"><Label>1<Label></td>
    <td style="text-align:left;"><Label>8<Label></td>
    <td style="text-align:left;"><Label>8<Label></td>
    <td style="text-align:left;"><Label>5<Label></td>
    <td style="text-align:left;"><Label>1<Label></td>
    <td style="text-align:left;"><Label>2<Label></td>
    <td style="text-align:left;"><Label>8<Label></td>
    <td style="text-align:left;"><Label>8<Label></td>
    <td style="text-align:left;"><Label>3<Label></td>
    <td style="text-align:left;"><Label>3<Label></td>
    <td style="text-align:left;"><Label>3<Label></td>
    <td style="text-align:left;"><Label>3<Label></td>
```

```html
        <td style="text-align:left;"><Label>7<Label></td>
        <td style="text-align:left;"><Label>5<Label></td>
        <td style="text-align:left;"><Label>6<Label></td>
        <td style="text-align:left;"><Label>6<Label></td>
        <td style="text-align:left;"><Label>6<Label></td>
        <td style="text-align:left;"><Label>5<Label></td>
        <td style="text-align:left;"><Label>5<Label></td>
        <td style="text-align:left;"><Label>8<Label></td>
        <td style="text-align:left;"><Label>4<Label></td>
        <td style="text-align:left;"><Label>4<Label></td>
        <td style="text-align:left;"><Label>2<Label></td>
        <td style="text-align:left;"><Label>3<Label></td>
        <td style="text-align:left;"><Label>2<Label></td>
        <td style="text-align:left;"><Label>5<Label></td>
        <td style="text-align:left;"><Label>2<Label></td>
        <td style="text-align:left;"><Label>2<Label></td>
        <td style="text-align:left;"><Label>1<Label></td>
        <td style="text-align:left;"><Label>3<Label></td>
        <td style="text-align:left;"><Label>4<Label></td>
        <td style="text-align:left;"><Label>1<Label></td>
        <td style="text-align:left;"><Label>4<Label></td>
        <td style="text-align:left;"><Label>4<Label></td>
        <td style="text-align:left;"><Label>8<Label></td>
        <td style="text-align:left;"><Label>7<Label></td>
        <td style="text-align:left;"><Label>1<Label></td>
        <td style="text-align:left;"><Label>1<Label></td>
        <td style="text-align:left;"><Label>2<Label></td>
</tr>
    <tr><th style="text-align:left;">QuantityPerUnit</th>
        <td style="text-align:left;"><Label>10 boxes x 20 bags<Label></td>
        <td style="text-align:left;"><Label>24 - 12 oz bottles<Label></td>
        <td style="text-align:left;"><Label>12 - 550 ml bottles<Label></td>
        <td style="text-align:left;"><Label>48 - 6 oz jars<Label></td>
        <td style="text-align:left;"><Label>36 boxes<Label></td>
        <td style="text-align:left;"><Label>12 - 8 oz jars<Label></td>
        <td style="text-align:left;"><Label>12 - 1 lb pkgs.<Label></td>
        <td style="text-align:left;"><Label>12 - 12 oz jars<Label></td>
        <td style="text-align:left;"><Label>18 - 500 g pkgs.<Label></td>
        <td style="text-align:left;"><Label>12 - 200 ml jars<Label></td>
        <td style="text-align:left;"><Label>1 kg pkg.<Label></td>
        <td style="text-align:left;"><Label>10 - 500 g pkgs.<Label></td>
        <td style="text-align:left;"><Label>2 kg box<Label></td>
        <td style="text-align:left;"><Label>40 - 100 g pkgs.<Label></td>
        <td style="text-align:left;"><Label>24 - 250 ml bottles<Label></td>
        <td style="text-align:left;"><Label>32 - 500 g boxes<Label></td>
        <td style="text-align:left;"><Label>20 - 1 kg tins<Label></td>
        <td style="text-align:left;"><Label>16 kg pkg.<Label></td>
        <td style="text-align:left;"><Label>10 boxes x 12 pieces<Label></td>
        <td style="text-align:left;"><Label>30 gift boxes<Label></td>
        <td style="text-align:left;"><Label>24 pkgs. x 4 pieces<Label></td>
        <td style="text-align:left;"><Label>24 - 500 g pkgs.<Label></td>
        <td style="text-align:left;"><Label>12 - 250 g pkgs.<Label></td>
        <td style="text-align:left;"><Label>12 - 355 ml cans<Label></td>
        <td style="text-align:left;"><Label>20 - 450 g glasses<Label></td>
        <td style="text-align:left;"><Label>100 - 250 g bags<Label></td>
        <td style="text-align:left;"><Label>100 - 100 g pieces<Label></td>
        <td style="text-align:left;"><Label>25 - 825 g cans<Label></td>
        <td style="text-align:left;"><Label>50 bags x 30 sausgs.<Label></td>
        <td style="text-align:left;"><Label>10 - 200 g glasses<Label></td>
        <td style="text-align:left;"><Label>12 - 100 g pkgs.<Label></td>
        <td style="text-align:left;"><Label>24 - 200 g pkgs.<Label></td>
        <td style="text-align:left;"><Label>500 g<Label></td>
        <td style="text-align:left;"><Label>24 - 12 oz bottles<Label></td>
        <td style="text-align:left;"><Label>24 - 12 oz bottles<Label></td>
        <td style="text-align:left;"><Label>24 - 250 g  jars<Label></td>
        <td style="text-align:left;"><Label>12 - 500 g pkgs.<Label></td>
```

```html
    <td style="text-align:left;"><Label>12 - 75 cl bottles<Label></td>
    <td style="text-align:left;"><Label>750 cc per bottle<Label></td>
    <td style="text-align:left;"><Label>24 - 4 oz tins<Label></td>
    <td style="text-align:left;"><Label>12 - 12 oz cans<Label></td>
    <td style="text-align:left;"><Label>32 - 1 kg pkgs.<Label></td>
    <td style="text-align:left;"><Label>16 - 500 g tins<Label></td>
    <td style="text-align:left;"><Label>20 - 2 kg bags<Label></td>
    <td style="text-align:left;"><Label>1k pkg.<Label></td>
    <td style="text-align:left;"><Label>4 - 450 g glasses<Label></td>
    <td style="text-align:left;"><Label>10 - 4 oz boxes<Label></td>
    <td style="text-align:left;"><Label>10 pkgs.<Label></td>
    <td style="text-align:left;"><Label>24 - 50 g pkgs.<Label></td>
    <td style="text-align:left;"><Label>12 - 100 g bars<Label></td>
    <td style="text-align:left;"><Label>50 - 300 g pkgs.<Label></td>
    <td style="text-align:left;"><Label>16 - 2 kg boxes<Label></td>
    <td style="text-align:left;"><Label>48 pieces<Label></td>
    <td style="text-align:left;"><Label>16 pies<Label></td>
    <td style="text-align:left;"><Label>24 boxes x 2 pies<Label></td>
    <td style="text-align:left;"><Label>24 - 250 g pkgs.<Label></td>
    <td style="text-align:left;"><Label>24 - 250 g pkgs.<Label></td>
    <td style="text-align:left;"><Label>24 pieces<Label></td>
    <td style="text-align:left;"><Label>5 kg pkg.<Label></td>
    <td style="text-align:left;"><Label>15 - 300 g rounds<Label></td>
    <td style="text-align:left;"><Label>24 - 500 ml bottles<Label></td>
    <td style="text-align:left;"><Label>48 pies<Label></td>
    <td style="text-align:left;"><Label>15 - 625 g jars<Label></td>
    <td style="text-align:left;"><Label>20 bags x 4 pieces<Label></td>
    <td style="text-align:left;"><Label>32 - 8 oz bottles<Label></td>
    <td style="text-align:left;"><Label>24 - 8 oz jars<Label></td>
    <td style="text-align:left;"><Label>24 - 12 oz bottles<Label></td>
    <td style="text-align:left;"><Label>10 boxes x 8 pieces<Label></td>
    <td style="text-align:left;"><Label>10 kg pkg.<Label></td>
    <td style="text-align:left;"><Label>24 - 355 ml bottles<Label></td>
    <td style="text-align:left;"><Label>10 - 500 g pkgs.<Label></td>
    <td style="text-align:left;"><Label>24 - 200 g pkgs.<Label></td>
    <td style="text-align:left;"><Label>24 - 150 g jars<Label></td>
    <td style="text-align:left;"><Label>5 kg pkg.<Label></td>
    <td style="text-align:left;"><Label>24 - 0.5 l bottles<Label></td>
    <td style="text-align:left;"><Label>500 ml<Label></td>
    <td style="text-align:left;"><Label>12 boxes<Label></td>
</tr>
    <tr><th style="text-align:left;">UnitPrice</th>
    <td style="text-align:left;"><Label>18<Label></td>
    <td style="text-align:left;"><Label>19<Label></td>
    <td style="text-align:left;"><Label>10<Label></td>
    <td style="text-align:left;"><Label>22<Label></td>
    <td style="text-align:left;"><Label>21.35<Label></td>
    <td style="text-align:left;"><Label>25<Label></td>
    <td style="text-align:left;"><Label>30<Label></td>
    <td style="text-align:left;"><Label>40<Label></td>
    <td style="text-align:left;"><Label>97<Label></td>
    <td style="text-align:left;"><Label>31<Label></td>
    <td style="text-align:left;"><Label>21<Label></td>
    <td style="text-align:left;"><Label>38<Label></td>
    <td style="text-align:left;"><Label>6<Label></td>
    <td style="text-align:left;"><Label>23.25<Label></td>
    <td style="text-align:left;"><Label>15.5<Label></td>
    <td style="text-align:left;"><Label>17.45<Label></td>
    <td style="text-align:left;"><Label>39<Label></td>
    <td style="text-align:left;"><Label>62.5<Label></td>
    <td style="text-align:left;"><Label>9.2<Label></td>
    <td style="text-align:left;"><Label>81<Label></td>
    <td style="text-align:left;"><Label>10<Label></td>
    <td style="text-align:left;"><Label>21<Label></td>
    <td style="text-align:left;"><Label>9<Label></td>
    <td style="text-align:left;"><Label>4.5<Label></td>
```

```
<td style="text-align:left;"><Label>14<Label></td>
<td style="text-align:left;"><Label>31.23<Label></td>
<td style="text-align:left;"><Label>43.9<Label></td>
<td style="text-align:left;"><Label>45.6<Label></td>
<td style="text-align:left;"><Label>123.79<Label></td>
<td style="text-align:left;"><Label>25.89<Label></td>
<td style="text-align:left;"><Label>12.5<Label></td>
<td style="text-align:left;"><Label>32<Label></td>
<td style="text-align:left;"><Label>2.5<Label></td>
<td style="text-align:left;"><Label>14<Label></td>
<td style="text-align:left;"><Label>18<Label></td>
<td style="text-align:left;"><Label>19<Label></td>
<td style="text-align:left;"><Label>26<Label></td>
<td style="text-align:left;"><Label>263.5<Label></td>
<td style="text-align:left;"><Label>18<Label></td>
<td style="text-align:left;"><Label>18.4<Label></td>
<td style="text-align:left;"><Label>9.65<Label></td>
<td style="text-align:left;"><Label>14<Label></td>
<td style="text-align:left;"><Label>46<Label></td>
<td style="text-align:left;"><Label>19.45<Label></td>
<td style="text-align:left;"><Label>9.5<Label></td>
<td style="text-align:left;"><Label>12<Label></td>
<td style="text-align:left;"><Label>9.5<Label></td>
<td style="text-align:left;"><Label>12.75<Label></td>
<td style="text-align:left;"><Label>20<Label></td>
<td style="text-align:left;"><Label>16.25<Label></td>
<td style="text-align:left;"><Label>53<Label></td>
<td style="text-align:left;"><Label>7<Label></td>
<td style="text-align:left;"><Label>32.8<Label></td>
<td style="text-align:left;"><Label>7.45<Label></td>
<td style="text-align:left;"><Label>24<Label></td>
<td style="text-align:left;"><Label>38<Label></td>
<td style="text-align:left;"><Label>19.5<Label></td>
<td style="text-align:left;"><Label>13.25<Label></td>
<td style="text-align:left;"><Label>55<Label></td>
<td style="text-align:left;"><Label>34<Label></td>
<td style="text-align:left;"><Label>28.5<Label></td>
<td style="text-align:left;"><Label>49.3<Label></td>
<td style="text-align:left;"><Label>43.9<Label></td>
<td style="text-align:left;"><Label>33.25<Label></td>
<td style="text-align:left;"><Label>21.05<Label></td>
<td style="text-align:left;"><Label>17<Label></td>
<td style="text-align:left;"><Label>14<Label></td>
<td style="text-align:left;"><Label>12.5<Label></td>
<td style="text-align:left;"><Label>36<Label></td>
<td style="text-align:left;"><Label>15<Label></td>
<td style="text-align:left;"><Label>21.5<Label></td>
<td style="text-align:left;"><Label>34.8<Label></td>
<td style="text-align:left;"><Label>15<Label></td>
<td style="text-align:left;"><Label>10<Label></td>
<td style="text-align:left;"><Label>7.75<Label></td>
<td style="text-align:left;"><Label>18<Label></td>
<td style="text-align:left;"><Label>13<Label></td>
</tr>
    <tr><th style="text-align:left;">UnitsInStock</th>
<td style="text-align:left;"><Label>39<Label></td>
<td style="text-align:left;"><Label>17<Label></td>
<td style="text-align:left;"><Label>13<Label></td>
<td style="text-align:left;"><Label>53<Label></td>
<td style="text-align:left;"><Label>0<Label></td>
<td style="text-align:left;"><Label>120<Label></td>
<td style="text-align:left;"><Label>15<Label></td>
<td style="text-align:left;"><Label>6<Label></td>
<td style="text-align:left;"><Label>29<Label></td>
<td style="text-align:left;"><Label>31<Label></td>
<td style="text-align:left;"><Label>22<Label></td>
```

```html
<td style="text-align:left;"><Label>86<Label></td>
<td style="text-align:left;"><Label>24<Label></td>
<td style="text-align:left;"><Label>35<Label></td>
<td style="text-align:left;"><Label>39<Label></td>
<td style="text-align:left;"><Label>29<Label></td>
<td style="text-align:left;"><Label>0<Label></td>
<td style="text-align:left;"><Label>42<Label></td>
<td style="text-align:left;"><Label>25<Label></td>
<td style="text-align:left;"><Label>40<Label></td>
<td style="text-align:left;"><Label>3<Label></td>
<td style="text-align:left;"><Label>104<Label></td>
<td style="text-align:left;"><Label>61<Label></td>
<td style="text-align:left;"><Label>20<Label></td>
<td style="text-align:left;"><Label>76<Label></td>
<td style="text-align:left;"><Label>15<Label></td>
<td style="text-align:left;"><Label>49<Label></td>
<td style="text-align:left;"><Label>26<Label></td>
<td style="text-align:left;"><Label>0<Label></td>
<td style="text-align:left;"><Label>10<Label></td>
<td style="text-align:left;"><Label>0<Label></td>
<td style="text-align:left;"><Label>9<Label></td>
<td style="text-align:left;"><Label>112<Label></td>
<td style="text-align:left;"><Label>111<Label></td>
<td style="text-align:left;"><Label>20<Label></td>
<td style="text-align:left;"><Label>112<Label></td>
<td style="text-align:left;"><Label>11<Label></td>
<td style="text-align:left;"><Label>17<Label></td>
<td style="text-align:left;"><Label>69<Label></td>
<td style="text-align:left;"><Label>123<Label></td>
<td style="text-align:left;"><Label>85<Label></td>
<td style="text-align:left;"><Label>26<Label></td>
<td style="text-align:left;"><Label>17<Label></td>
<td style="text-align:left;"><Label>27<Label></td>
<td style="text-align:left;"><Label>5<Label></td>
<td style="text-align:left;"><Label>95<Label></td>
<td style="text-align:left;"><Label>36<Label></td>
<td style="text-align:left;"><Label>15<Label></td>
<td style="text-align:left;"><Label>10<Label></td>
<td style="text-align:left;"><Label>65<Label></td>
<td style="text-align:left;"><Label>20<Label></td>
<td style="text-align:left;"><Label>38<Label></td>
<td style="text-align:left;"><Label>0<Label></td>
<td style="text-align:left;"><Label>21<Label></td>
<td style="text-align:left;"><Label>115<Label></td>
<td style="text-align:left;"><Label>21<Label></td>
<td style="text-align:left;"><Label>36<Label></td>
<td style="text-align:left;"><Label>62<Label></td>
<td style="text-align:left;"><Label>79<Label></td>
<td style="text-align:left;"><Label>19<Label></td>
<td style="text-align:left;"><Label>113<Label></td>
<td style="text-align:left;"><Label>17<Label></td>
<td style="text-align:left;"><Label>24<Label></td>
<td style="text-align:left;"><Label>22<Label></td>
<td style="text-align:left;"><Label>76<Label></td>
<td style="text-align:left;"><Label>4<Label></td>
<td style="text-align:left;"><Label>52<Label></td>
<td style="text-align:left;"><Label>6<Label></td>
<td style="text-align:left;"><Label>26<Label></td>
<td style="text-align:left;"><Label>15<Label></td>
<td style="text-align:left;"><Label>26<Label></td>
<td style="text-align:left;"><Label>14<Label></td>
<td style="text-align:left;"><Label>101<Label></td>
<td style="text-align:left;"><Label>4<Label></td>
<td style="text-align:left;"><Label>125<Label></td>
<td style="text-align:left;"><Label>57<Label></td>
<td style="text-align:left;"><Label>32<Label></td>
```

```html
</tr>
    <tr><th style="text-align:left;">UnitsOnOrder</th>
    <td style="text-align:left;"><Label>0<Label></td>
    <td style="text-align:left;"><Label>40<Label></td>
    <td style="text-align:left;"><Label>70<Label></td>
    <td style="text-align:left;"><Label>0<Label></td>
    <td style="text-align:left;"><Label>0<Label></td>
    <td style="text-align:left;"><Label>0<Label></td>
    <td style="text-align:left;"><Label>0<Label></td>
    <td style="text-align:left;"><Label>0<Label></td>
    <td style="text-align:left;"><Label>0<Label></td>
    <td style="text-align:left;"><Label>0<Label></td>
    <td style="text-align:left;"><Label>30<Label></td>
    <td style="text-align:left;"><Label>0<Label></td>
    <td style="text-align:left;"><Label>0<Label></td>
    <td style="text-align:left;"><Label>0<Label></td>
    <td style="text-align:left;"><Label>0<Label></td>
    <td style="text-align:left;"><Label>0<Label></td>
    <td style="text-align:left;"><Label>0<Label></td>
    <td style="text-align:left;"><Label>0<Label></td>
    <td style="text-align:left;"><Label>0<Label></td>
    <td style="text-align:left;"><Label>40<Label></td>
    <td style="text-align:left;"><Label>0<Label></td>
    <td style="text-align:left;"><Label>0<Label></td>
    <td style="text-align:left;"><Label>0<Label></td>
    <td style="text-align:left;"><Label>0<Label></td>
    <td style="text-align:left;"><Label>0<Label></td>
    <td style="text-align:left;"><Label>0<Label></td>
    <td style="text-align:left;"><Label>0<Label></td>
    <td style="text-align:left;"><Label>0<Label></td>
    <td style="text-align:left;"><Label>70<Label></td>
    <td style="text-align:left;"><Label>40<Label></td>
    <td style="text-align:left;"><Label>0<Label></td>
    <td style="text-align:left;"><Label>0<Label></td>
    <td style="text-align:left;"><Label>0<Label></td>
    <td style="text-align:left;"><Label>0<Label></td>
    <td style="text-align:left;"><Label>50<Label></td>
    <td style="text-align:left;"><Label>0<Label></td>
    <td style="text-align:left;"><Label>0<Label></td>
    <td style="text-align:left;"><Label>0<Label></td>
    <td style="text-align:left;"><Label>0<Label></td>
    <td style="text-align:left;"><Label>0<Label></td>
    <td style="text-align:left;"><Label>10<Label></td>
    <td style="text-align:left;"><Label>0<Label></td>
    <td style="text-align:left;"><Label>70<Label></td>
    <td style="text-align:left;"><Label>0<Label></td>
    <td style="text-align:left;"><Label>0<Label></td>
    <td style="text-align:left;"><Label>70<Label></td>
    <td style="text-align:left;"><Label>60<Label></td>
    <td style="text-align:left;"><Label>0<Label></td>
    <td style="text-align:left;"><Label>0<Label></td>
    <td style="text-align:left;"><Label>0<Label></td>
    <td style="text-align:left;"><Label>0<Label></td>
    <td style="text-align:left;"><Label>0<Label></td>
    <td style="text-align:left;"><Label>0<Label></td>
    <td style="text-align:left;"><Label>10<Label></td>
    <td style="text-align:left;"><Label>0<Label></td>
    <td style="text-align:left;"><Label>0<Label></td>
    <td style="text-align:left;"><Label>0<Label></td>
    <td style="text-align:left;"><Label>0<Label></td>
    <td style="text-align:left;"><Label>0<Label></td>
    <td style="text-align:left;"><Label>0<Label></td>
    <td style="text-align:left;"><Label>0<Label></td>
    <td style="text-align:left;"><Label>80<Label></td>
```

```html
    <td style="text-align:left;"><Label>0<Label></td>
    <td style="text-align:left;"><Label>100<Label></td>
    <td style="text-align:left;"><Label>0<Label></td>
    <td style="text-align:left;"><Label>10<Label></td>
    <td style="text-align:left;"><Label>0<Label></td>
    <td style="text-align:left;"><Label>10<Label></td>
    <td style="text-align:left;"><Label>0<Label></td>
    <td style="text-align:left;"><Label>0<Label></td>
    <td style="text-align:left;"><Label>0<Label></td>
    <td style="text-align:left;"><Label>20<Label></td>
    <td style="text-align:left;"><Label>0<Label></td>
    <td style="text-align:left;"><Label>0<Label></td>
    <td style="text-align:left;"><Label>0<Label></td>
</tr>
        <tr><th style="text-align:left;">ReorderLevel</th>
    <td style="text-align:left;"><Label>10<Label></td>
    <td style="text-align:left;"><Label>25<Label></td>
    <td style="text-align:left;"><Label>25<Label></td>
    <td style="text-align:left;"><Label>0<Label></td>
    <td style="text-align:left;"><Label>0<Label></td>
    <td style="text-align:left;"><Label>25<Label></td>
    <td style="text-align:left;"><Label>10<Label></td>
    <td style="text-align:left;"><Label>0<Label></td>
    <td style="text-align:left;"><Label>0<Label></td>
    <td style="text-align:left;"><Label>0<Label></td>
    <td style="text-align:left;"><Label>30<Label></td>
    <td style="text-align:left;"><Label>0<Label></td>
    <td style="text-align:left;"><Label>5<Label></td>
    <td style="text-align:left;"><Label>0<Label></td>
    <td style="text-align:left;"><Label>5<Label></td>
    <td style="text-align:left;"><Label>10<Label></td>
    <td style="text-align:left;"><Label>0<Label></td>
    <td style="text-align:left;"><Label>0<Label></td>
    <td style="text-align:left;"><Label>5<Label></td>
    <td style="text-align:left;"><Label>0<Label></td>
    <td style="text-align:left;"><Label>5<Label></td>
    <td style="text-align:left;"><Label>25<Label></td>
    <td style="text-align:left;"><Label>25<Label></td>
    <td style="text-align:left;"><Label>0<Label></td>
    <td style="text-align:left;"><Label>30<Label></td>
    <td style="text-align:left;"><Label>0<Label></td>
    <td style="text-align:left;"><Label>30<Label></td>
    <td style="text-align:left;"><Label>0<Label></td>
    <td style="text-align:left;"><Label>0<Label></td>
    <td style="text-align:left;"><Label>15<Label></td>
    <td style="text-align:left;"><Label>20<Label></td>
    <td style="text-align:left;"><Label>25<Label></td>
    <td style="text-align:left;"><Label>20<Label></td>
    <td style="text-align:left;"><Label>15<Label></td>
    <td style="text-align:left;"><Label>15<Label></td>
    <td style="text-align:left;"><Label>20<Label></td>
    <td style="text-align:left;"><Label>25<Label></td>
    <td style="text-align:left;"><Label>15<Label></td>
    <td style="text-align:left;"><Label>5<Label></td>
    <td style="text-align:left;"><Label>30<Label></td>
    <td style="text-align:left;"><Label>10<Label></td>
    <td style="text-align:left;"><Label>0<Label></td>
    <td style="text-align:left;"><Label>25<Label></td>
    <td style="text-align:left;"><Label>15<Label></td>
    <td style="text-align:left;"><Label>15<Label></td>
    <td style="text-align:left;"><Label>0<Label></td>
    <td style="text-align:left;"><Label>0<Label></td>
    <td style="text-align:left;"><Label>25<Label></td>
    <td style="text-align:left;"><Label>15<Label></td>
    <td style="text-align:left;"><Label>30<Label></td>
    <td style="text-align:left;"><Label>10<Label></td>
```

```html
<td style="text-align:left;"><Label>25<Label></td>
<td style="text-align:left;"><Label>0<Label></td>
<td style="text-align:left;"><Label>10<Label></td>
<td style="text-align:left;"><Label>20<Label></td>
<td style="text-align:left;"><Label>30<Label></td>
<td style="text-align:left;"><Label>20<Label></td>
<td style="text-align:left;"><Label>20<Label></td>
<td style="text-align:left;"><Label>0<Label></td>
<td style="text-align:left;"><Label>0<Label></td>
<td style="text-align:left;"><Label>25<Label></td>
<td style="text-align:left;"><Label>0<Label></td>
<td style="text-align:left;"><Label>5<Label></td>
<td style="text-align:left;"><Label>30<Label></td>
<td style="text-align:left;"><Label>0<Label></td>
<td style="text-align:left;"><Label>20<Label></td>
<td style="text-align:left;"><Label>10<Label></td>
<td style="text-align:left;"><Label>15<Label></td>
<td style="text-align:left;"><Label>15<Label></td>
<td style="text-align:left;"><Label>30<Label></td>
<td style="text-align:left;"><Label>0<Label></td>
<td style="text-align:left;"><Label>0<Label></td>
<td style="text-align:left;"><Label>5<Label></td>
<td style="text-align:left;"><Label>5<Label></td>
<td style="text-align:left;"><Label>25<Label></td>
<td style="text-align:left;"><Label>20<Label></td>
<td style="text-align:left;"><Label>15<Label></td>
</tr>
    <tr><th style="text-align:left;">Discontinued</th>
<td style="text-align:left;"><Label>False<Label></td>
<td style="text-align:left;"><Label>False<Label></td>
<td style="text-align:left;"><Label>False<Label></td>
<td style="text-align:left;"><Label>False<Label></td>
<td style="text-align:left;"><Label>True<Label></td>
<td style="text-align:left;"><Label>False<Label></td>
<td style="text-align:left;"><Label>False<Label></td>
<td style="text-align:left;"><Label>False<Label></td>
<td style="text-align:left;"><Label>True<Label></td>
<td style="text-align:left;"><Label>False<Label></td>
<td style="text-align:left;"><Label>False<Label></td>
<td style="text-align:left;"><Label>False<Label></td>
<td style="text-align:left;"><Label>False<Label></td>
<td style="text-align:left;"><Label>False<Label></td>
<td style="text-align:left;"><Label>False<Label></td>
<td style="text-align:left;"><Label>True<Label></td>
<td style="text-align:left;"><Label>False<Label></td>
<td style="text-align:left;"><Label>False<Label></td>
<td style="text-align:left;"><Label>False<Label></td>
<td style="text-align:left;"><Label>False<Label></td>
<td style="text-align:left;"><Label>False<Label></td>
<td style="text-align:left;"><Label>False<Label></td>
<td style="text-align:left;"><Label>True<Label></td>
<td style="text-align:left;"><Label>False<Label></td>
<td style="text-align:left;"><Label>False<Label></td>
<td style="text-align:left;"><Label>False<Label></td>
<td style="text-align:left;"><Label>True<Label></td>
<td style="text-align:left;"><Label>True<Label></td>
<td style="text-align:left;"><Label>False<Label></td>
<td style="text-align:left;"><Label>False<Label></td>
<td style="text-align:left;"><Label>False<Label></td>
<td style="text-align:left;"><Label>False<Label></td>
<td style="text-align:left;"><Label>False<Label></td>
<td style="text-align:left;"><Label>False<Label></td>
<td style="text-align:left;"><Label>False<Label></td>
<td style="text-align:left;"><Label>False<Label></td>
<td style="text-align:left;"><Label>False<Label></td>
```

```
                    <td style="text-align:left;"><Label>False<Label></td>
                    <td style="text-align:left;"><Label>False<Label></td>
                    <td style="text-align:left;"><Label>False<Label></td>
                    <td style="text-align:left;"><Label>True<Label></td>
                    <td style="text-align:left;"><Label>False<Label></td>
                    <td style="text-align:left;"><Label>False<Label></td>
                    <td style="text-align:left;"><Label>False<Label></td>
                    <td style="text-align:left;"><Label>False<Label></td>
                    <td style="text-align:left;"><Label>False<Label></td>
                    <td style="text-align:left;"><Label>False<Label></td>
                    <td style="text-align:left;"><Label>False<Label></td>
                    <td style="text-align:left;"><Label>False<Label></td>
                    <td style="text-align:left;"><Label>False<Label></td>
                    <td style="text-align:left;"><Label>True<Label></td>
                    <td style="text-align:left;"><Label>False<Label></td>
                    <td style="text-align:left;"><Label>False<Label></td>
                    <td style="text-align:left;"><Label>False<Label></td>
                    <td style="text-align:left;"><Label>False<Label></td>
                    <td style="text-align:left;"><Label>False<Label></td>
                    <td style="text-align:left;"><Label>False<Label></td>
                    <td style="text-align:left;"><Label>False<Label></td>
                    <td style="text-align:left;"><Label>False<Label></td>
                    <td style="text-align:left;"><Label>False<Label></td>
                    <td style="text-align:left;"><Label>False<Label></td>
                    <td style="text-align:left;"><Label>False<Label></td>
                    <td style="text-align:left;"><Label>False<Label></td>
                    <td style="text-align:left;"><Label>False<Label></td>
                    <td style="text-align:left;"><Label>False<Label></td>
                    <td style="text-align:left;"><Label>False<Label></td>
                    <td style="text-align:left;"><Label>False<Label></td>
                    <td style="text-align:left;"><Label>False<Label></td>
                    <td style="text-align:left;"><Label>False<Label></td>
                    <td style="text-align:left;"><Label>False<Label></td>
                    <td style="text-align:left;"><Label>False<Label></td>
                    <td style="text-align:left;"><Label>False<Label></td>
                </tr>
                </table>

        </div>
    </form>
</body>
</html>
```

And the output:

Property Name	Row0	Row1	Row2	Row3	Row4	Row5	Row6
ProductID	1	2	3	4	5	6	7
ProductName	Chai	Chang	Aniseed Syrup	Chef Anton's Cajun Seasoning	Chef Anton's Gumbo Mix	Grandma's Boysenberry Spread	Uncle Bob's Organic Dried Pears
SupplierID	1	1	1	2	2	3	3
CategoryID	1	1	2	2	2	2	7
QuantityPerUnit	10 boxes x 20 bags	24 - 12 oz bottles	12 - 550 ml bottles	48 - 6 oz jars	36 boxes	12 - 8 oz jars	12 - 1 lb pkgs.
UnitPrice	18	19	10	22	21.35	25	30
UnitsInStock	39	17	13	53	0	120	15
UnitsOnOrder	0	40	70	0	0	0	0
ReorderLevel	10	25	25	0	0	25	10
Discontinued	False	False	False	False	True	False	False

Okay, so now we have both horizontal and vertical formats along with all the code to make this work both inside the ASP Form and externally.

Below are some stylesheets you can add use with your ASP:

Basic:

```
txtstream.WriteLine("<style type='text/css'>")
txtstream.WriteLine("th")
txtstream.WriteLine("{")
txtstream.WriteLine("    COLOR: Darkred;")
txtstream.WriteLine("}")
txtstream.WriteLine("td")
txtstream.WriteLine("{")
txtstream.WriteLine("    COLOR: navy;")
txtstream.WriteLine("}")
txtstream.WriteLine("</style>")
```

Table:

```
txtstream.WriteLine("<style type=text/css>")
txtstream.WriteLine("#itsthetable {")
txtstream.WriteLine("    font-family: Georgia, \"""Times New Roman\"""", Times, serif;")
txtstream.WriteLine("    color: #036;")
txtstream.WriteLine("}")

txtstream.WriteLine("caption {")
txtstream.WriteLine("    font-size: 48px;")
txtstream.WriteLine("    color: #036;")
txtstream.WriteLine("    font-weight: bolder;")
txtstream.WriteLine("    font-variant: small-caps;")
txtstream.WriteLine("}")

txtstream.WriteLine("th {")
txtstream.WriteLine("    font-size: 12px;")
txtstream.WriteLine("    color: #FFF;")
txtstream.WriteLine("    background-color: #06C;")
txtstream.WriteLine("    padding: 8px 4px;")
txtstream.WriteLine("    border-bottom: 1px solid #015ebc;")
txtstream.WriteLine("}")

txtstream.WriteLine("table {")
txtstream.WriteLine("    margin: 0;")
txtstream.WriteLine("    padding: 0;")
txtstream.WriteLine("    border-collapse: collapse;")
txtstream.WriteLine("    border: 1px solid #06C;")
txtstream.WriteLine("    width: 100%")
txtstream.WriteLine("}")

txtstream.WriteLine("#itsthetable th a:link, #itsthetable th a:visited {")
txtstream.WriteLine("    color: #FFF;")
txtstream.WriteLine("    text-decoration: none;")
txtstream.WriteLine("    border-left: 5px solid #FFF;")
txtstream.WriteLine("    padding-left: 3px;")
txtstream.WriteLine("}")

txtstream.WriteLine("th a:hover, #itsthetable th a:active {")
txtstream.WriteLine("    color: #F90;")
txtstream.WriteLine("    text-decoration: line-through;")
txtstream.WriteLine("    border-left: 5px solid #F90;")
txtstream.WriteLine("    padding-left: 3px;")
txtstream.WriteLine("}")
```

```
txtstream.WriteLine("tbody th:hover {")
txtstream.WriteLine("    background-image: url(imgs/tbody_hover.gif);")
txtstream.WriteLine("    background-position: bottom;")
txtstream.WriteLine("    background-repeat: repeat-x;")
txtstream.WriteLine("}")

txtstream.WriteLine("td {")
txtstream.WriteLine("    background-color: #f2f2f2;")
txtstream.WriteLine("    padding: 4px;")
txtstream.WriteLine("    font-size: 12px;")
txtstream.WriteLine("}")

txtstream.WriteLine("#itsthetable td:hover {")
txtstream.WriteLine("    background-color: #f8f8f8;")

txtstream.WriteLine("}")

txtstream.WriteLine("#itsthetable td a:link, #itsthetable td a:visited {")
txtstream.WriteLine("    color: #039;")
txtstream.WriteLine("    text-decoration: none;")
txtstream.WriteLine("    border-left: 3px solid #039;")
txtstream.WriteLine("    padding-left: 3px;")
txtstream.WriteLine("}")

txtstream.WriteLine("#itsthetable td a:hover, #itsthetable td a:active {")
txtstream.WriteLine("    color: #06C;")
txtstream.WriteLine("    text-decoration: line-through;")
txtstream.WriteLine("    border-left: 3px solid #06C;")
txtstream.WriteLine("    padding-left: 3px;")
txtstream.WriteLine("}")

txtstream.WriteLine("#itsthetable th {")
txtstream.WriteLine("    text-align: left;")
txtstream.WriteLine("    width: 150px;")
txtstream.WriteLine("}")

txtstream.WriteLine("#itsthetable tr {")
txtstream.WriteLine("    border-bottom: 1px solid #CCC;")
txtstream.WriteLine("}")

txtstream.WriteLine("#itsthetable thead th {")
txtstream.WriteLine("    background-image: url(imgs/thead_back.gif);")
txtstream.WriteLine("    background-repeat: repeat-x;")
txtstream.WriteLine("    background-color: #06C;")
txtstream.WriteLine("    height: 30px;")
txtstream.WriteLine("    font-size: 18px;")
txtstream.WriteLine("    text-align: center;")
txtstream.WriteLine("    text-shadow: #333 2px 2px;")
txtstream.WriteLine("    border: 2px;")
txtstream.WriteLine("}")

txtstream.WriteLine("#itsthetable tfoot th {")
txtstream.WriteLine("    background-image: url(imgs/tfoot_back.gif);")
txtstream.WriteLine("    background-repeat: repeat-x;")
txtstream.WriteLine("    background-color: #036;")
txtstream.WriteLine("    height: 30px;")
txtstream.WriteLine("    font-size: 28px;")
txtstream.WriteLine("    text-align: center;")
txtstream.WriteLine("    text-shadow: #333 2px 2px;")
txtstream.WriteLine("}")

txtstream.WriteLine("#itsthetable tfoot td {")
txtstream.WriteLine("    background-image: url(imgs/tfoot_back.gif);")
txtstream.WriteLine("    background-repeat: repeat-x;")
txtstream.WriteLine("    background-color: #036;")
txtstream.WriteLine("    color: FFF;")
```

```
txtstream.WriteLine("        height: 30px;")
txtstream.WriteLine("        font-size: 24px;")
txtstream.WriteLine("        text-align: left;")
txtstream.WriteLine("        text-shadow: #333 2px 2px;")
txtstream.WriteLine("}")

txtstream.WriteLine("tbody td a[href=\""http:www.csslab.cl/\""] {")
txtstream.WriteLine("        font-weight: bolder;")
txtstream.WriteLine("}")
txtstream.WriteLine("</style>")
```

BlackAndWhiteText:

```
txtstream.WriteLine("<style type='text/css'>")
txtstream.WriteLine("th")
txtstream.WriteLine("{")
txtstream.WriteLine("    COLOR: white;")
txtstream.WriteLine("    BACKGROUND-COLOR: black;")
txtstream.WriteLine("    FONT-FAMILY:font-family: Cambria, serif;")
txtstream.WriteLine("    FONT-SIZE: 12px;")
txtstream.WriteLine("    text-align: left;")
txtstream.WriteLine("    white-Space: nowrap;")
txtstream.WriteLine("}")
txtstream.WriteLine("td")
txtstream.WriteLine("{")
txtstream.WriteLine("    COLOR: white;")
txtstream.WriteLine("    BACKGROUND-COLOR: black;")
txtstream.WriteLine("    FONT-FAMILY: Cambria, serif;")
txtstream.WriteLine("    FONT-SIZE: 12px;")
txtstream.WriteLine("    text-align: left;")
txtstream.WriteLine("    white-Space: nowrap;")
txtstream.WriteLine("}")
txtstream.WriteLine("div")
txtstream.WriteLine("{")
txtstream.WriteLine("    COLOR: white;")
txtstream.WriteLine("    BACKGROUND-COLOR: black;")
txtstream.WriteLine("    FONT-FAMILY: Cambria, serif;")
txtstream.WriteLine("    FONT-SIZE: 10px;")
txtstream.WriteLine("    text-align: left;")
txtstream.WriteLine("    white-Space: nowrap;")
txtstream.WriteLine("}")
txtstream.WriteLine("span")
txtstream.WriteLine("{")
txtstream.WriteLine("    COLOR: white;")
txtstream.WriteLine("    BACKGROUND-COLOR: black;")
txtstream.WriteLine("    FONT-FAMILY: Cambria, serif;")
txtstream.WriteLine("    FONT-SIZE: 10px;")
txtstream.WriteLine("    text-align: left;")
txtstream.WriteLine("    white-Space: nowrap;")
txtstream.WriteLine("    display:inline-block;")
txtstream.WriteLine("    width: 100%;")
txtstream.WriteLine("}")
txtstream.WriteLine("textarea")
txtstream.WriteLine("{")
txtstream.WriteLine("    COLOR: white;")
txtstream.WriteLine("    BACKGROUND-COLOR: black;")
txtstream.WriteLine("    FONT-FAMILY: Cambria, serif;")
txtstream.WriteLine("    FONT-SIZE: 10px;")
txtstream.WriteLine("    text-align: left;")
txtstream.WriteLine("    white-Space: nowrap;")
txtstream.WriteLine("    width: 100%;")
txtstream.WriteLine("}")
txtstream.WriteLine("select")
txtstream.WriteLine("{")
```

```
txtstream.WriteLine("   COLOR: white;")
txtstream.WriteLine("   BACKGROUND-COLOR: black;")
txtstream.WriteLine("   FONT-FAMILY: Cambria, serif;")
txtstream.WriteLine("   FONT-SIZE: 10px;")
txtstream.WriteLine("   text-align: left;")
txtstream.WriteLine("   white-Space: nowrap;")
txtstream.WriteLine("   width: 100%;")
txtstream.WriteLine("}")
txtstream.WriteLine("input")
txtstream.WriteLine("{")
txtstream.WriteLine("   COLOR: white;")
txtstream.WriteLine("   BACKGROUND-COLOR: black;")
txtstream.WriteLine("   FONT-FAMILY: Cambria, serif;")
txtstream.WriteLine("   FONT-SIZE: 12px;")
txtstream.WriteLine("   text-align: left;")
txtstream.WriteLine("   display:table-cell;")
txtstream.WriteLine("   white-Space: nowrap;")
txtstream.WriteLine("}")
txtstream.WriteLine("h1 {")
txtstream.WriteLine("color: antiquewhite;")
txtstream.WriteLine("text-shadow: 1px 1px 1px black;")
txtstream.WriteLine("padding: 3px;")
txtstream.WriteLine("text-align: center;")
txtstream.WriteLine("box-shadow: in2px 2px 5px rgba(0,0,0,0.5), in-2px -2px 5px
rgba(255,255,255,0.5);")
txtstream.WriteLine("}")
txtstream.WriteLine("</style>")
```

ColoredText

```
txtstream.WriteLine("<style type='text/css'>")
txtstream.WriteLine("th")
txtstream.WriteLine("{")
txtstream.WriteLine("   COLOR: darkred;")
txtstream.WriteLine("   BACKGROUND-COLOR: #eeeeee;")
txtstream.WriteLine("   FONT-FAMILY:font-family: Cambria, serif;")
txtstream.WriteLine("   FONT-SIZE: 12px;")
txtstream.WriteLine("   text-align: left;")
txtstream.WriteLine("   white-Space: nowrap;")
txtstream.WriteLine("}")
txtstream.WriteLine("td")
txtstream.WriteLine("{")
txtstream.WriteLine("   COLOR: navy;")
txtstream.WriteLine("   BACKGROUND-COLOR: #eeeeee;")
txtstream.WriteLine("   FONT-FAMILY: Cambria, serif;")
txtstream.WriteLine("   FONT-SIZE: 12px;")
txtstream.WriteLine("   text-align: left;")
txtstream.WriteLine("   white-Space: nowrap;")
txtstream.WriteLine("}")
txtstream.WriteLine("div")
txtstream.WriteLine("{")
txtstream.WriteLine("   COLOR: white;")
txtstream.WriteLine("   BACKGROUND-COLOR: navy;")
txtstream.WriteLine("   FONT-FAMILY: Cambria, serif;")
txtstream.WriteLine("   FONT-SIZE: 10px;")
txtstream.WriteLine("   text-align: left;")
txtstream.WriteLine("   white-Space: nowrap;")
txtstream.WriteLine("}")
txtstream.WriteLine("span")
txtstream.WriteLine("{")
txtstream.WriteLine("   COLOR: white;")
txtstream.WriteLine("   BACKGROUND-COLOR: navy;")
txtstream.WriteLine("   FONT-FAMILY: Cambria, serif;")
txtstream.WriteLine("   FONT-SIZE: 10px;")
txtstream.WriteLine("   text-align: left;")
txtstream.WriteLine("   white-Space: nowrap;")
```

```
txtstream.WriteLine("    display:inline-block;")
txtstream.WriteLine("    width: 100%;")
txtstream.WriteLine("}")
txtstream.WriteLine("textarea")
txtstream.WriteLine("{")
txtstream.WriteLine("    COLOR: white;")
txtstream.WriteLine("    BACKGROUND-COLOR: navy;")
txtstream.WriteLine("    FONT-FAMILY: Cambria, serif;")
txtstream.WriteLine("    FONT-SIZE: 10px;")
txtstream.WriteLine("    text-align: left;")
txtstream.WriteLine("    white-Space: nowrap;")
txtstream.WriteLine("    width: 100%;")
txtstream.WriteLine("}")
txtstream.WriteLine("select")
txtstream.WriteLine("{")
txtstream.WriteLine("    COLOR: white;")
txtstream.WriteLine("    BACKGROUND-COLOR: navy;")
txtstream.WriteLine("    FONT-FAMILY: Cambria, serif;")
txtstream.WriteLine("    FONT-SIZE: 10px;")
txtstream.WriteLine("    text-align: left;")
txtstream.WriteLine("    white-Space: nowrap;")
txtstream.WriteLine("    width: 100%;")
txtstream.WriteLine("}")
txtstream.WriteLine("input")
txtstream.WriteLine("{")
txtstream.WriteLine("    COLOR: white;")
txtstream.WriteLine("    BACKGROUND-COLOR: navy;")
txtstream.WriteLine("    FONT-FAMILY: Cambria, serif;")
txtstream.WriteLine("    FONT-SIZE: 12px;")
txtstream.WriteLine("    text-align: left;")
txtstream.WriteLine("    display:table-cell;")
txtstream.WriteLine("    white-Space: nowrap;")
txtstream.WriteLine("}")
txtstream.WriteLine("h1 {")
txtstream.WriteLine("color: antiquewhite;")
txtstream.WriteLine("text-shadow: 1px 1px 1px black;")
txtstream.WriteLine("padding: 3px;")
txtstream.WriteLine("text-align: center;")
txtstream.WriteLine("box-shadow: in2px 2px 5px rgba(0,0,0,0.5), in-2px -2px 5px
rgba(255,255,255,0.5);")
txtstream.WriteLine("}")
txtstream.WriteLine("</style>")


OscillatingRowColors:


txtstream.WriteLine("<style type='text/css'> ")
txtstream.WriteLine("th")
txtstream.WriteLine("{")
txtstream.WriteLine("    COLOR: white;")
txtstream.WriteLine("    BACKGROUND-COLOR: navy;")
txtstream.WriteLine("    FONT-FAMILY:font-family: Cambria, serif;")
txtstream.WriteLine("    FONT-SIZE: 12px;")
txtstream.WriteLine("    text-align: left;")
txtstream.WriteLine("    white-Space: nowrap;")
txtstream.WriteLine("}")
txtstream.WriteLine("td")
txtstream.WriteLine("{")
txtstream.WriteLine("    COLOR: navy;")
txtstream.WriteLine("    FONT-FAMILY: Cambria, serif;")
txtstream.WriteLine("    FONT-SIZE: 12px;")
txtstream.WriteLine("    text-align: left;")
txtstream.WriteLine("    white-Space: nowrap;")
txtstream.WriteLine("}")
txtstream.WriteLine("div")
```

```
txtstream.WriteLine("{")
txtstream.WriteLine("    COLOR: navy;")
txtstream.WriteLine("    FONT-FAMILY: Cambria, serif;")
txtstream.WriteLine("    FONT-SIZE: 12px;")
txtstream.WriteLine("    text-align: left;")
txtstream.WriteLine("    white-Space: nowrap;")
txtstream.WriteLine("}")
txtstream.WriteLine("span")
txtstream.WriteLine("{")
txtstream.WriteLine("    COLOR: navy;")
txtstream.WriteLine("    FONT-FAMILY: Cambria, serif;")
txtstream.WriteLine("    FONT-SIZE: 12px;")
txtstream.WriteLine("    text-align: left;")
txtstream.WriteLine("    white-Space: nowrap;")
txtstream.WriteLine("    width: 100%;")
txtstream.WriteLine("}")
txtstream.WriteLine("textarea")
txtstream.WriteLine("{")
txtstream.WriteLine("    COLOR: navy;")
txtstream.WriteLine("    FONT-FAMILY: Cambria, serif;")
txtstream.WriteLine("    FONT-SIZE: 12px;")
txtstream.WriteLine("    text-align: left;")
txtstream.WriteLine("    white-Space: nowrap;")
txtstream.WriteLine("    display:inline-block;")
txtstream.WriteLine("    width: 100%;")
txtstream.WriteLine("}")
txtstream.WriteLine("select")
txtstream.WriteLine("{")
txtstream.WriteLine("    COLOR: navy;")
txtstream.WriteLine("    FONT-FAMILY: Cambria, serif;")
txtstream.WriteLine("    FONT-SIZE: 10px;")
txtstream.WriteLine("    text-align: left;")
txtstream.WriteLine("    white-Space: nowrap;")
txtstream.WriteLine("    display:inline-block;")
txtstream.WriteLine("    width: 100%;")
txtstream.WriteLine("}")
txtstream.WriteLine("input")
txtstream.WriteLine("{")
txtstream.WriteLine("    COLOR: navy;")
txtstream.WriteLine("    FONT-FAMILY: Cambria, serif;")
txtstream.WriteLine("    FONT-SIZE: 12px;")
txtstream.WriteLine("    text-align: left;")
txtstream.WriteLine("    display:table-cell;")
txtstream.WriteLine("    white-Space: nowrap;")
txtstream.WriteLine("}")
txtstream.WriteLine("h1 {")
txtstream.WriteLine("color: antiquewhite;")
txtstream.WriteLine("text-shadow: 1px 1px 1px black;")
txtstream.WriteLine("padding: 3px;")
txtstream.WriteLine("text-align: center;")
txtstream.WriteLine("box-shadow: in2px 2px 5px rgba(0,0,0,0.5), in-2px -2px 5px
rgba(255,255,255,0.5);")
txtstream.WriteLine("}")
txtstream.WriteLine("tr:nth-child(even){background-color:#f2f2f2;}")
txtstream.WriteLine("tr:nth-child(odd){background-color:#cccccc; color:#f2f2f2;}")
txtstream.WriteLine("</style>")
```

GhostDecorated:

```
txtstream.WriteLine("<style type='text/css'>")
txtstream.WriteLine("th")
txtstream.WriteLine("{")
txtstream.WriteLine("    COLOR: black;")
txtstream.WriteLine("    BACKGROUND-COLOR: white;")
txtstream.WriteLine("    FONT-FAMILY:font-family: Cambria, serif;")
```

```
txtstream.WriteLine("    FONT-SIZE: 12px;")
txtstream.WriteLine("    text-align: left;")
txtstream.WriteLine("    white-Space: nowrap;")
txtstream.WriteLine("}")
txtstream.WriteLine("td")
txtstream.WriteLine("{")
txtstream.WriteLine("    COLOR: black;")
txtstream.WriteLine("    BACKGROUND-COLOR: white;")
txtstream.WriteLine("    FONT-FAMILY: Cambria, serif;")
txtstream.WriteLine("    FONT-SIZE: 12px;")
txtstream.WriteLine("    text-align: left;")
txtstream.WriteLine("    white-Space: nowrap;")
txtstream.WriteLine("}")
txtstream.WriteLine("div")
txtstream.WriteLine("{")
txtstream.WriteLine("    COLOR: black;")
txtstream.WriteLine("    BACKGROUND-COLOR: white;")
txtstream.WriteLine("    FONT-FAMILY: Cambria, serif;")
txtstream.WriteLine("    FONT-SIZE: 10px;")
txtstream.WriteLine("    text-align: left;")
txtstream.WriteLine("    white-Space: nowrap;")
txtstream.WriteLine("}")
txtstream.WriteLine("span")
txtstream.WriteLine("{")
txtstream.WriteLine("    COLOR: black;")
txtstream.WriteLine("    BACKGROUND-COLOR: white;")
txtstream.WriteLine("    FONT-FAMILY: Cambria, serif;")
txtstream.WriteLine("    FONT-SIZE: 10px;")
txtstream.WriteLine("    text-align: left;")
txtstream.WriteLine("    white-Space: nowrap;")
txtstream.WriteLine("    display:inline-block;")
txtstream.WriteLine("    width: 100%;")
txtstream.WriteLine("}")
txtstream.WriteLine("textarea")
txtstream.WriteLine("{")
txtstream.WriteLine("    COLOR: black;")
txtstream.WriteLine("    BACKGROUND-COLOR: white;")
txtstream.WriteLine("    FONT-FAMILY: Cambria, serif;")
txtstream.WriteLine("    FONT-SIZE: 10px;")
txtstream.WriteLine("    text-align: left;")
txtstream.WriteLine("    white-Space: nowrap;")
txtstream.WriteLine("    width: 100%;")
txtstream.WriteLine("}")
txtstream.WriteLine("select")
txtstream.WriteLine("{")
txtstream.WriteLine("    COLOR: black;")
txtstream.WriteLine("    BACKGROUND-COLOR: white;")
txtstream.WriteLine("    FONT-FAMILY: Cambria, serif;")
txtstream.WriteLine("    FONT-SIZE: 10px;")
txtstream.WriteLine("    text-align: left;")
txtstream.WriteLine("    white-Space: nowrap;")
txtstream.WriteLine("    width: 100%;")
txtstream.WriteLine("}")
txtstream.WriteLine("input")
txtstream.WriteLine("{")
txtstream.WriteLine("    COLOR: black;")
txtstream.WriteLine("    BACKGROUND-COLOR: white;")
txtstream.WriteLine("    FONT-FAMILY: Cambria, serif;")
txtstream.WriteLine("    FONT-SIZE: 12px;")
txtstream.WriteLine("    text-align: left;")
txtstream.WriteLine("    display:table-cell;")
txtstream.WriteLine("    white-Space: nowrap;")
txtstream.WriteLine("}")
txtstream.WriteLine("h1 {")
txtstream.WriteLine("color: antiquewhite;")
txtstream.WriteLine("text-shadow: 1px 1px 1px black;")
```

```
        txtstream.WriteLine("padding: 3px;")
        txtstream.WriteLine("text-align: center;")
        txtstream.WriteLine("box-shadow: in2px 2px 5px rgba(0,0,0,0.5), in-2px -2px 5px
rgba(255,255,255,0.5);")
        txtstream.WriteLine("}")
        txtstream.WriteLine("</style>")

   3D:


        txtstream.WriteLine("<style type='text/css'>")
        txtstream.WriteLine("body")
        txtstream.WriteLine("{")
        txtstream.WriteLine("   PADDING-RIGHT: 0px;")
        txtstream.WriteLine("   PADDING-LEFT: 0px;")
        txtstream.WriteLine("   PADDING-BOTTOM: 0px;")
        txtstream.WriteLine("   MARGIN: 0px;")
        txtstream.WriteLine("   COLOR: #333;")
        txtstream.WriteLine("   PADDING-TOP: 0px;")
        txtstream.WriteLine("   FONT-FAMILY: verdana, arial, helvetica, sans-serif;")
        txtstream.WriteLine("}")
        txtstream.WriteLine("table")
        txtstream.WriteLine("{")
        txtstream.WriteLine("   BORDER-RIGHT: #999999 3px solid;")
        txtstream.WriteLine("   PADDING-RIGHT: 6px;")
        txtstream.WriteLine("   PADDING-LEFT: 6px;")
        txtstream.WriteLine("   FONT-WEIGHT: Bold;")
        txtstream.WriteLine("   FONT-SIZE: 14px;")
        txtstream.WriteLine("   PADDING-BOTTOM: 6px;")
        txtstream.WriteLine("   COLOR: Peru;")
        txtstream.WriteLine("   LINE-HEIGHT: 14px;")
        txtstream.WriteLine("   PADDING-TOP: 6px;")
        txtstream.WriteLine("   BORDER-BOTTOM: #999 1px solid;")
        txtstream.WriteLine("   BACKGROUND-COLOR: #eeeeee;")
        txtstream.WriteLine("   FONT-FAMILY: verdana, arial, helvetica, sans-serif;")
        txtstream.WriteLine("   FONT-SIZE: 12px;")
        txtstream.WriteLine("}")
        txtstream.WriteLine("th")
        txtstream.WriteLine("{")
        txtstream.WriteLine("   BORDER-RIGHT: #999999 3px solid;")
        txtstream.WriteLine("   PADDING-RIGHT: 6px;")
        txtstream.WriteLine("   PADDING-LEFT: 6px;")
        txtstream.WriteLine("   FONT-WEIGHT: Bold;")
        txtstream.WriteLine("   FONT-SIZE: 14px;")
        txtstream.WriteLine("   PADDING-BOTTOM: 6px;")
        txtstream.WriteLine("   COLOR: darkred;")
        txtstream.WriteLine("   LINE-HEIGHT: 14px;")
        txtstream.WriteLine("   PADDING-TOP: 6px;")
        txtstream.WriteLine("   BORDER-BOTTOM: #999 1px solid;")
        txtstream.WriteLine("   BACKGROUND-COLOR: #eeeeee;")
        txtstream.WriteLine("   FONT-FAMILY:font-family: Cambria, serif;")
        txtstream.WriteLine("   FONT-SIZE: 12px;")
        txtstream.WriteLine("   text-align: left;")
        txtstream.WriteLine("   white-Space: nowrap;")
        txtstream.WriteLine("}")
        txtstream.WriteLine(".th")
        txtstream.WriteLine("{")
        txtstream.WriteLine("   BORDER-RIGHT: #999999 2px solid;")
        txtstream.WriteLine("   PADDING-RIGHT: 6px;")
        txtstream.WriteLine("   PADDING-LEFT: 6px;")
        txtstream.WriteLine("   FONT-WEIGHT: Bold;")
        txtstream.WriteLine("   PADDING-BOTTOM: 6px;")
        txtstream.WriteLine("   COLOR: black;")
        txtstream.WriteLine("   PADDING-TOP: 6px;")
        txtstream.WriteLine("   BORDER-BOTTOM: #999 2px solid;")
        txtstream.WriteLine("   BACKGROUND-COLOR: #eeeeee;")
```

```
txtstream.WriteLine("    FONT-FAMILY: Cambria, serif;")
txtstream.WriteLine("    FONT-SIZE: 10px;")
txtstream.WriteLine("    text-align: right;")
txtstream.WriteLine("    white-Space: nowrap;")
txtstream.WriteLine("}")
txtstream.WriteLine("td")
txtstream.WriteLine("{")
txtstream.WriteLine("    BORDER-RIGHT: #999999 3px solid;")
txtstream.WriteLine("    PADDING-RIGHT: 6px;")
txtstream.WriteLine("    PADDING-LEFT: 6px;")
txtstream.WriteLine("    FONT-WEIGHT: Normal;")
txtstream.WriteLine("    PADDING-BOTTOM: 6px;")
txtstream.WriteLine("    COLOR: navy;")
txtstream.WriteLine("    LINE-HEIGHT: 14px;")
txtstream.WriteLine("    PADDING-TOP: 6px;")
txtstream.WriteLine("    BORDER-BOTTOM: #999 1px solid;")
txtstream.WriteLine("    BACKGROUND-COLOR: #eeeeee;")
txtstream.WriteLine("    FONT-FAMILY: Cambria, serif;")
txtstream.WriteLine("    FONT-SIZE: 12px;")
txtstream.WriteLine("    text-align: left;")
txtstream.WriteLine("    white-Space: nowrap;")
txtstream.WriteLine("}")
txtstream.WriteLine("div")
txtstream.WriteLine("{")
txtstream.WriteLine("    BORDER-RIGHT: #999999 3px solid;")
txtstream.WriteLine("    PADDING-RIGHT: 6px;")
txtstream.WriteLine("    PADDING-LEFT: 6px;")
txtstream.WriteLine("    FONT-WEIGHT: Normal;")
txtstream.WriteLine("    PADDING-BOTTOM: 6px;")
txtstream.WriteLine("    COLOR: white;")
txtstream.WriteLine("    PADDING-TOP: 6px;")
txtstream.WriteLine("    BORDER-BOTTOM: #999 1px solid;")
txtstream.WriteLine("    BACKGROUND-COLOR: navy;")
txtstream.WriteLine("    FONT-FAMILY: Cambria, serif;")
txtstream.WriteLine("    FONT-SIZE: 10px;")
txtstream.WriteLine("    text-align: left;")
txtstream.WriteLine("    white-Space: nowrap;")
txtstream.WriteLine("}")
txtstream.WriteLine("span")
txtstream.WriteLine("{")
txtstream.WriteLine("    BORDER-RIGHT: #999999 3px solid;")
txtstream.WriteLine("    PADDING-RIGHT: 3px;")
txtstream.WriteLine("    PADDING-LEFT: 3px;")
txtstream.WriteLine("    FONT-WEIGHT: Normal;")
txtstream.WriteLine("    PADDING-BOTTOM: 3px;")
txtstream.WriteLine("    COLOR: white;")
txtstream.WriteLine("    PADDING-TOP: 3px;")
txtstream.WriteLine("    BORDER-BOTTOM: #999 1px solid;")
txtstream.WriteLine("    BACKGROUND-COLOR: navy;")
txtstream.WriteLine("    FONT-FAMILY: Cambria, serif;")
txtstream.WriteLine("    FONT-SIZE: 10px;")
txtstream.WriteLine("    text-align: left;")
txtstream.WriteLine("    white-Space: nowrap;")
txtstream.WriteLine("    display:inline-block;")
txtstream.WriteLine("    width: 100%;")
txtstream.WriteLine("}")
txtstream.WriteLine("textarea")
txtstream.WriteLine("{")
txtstream.WriteLine("    BORDER-RIGHT: #999999 3px solid;")
txtstream.WriteLine("    PADDING-RIGHT: 3px;")
txtstream.WriteLine("    PADDING-LEFT: 3px;")
txtstream.WriteLine("    FONT-WEIGHT: Normal;")
txtstream.WriteLine("    PADDING-BOTTOM: 3px;")
txtstream.WriteLine("    COLOR: white;")
txtstream.WriteLine("    PADDING-TOP: 3px;")
txtstream.WriteLine("    BORDER-BOTTOM: #999 1px solid;")
```

```
txtstream.WriteLine("    BACKGROUND-COLOR: navy;")
txtstream.WriteLine("    FONT-FAMILY: Cambria, serif;")
txtstream.WriteLine("    FONT-SIZE: 10px;")
txtstream.WriteLine("    text-align: left;")
txtstream.WriteLine("    white-Space: nowrap;")
txtstream.WriteLine("    width: 100%;")
txtstream.WriteLine("}")
txtstream.WriteLine("select")
txtstream.WriteLine("{")
txtstream.WriteLine("    BORDER-RIGHT: #999999 3px solid;")
txtstream.WriteLine("    PADDING-RIGHT: 6px;")
txtstream.WriteLine("    PADDING-LEFT: 6px;")
txtstream.WriteLine("    FONT-WEIGHT: Normal;")
txtstream.WriteLine("    PADDING-BOTTOM: 6px;")
txtstream.WriteLine("    COLOR: white;")
txtstream.WriteLine("    PADDING-TOP: 6px;")
txtstream.WriteLine("    BORDER-BOTTOM: #999 1px solid;")
txtstream.WriteLine("    BACKGROUND-COLOR: navy;")
txtstream.WriteLine("    FONT-FAMILY: Cambria, serif;")
txtstream.WriteLine("    FONT-SIZE: 10px;")
txtstream.WriteLine("    text-align: left;")
txtstream.WriteLine("    white-Space: nowrap;")
txtstream.WriteLine("    width: 100%;")
txtstream.WriteLine("}")
txtstream.WriteLine("input")
txtstream.WriteLine("{")
txtstream.WriteLine("    BORDER-RIGHT: #999999 3px solid;")
txtstream.WriteLine("    PADDING-RIGHT: 3px;")
txtstream.WriteLine("    PADDING-LEFT: 3px;")
txtstream.WriteLine("    FONT-WEIGHT: Bold;")
txtstream.WriteLine("    PADDING-BOTTOM: 3px;")
txtstream.WriteLine("    COLOR: white;")
txtstream.WriteLine("    PADDING-TOP: 3px;")
txtstream.WriteLine("    BORDER-BOTTOM: #999 1px solid;")
txtstream.WriteLine("    BACKGROUND-COLOR: navy;")
txtstream.WriteLine("    FONT-FAMILY: Cambria, serif;")
txtstream.WriteLine("    FONT-SIZE: 12px;")
txtstream.WriteLine("    text-align: left;")
txtstream.WriteLine("    display:table-cell;")
txtstream.WriteLine("    white-Space: nowrap;")
txtstream.WriteLine("    width: 100%;")
txtstream.WriteLine("}")
txtstream.WriteLine("h1 {")
txtstream.WriteLine("color: antiquewhite;")
txtstream.WriteLine("text-shadow: 1px 1px 1px black;")
txtstream.WriteLine("padding: 3px;")
txtstream.WriteLine("text-align: center;")
txtstream.WriteLine("box-shadow: in2px 2px 5px rgba(0,0,0,0.5), in-2px -2px 5px
rgba(255,255,255,0.5);")
txtstream.WriteLine("}")
txtstream.WriteLine("</style>")
```

ShadowBox:

```
txtstream.WriteLine("<style type='text/css'>")
txtstream.WriteLine("body")
txtstream.WriteLine("{")
txtstream.WriteLine("    PADDING-RIGHT: 0px;")
txtstream.WriteLine("    PADDING-LEFT: 0px;")
txtstream.WriteLine("    PADDING-BOTTOM: 0px;")
txtstream.WriteLine("    MARGIN: 0px;")
txtstream.WriteLine("    COLOR: #333;")
txtstream.WriteLine("    PADDING-TOP: 0px;")
txtstream.WriteLine("    FONT-FAMILY: verdana, arial, helvetica, sans-serif;")
txtstream.WriteLine("}")
txtstream.WriteLine("table")
```

```
txtstream.WriteLine("{")
txtstream.WriteLine("    BORDER-RIGHT: #999999 1px solid;")
txtstream.WriteLine("    PADDING-RIGHT: 1px;")
txtstream.WriteLine("    PADDING-LEFT: 1px;")
txtstream.WriteLine("    PADDING-BOTTOM: 1px;")
txtstream.WriteLine("    LINE-HEIGHT: 8px;")
txtstream.WriteLine("    PADDING-TOP: 1px;")
txtstream.WriteLine("    BORDER-BOTTOM: #999 1px solid;")
txtstream.WriteLine("    BACKGROUND-COLOR: #eeeeee;")
txtstream.WriteLine("    filter:progid:DXImageTransform.Microsoft.Shadow(color='silver',
Direction=135, Strength=16)")
txtstream.WriteLine("}")
txtstream.WriteLine("th")
txtstream.WriteLine("{")
txtstream.WriteLine("    BORDER-RIGHT: #999999 3px solid;")
txtstream.WriteLine("    PADDING-RIGHT: 6px;")
txtstream.WriteLine("    PADDING-LEFT: 6px;")
txtstream.WriteLine("    FONT-WEIGHT: Bold;")
txtstream.WriteLine("    FONT-SIZE: 14px;")
txtstream.WriteLine("    PADDING-BOTTOM: 6px;")
txtstream.WriteLine("    COLOR: darkred;")
txtstream.WriteLine("    LINE-HEIGHT: 14px;")
txtstream.WriteLine("    PADDING-TOP: 6px;")
txtstream.WriteLine("    BORDER-BOTTOM: #999 1px solid;")
txtstream.WriteLine("    BACKGROUND-COLOR: #eeeeee;")
txtstream.WriteLine("    FONT-FAMILY: Cambria, serif;")
txtstream.WriteLine("    FONT-SIZE: 12px;")
txtstream.WriteLine("    text-align: left;")
txtstream.WriteLine("    white-Space: nowrap;")
txtstream.WriteLine("}")
txtstream.WriteLine(".th")
txtstream.WriteLine("{")
txtstream.WriteLine("    BORDER-RIGHT: #999999 2px solid;")
txtstream.WriteLine("    PADDING-RIGHT: 6px;")
txtstream.WriteLine("    PADDING-LEFT: 6px;")
txtstream.WriteLine("    FONT-WEIGHT: Bold;")
txtstream.WriteLine("    PADDING-BOTTOM: 6px;")
txtstream.WriteLine("    COLOR: black;")
txtstream.WriteLine("    PADDING-TOP: 6px;")
txtstream.WriteLine("    BORDER-BOTTOM: #999 2px solid;")
txtstream.WriteLine("    BACKGROUND-COLOR: #eeeeee;")
txtstream.WriteLine("    FONT-FAMILY: Cambria, serif;")
txtstream.WriteLine("    FONT-SIZE: 10px;")
txtstream.WriteLine("    text-align: right;")
txtstream.WriteLine("    white-Space: nowrap;")
txtstream.WriteLine("}")
txtstream.WriteLine("td")
txtstream.WriteLine("{")
txtstream.WriteLine("    BORDER-RIGHT: #999999 3px solid;")
txtstream.WriteLine("    PADDING-RIGHT: 6px;")
txtstream.WriteLine("    PADDING-LEFT: 6px;")
txtstream.WriteLine("    FONT-WEIGHT: Normal;")
txtstream.WriteLine("    PADDING-BOTTOM: 6px;")
txtstream.WriteLine("    COLOR: navy;")
txtstream.WriteLine("    LINE-HEIGHT: 14px;")
txtstream.WriteLine("    PADDING-TOP: 6px;")
txtstream.WriteLine("    BORDER-BOTTOM: #999 1px solid;")
txtstream.WriteLine("    BACKGROUND-COLOR: #eeeeee;")
txtstream.WriteLine("    FONT-FAMILY: Cambria, serif;")
txtstream.WriteLine("    FONT-SIZE: 12px;")
txtstream.WriteLine("    text-align: left;")
txtstream.WriteLine("    white-Space: nowrap;")
txtstream.WriteLine("}")
txtstream.WriteLine("div")
txtstream.WriteLine("{")
txtstream.WriteLine("    BORDER-RIGHT: #999999 3px solid;")
```

```
txtstream.WriteLine("    PADDING-RIGHT: 6px;")
txtstream.WriteLine("    PADDING-LEFT: 6px;")
txtstream.WriteLine("    FONT-WEIGHT: Normal;")
txtstream.WriteLine("    PADDING-BOTTOM: 6px;")
txtstream.WriteLine("    COLOR: white;")
txtstream.WriteLine("    PADDING-TOP: 6px;")
txtstream.WriteLine("    BORDER-BOTTOM: #999 1px solid;")
txtstream.WriteLine("    BACKGROUND-COLOR: navy;")
txtstream.WriteLine("    FONT-FAMILY: Cambria, serif;")
txtstream.WriteLine("    FONT-SIZE: 10px;")
txtstream.WriteLine("    text-align: left;")
txtstream.WriteLine("    white-Space: nowrap;")
txtstream.WriteLine("}")
txtstream.WriteLine("span")
txtstream.WriteLine("{")
txtstream.WriteLine("    BORDER-RIGHT: #999999 3px solid;")
txtstream.WriteLine("    PADDING-RIGHT: 3px;")
txtstream.WriteLine("    PADDING-LEFT: 3px;")
txtstream.WriteLine("    FONT-WEIGHT: Normal;")
txtstream.WriteLine("    PADDING-BOTTOM: 3px;")
txtstream.WriteLine("    COLOR: white;")
txtstream.WriteLine("    PADDING-TOP: 3px;")
txtstream.WriteLine("    BORDER-BOTTOM: #999 1px solid;")
txtstream.WriteLine("    BACKGROUND-COLOR: navy;")
txtstream.WriteLine("    FONT-FAMILY: Cambria, serif;")
txtstream.WriteLine("    FONT-SIZE: 10px;")
txtstream.WriteLine("    text-align: left;")
txtstream.WriteLine("    white-Space: nowrap;")
txtstream.WriteLine("    display: inline-block;")
txtstream.WriteLine("    width: 100%;")
txtstream.WriteLine("}")
txtstream.WriteLine("textarea")
txtstream.WriteLine("{")
txtstream.WriteLine("    BORDER-RIGHT: #999999 3px solid;")
txtstream.WriteLine("    PADDING-RIGHT: 3px;")
txtstream.WriteLine("    PADDING-LEFT: 3px;")
txtstream.WriteLine("    FONT-WEIGHT: Normal;")
txtstream.WriteLine("    PADDING-BOTTOM: 3px;")
txtstream.WriteLine("    COLOR: white;")
txtstream.WriteLine("    PADDING-TOP: 3px;")
txtstream.WriteLine("    BORDER-BOTTOM: #999 1px solid;")
txtstream.WriteLine("    BACKGROUND-COLOR: navy;")
txtstream.WriteLine("    FONT-FAMILY: Cambria, serif;")
txtstream.WriteLine("    FONT-SIZE: 10px;")
txtstream.WriteLine("    text-align: left;")
txtstream.WriteLine("    white-Space: nowrap;")
txtstream.WriteLine("    width: 100%;")
txtstream.WriteLine("}")
txtstream.WriteLine("select")
txtstream.WriteLine("{")
txtstream.WriteLine("    BORDER-RIGHT: #999999 3px solid;")
txtstream.WriteLine("    PADDING-RIGHT: 6px;")
txtstream.WriteLine("    PADDING-LEFT: 6px;")
txtstream.WriteLine("    FONT-WEIGHT: Normal;")
txtstream.WriteLine("    PADDING-BOTTOM: 6px;")
txtstream.WriteLine("    COLOR: white;")
txtstream.WriteLine("    PADDING-TOP: 6px;")
txtstream.WriteLine("    BORDER-BOTTOM: #999 1px solid;")
txtstream.WriteLine("    BACKGROUND-COLOR: navy;")
txtstream.WriteLine("    FONT-FAMILY: Cambria, serif;")
txtstream.WriteLine("    FONT-SIZE: 10px;")
txtstream.WriteLine("    text-align: left;")
txtstream.WriteLine("    white-Space: nowrap;")
txtstream.WriteLine("    width: 100%;")
txtstream.WriteLine("}")
txtstream.WriteLine("input")
```

```
txtstream.WriteLine("{")
txtstream.WriteLine("    BORDER-RIGHT: #999999 3px solid;")
txtstream.WriteLine("    PADDING-RIGHT: 3px;")
txtstream.WriteLine("    PADDING-LEFT: 3px;")
txtstream.WriteLine("    FONT-WEIGHT: Bold;")
txtstream.WriteLine("    PADDING-BOTTOM: 3px;")
txtstream.WriteLine("    COLOR: white;")
txtstream.WriteLine("    PADDING-TOP: 3px;")
txtstream.WriteLine("    BORDER-BOTTOM: #999 1px solid;")
txtstream.WriteLine("    BACKGROUND-COLOR: navy;")
txtstream.WriteLine("    FONT-FAMILY: Cambria, serif;")
txtstream.WriteLine("    FONT-SIZE: 12px;")
txtstream.WriteLine("    text-align: left;")
txtstream.WriteLine("    display: table-cell;")
txtstream.WriteLine("    white-Space: nowrap;")
txtstream.WriteLine("    width: 100%;")
txtstream.WriteLine("}")
txtstream.WriteLine("h1 {")
txtstream.WriteLine("color: antiquewhite;")
txtstream.WriteLine("text-shadow: 1px 1px 1px black;")
txtstream.WriteLine("padding: 3px;")
txtstream.WriteLine("text-align: center;")
txtstream.WriteLine("box-shadow: in2px 2px 5px rgba(0,0,0,0.5), in-2px -2px 5px
rgba(255,255,255,0.5);")
txtstream.WriteLine("}")
txtstream.WriteLine("</style>")

        Case "Customized"

txtstream.WriteLine("<style type='text/css'>")
txtstream.WriteLine("body")
txtstream.WriteLine("{")
txtstream.WriteLine("    PADDING-RIGHT: 0px;")
txtstream.WriteLine("    PADDING-LEFT: 0px;")
txtstream.WriteLine("    PADDING-BOTTOM: 0px;")
txtstream.WriteLine("    MARGIN: 0px;")
txtstream.WriteLine("    COLOR: #333;")
txtstream.WriteLine("    PADDING-TOP: 0px;")
txtstream.WriteLine("    FONT-FAMILY: verdana, arial, helvetica, sans-serif;")
txtstream.WriteLine("}")
txtstream.WriteLine("Table")
txtstream.WriteLine("{")
txtstream.WriteLine("    BORDER-RIGHT: #999999 1px solid;")
txtstream.WriteLine("    PADDING-RIGHT: 1px;")
txtstream.WriteLine("    PADDING-LEFT: 1px;")
txtstream.WriteLine("    PADDING-BOTTOM: 1px;")
txtstream.WriteLine("    LINE-HEIGHT: 8px;")
txtstream.WriteLine("    PADDING-TOP: 1px;")
txtstream.WriteLine("    BORDER-BOTTOM: #999 1px solid;")
txtstream.WriteLine("    BACKGROUND-COLOR: #eeeeee;")
txtstream.WriteLine("    filter:progid:DXImageTransform.Microsoft.Shadow(color='silver',
Direction=135, Strength=16)")
txtstream.WriteLine("}")
txtstream.WriteLine("th")
txtstream.WriteLine("{")
txtstream.WriteLine("    BORDER-RIGHT: #999999 3px solid;")
txtstream.WriteLine("    PADDING-RIGHT: 6px;")
txtstream.WriteLine("    PADDING-LEFT: 6px;")
txtstream.WriteLine("    FONT-WEIGHT: Bold;")
txtstream.WriteLine("    FONT-SIZE: 14px;")
txtstream.WriteLine("    PADDING-BOTTOM: 6px;")
txtstream.WriteLine("    COLOR: darkred;")
txtstream.WriteLine("    LINE-HEIGHT: 14px;")
txtstream.WriteLine("    PADDING-TOP: 6px;")
txtstream.WriteLine("    BORDER-BOTTOM: #999 1px solid;")
txtstream.WriteLine("    BACKGROUND-COLOR: #eeeeee;")
```

```
txtstream.WriteLine("   FONT-FAMILY: Cambria, serif;")
txtstream.WriteLine("   FONT-SIZE: 12px;")
txtstream.WriteLine("   text-align: left;")
txtstream.WriteLine("   white-Space: nowrap;")
txtstream.WriteLine("}")
txtstream.WriteLine(".th")
txtstream.WriteLine("{")
txtstream.WriteLine("   BORDER-RIGHT: #999999 2px solid;")
txtstream.WriteLine("   PADDING-RIGHT: 6px;")
txtstream.WriteLine("   PADDING-LEFT: 6px;")
txtstream.WriteLine("   FONT-WEIGHT: Bold;")
txtstream.WriteLine("   PADDING-BOTTOM: 6px;")
txtstream.WriteLine("   COLOR: black;")
txtstream.WriteLine("   PADDING-TOP: 6px;")
txtstream.WriteLine("   BORDER-BOTTOM: #999 2px solid;")
txtstream.WriteLine("   BACKGROUND-COLOR: #eeeeee;")
txtstream.WriteLine("   FONT-FAMILY: Cambria, serif;")
txtstream.WriteLine("   FONT-SIZE: 10px;")
txtstream.WriteLine("   text-align: right;")
txtstream.WriteLine("   white-Space: nowrap;")
txtstream.WriteLine("}")
txtstream.WriteLine("td")
txtstream.WriteLine("{")
txtstream.WriteLine("   BORDER-RIGHT: #999999 3px solid;")
txtstream.WriteLine("   PADDING-RIGHT: 6px;")
txtstream.WriteLine("   PADDING-LEFT: 6px;")
txtstream.WriteLine("   FONT-WEIGHT: Normal;")
txtstream.WriteLine("   PADDING-BOTTOM: 6px;")
txtstream.WriteLine("   COLOR: navy;")
txtstream.WriteLine("   LINE-HEIGHT: 14px;")
txtstream.WriteLine("   PADDING-TOP: 6px;")
txtstream.WriteLine("   BORDER-BOTTOM: #999 1px solid;")
txtstream.WriteLine("   BACKGROUND-COLOR: #eeeeee;")
txtstream.WriteLine("   FONT-FAMILY: Cambria, serif;")
txtstream.WriteLine("   FONT-SIZE: 12px;")
txtstream.WriteLine("   text-align: left;")
txtstream.WriteLine("   white-Space: nowrap;")
txtstream.WriteLine("}")
txtstream.WriteLine("div")
txtstream.WriteLine("{")
txtstream.WriteLine("   BORDER-RIGHT: #999999 3px solid;")
txtstream.WriteLine("   PADDING-RIGHT: 6px;")
txtstream.WriteLine("   PADDING-LEFT: 6px;")
txtstream.WriteLine("   FONT-WEIGHT: Normal;")
txtstream.WriteLine("   PADDING-BOTTOM: 6px;")
txtstream.WriteLine("   COLOR: white;")
txtstream.WriteLine("   PADDING-TOP: 6px;")
txtstream.WriteLine("   BORDER-BOTTOM: #999 1px solid;")
txtstream.WriteLine("   BACKGROUND-COLOR: navy;")
txtstream.WriteLine("   FONT-FAMILY: Cambria, serif;")
txtstream.WriteLine("   FONT-SIZE: 10px;")
txtstream.WriteLine("   text-align: left;")
txtstream.WriteLine("   white-Space: nowrap;")
txtstream.WriteLine("}")
txtstream.WriteLine("span")
txtstream.WriteLine("{")
txtstream.WriteLine("   BORDER-RIGHT: #999999 3px solid;")
txtstream.WriteLine("   PADDING-RIGHT: 3px;")
txtstream.WriteLine("   PADDING-LEFT: 3px;")
txtstream.WriteLine("   FONT-WEIGHT: Normal;")
txtstream.WriteLine("   PADDING-BOTTOM: 3px;")
txtstream.WriteLine("   COLOR: white;")
txtstream.WriteLine("   PADDING-TOP: 3px;")
txtstream.WriteLine("   BORDER-BOTTOM: #999 1px solid;")
txtstream.WriteLine("   BACKGROUND-COLOR: navy;")
txtstream.WriteLine("   FONT-FAMILY: Cambria, serif;")
```

```
txtstream.WriteLine("    FONT-SIZE: 10px;")
txtstream.WriteLine("    text-align: left;")
txtstream.WriteLine("    white-Space: nowrap;")
txtstream.WriteLine("    display: inline-block;")
txtstream.WriteLine("    width: 100%;")
txtstream.WriteLine("}")
txtstream.WriteLine("textarea")
txtstream.WriteLine("{")
txtstream.WriteLine("    BORDER-RIGHT: #999999 3px solid;")
txtstream.WriteLine("    PADDING-RIGHT: 3px;")
txtstream.WriteLine("    PADDING-LEFT: 3px;")
txtstream.WriteLine("    FONT-WEIGHT: Normal;")
txtstream.WriteLine("    PADDING-BOTTOM: 3px;")
txtstream.WriteLine("    COLOR: white;")
txtstream.WriteLine("    PADDING-TOP: 3px;")
txtstream.WriteLine("    BORDER-BOTTOM: #999 1px solid;")
txtstream.WriteLine("    BACKGROUND-COLOR: navy;")
txtstream.WriteLine("    FONT-FAMILY: Cambria, serif;")
txtstream.WriteLine("    FONT-SIZE: 12px;")
txtstream.WriteLine("    text-align: left;")
txtstream.WriteLine("    width: 100%;")
txtstream.WriteLine("}")
txtstream.WriteLine("select")
txtstream.WriteLine("{")
txtstream.WriteLine("    BORDER-RIGHT: #999999 1px solid;")
txtstream.WriteLine("    PADDING-RIGHT: 1px;")
txtstream.WriteLine("    PADDING-LEFT: 1px;")
txtstream.WriteLine("    FONT-WEIGHT: Normal;")
txtstream.WriteLine("    PADDING-BOTTOM: 1px;")
txtstream.WriteLine("    COLOR: white;")
txtstream.WriteLine("    PADDING-TOP: 1px;")
txtstream.WriteLine("    BORDER-BOTTOM: #999 1px solid;")
txtstream.WriteLine("    BACKGROUND-COLOR: navy;")
txtstream.WriteLine("    FONT-FAMILY: Cambria, serif;")
txtstream.WriteLine("    FONT-SIZE: 12px;")
txtstream.WriteLine("    text-align: left;")
txtstream.WriteLine("    white-Space: nowrap;")
txtstream.WriteLine("    width: 450px;")
txtstream.WriteLine("}")
txtstream.WriteLine("select1")
txtstream.WriteLine("{")
txtstream.WriteLine("    BORDER-RIGHT: #999999 1px solid;")
txtstream.WriteLine("    PADDING-RIGHT: 1px;")
txtstream.WriteLine("    PADDING-LEFT: 1px;")
txtstream.WriteLine("    FONT-WEIGHT: Normal;")
txtstream.WriteLine("    PADDING-BOTTOM: 1px;")
txtstream.WriteLine("    COLOR: white;")
txtstream.WriteLine("    PADDING-TOP: 1px;")
txtstream.WriteLine("    BORDER-BOTTOM: #999 1px solid;")
txtstream.WriteLine("    BACKGROUND-COLOR: navy;")
txtstream.WriteLine("    FONT-FAMILY: Cambria, serif;")
txtstream.WriteLine("    FONT-SIZE: 12px;")
txtstream.WriteLine("    text-align: left;")
txtstream.WriteLine("    white-Space: nowrap;")
txtstream.WriteLine("    width: 450px;")
txtstream.WriteLine("}")
txtstream.WriteLine("select2")
txtstream.WriteLine("{")
txtstream.WriteLine("    BORDER-RIGHT: #999999 1px solid;")
txtstream.WriteLine("    PADDING-RIGHT: 1px;")
txtstream.WriteLine("    PADDING-LEFT: 1px;")
txtstream.WriteLine("    FONT-WEIGHT: Normal;")
txtstream.WriteLine("    PADDING-BOTTOM: 1px;")
txtstream.WriteLine("    COLOR: white;")
txtstream.WriteLine("    PADDING-TOP: 1px;")
txtstream.WriteLine("    BORDER-BOTTOM: #999 1px solid;")
```

```
txtstream.WriteLine("    BACKGROUND-COLOR: navy;")
txtstream.WriteLine("    FONT-FAMILY: Cambria, serif;")
txtstream.WriteLine("    FONT-SIZE: 12px;")
txtstream.WriteLine("    text-align: left;")
txtstream.WriteLine("    white-Space: nowrap;")
txtstream.WriteLine("    width: 450px;")
txtstream.WriteLine("}")
txtstream.WriteLine("select3")
txtstream.WriteLine("{")
txtstream.WriteLine("    BORDER-RIGHT: #999999 1px solid;")
txtstream.WriteLine("    PADDING-RIGHT: 1px;")
txtstream.WriteLine("    PADDING-LEFT: 1px;")
txtstream.WriteLine("    FONT-WEIGHT: Normal;")
txtstream.WriteLine("    PADDING-BOTTOM: 1px;")
txtstream.WriteLine("    COLOR: white;")
txtstream.WriteLine("    PADDING-TOP: 1px;")
txtstream.WriteLine("    BORDER-BOTTOM: #999 1px solid;")
txtstream.WriteLine("    BACKGROUND-COLOR: navy;")
txtstream.WriteLine("    FONT-FAMILY: Cambria, serif;")
txtstream.WriteLine("    FONT-SIZE: 12px;")
txtstream.WriteLine("    text-align: left;")
txtstream.WriteLine("    white-Space: nowrap;")
txtstream.WriteLine("    width: 100px;")
txtstream.WriteLine("}")
txtstream.WriteLine("select4")
txtstream.WriteLine("{")
txtstream.WriteLine("    BORDER-RIGHT: #999999 1px solid;")
txtstream.WriteLine("    PADDING-RIGHT: 1px;")
txtstream.WriteLine("    PADDING-LEFT: 1px;")
txtstream.WriteLine("    FONT-WEIGHT: Normal;")
txtstream.WriteLine("    PADDING-BOTTOM: 1px;")
txtstream.WriteLine("    COLOR: white;")
txtstream.WriteLine("    PADDING-TOP: 1px;")
txtstream.WriteLine("    BORDER-BOTTOM: #999 1px solid;")
txtstream.WriteLine("    BACKGROUND-COLOR: navy;")
txtstream.WriteLine("    FONT-FAMILY: Cambria, serif;")
txtstream.WriteLine("    FONT-SIZE: 12px;")
txtstream.WriteLine("    text-align: left;")
txtstream.WriteLine("    white-Space: nowrap;")
txtstream.WriteLine("    width: 254px;")
txtstream.WriteLine("}")
txtstream.WriteLine("input")
txtstream.WriteLine("{")
txtstream.WriteLine("    BORDER-RIGHT: #999999 3px solid;")
txtstream.WriteLine("    PADDING-RIGHT: 3px;")
txtstream.WriteLine("    PADDING-LEFT: 3px;")
txtstream.WriteLine("    FONT-WEIGHT: Bold;")
txtstream.WriteLine("    PADDING-BOTTOM: 3px;")
txtstream.WriteLine("    COLOR: white;")
txtstream.WriteLine("    PADDING-TOP: 3px;")
txtstream.WriteLine("    BORDER-BOTTOM: #999 1px solid;")
txtstream.WriteLine("    BACKGROUND-COLOR: navy;")
txtstream.WriteLine("    FONT-FAMILY: Cambria, serif;")
txtstream.WriteLine("    FONT-SIZE: 12px;")
txtstream.WriteLine("    text-align: left;")
txtstream.WriteLine("    display: table-cell;")
txtstream.WriteLine("    white-Space: nowrap;")
txtstream.WriteLine("    width: 100%;")
txtstream.WriteLine("}")
txtstream.WriteLine("</style>")
```

www.ingramcontent.com/pod-product-compliance
Lightning Source LLC
Chambersburg PA
CBHW031245050326
40690CB00007B/954